Applications and Innovations in Intelligent Systems XIV

T0142929

Richard Ellis, Tony Allen and
Andrew Tuson (Eds)

Applications and Innovations in Intelligent Systems XIV

Proceedings of AI-2006, the Twenty-sixth SGAI International Conference on Innovative Techniques and Applications of Artificial Intelligence

 Springer

Richard Ellis, BSc, MSc
Stratum Management Ltd, UK

Dr Tony Allen, PhD
Nottingham Trent University, UK

Dr Andrew Tuson, MA, MSc, PhD, MBCS
Department of Computing, City University, London

British Library Cataloguing in Publication Data
A catalogue record for this book is available from the British Library

ISBN-10: 1-84628-665-4   Printed on acid-free paper
ISBN-13: 978-1-84628-665-0

9 8 7 6 5 4 3 2 1

Springer Science+Business Media
springer.com

APPLICATION PROGRAMME CHAIR'S INTRODUCTION

RICHARD ELLIS
Managing Director, Stratum Management Ltd, UK

The papers in this volume are the refereed application papers presented at AI-2006, the Twenty-sixth SGAI International Conference on Innovative Techniques and Applications of Artificial Intelligence, held in Cambridge in December 2006. The conference was organised by SGAI, the British Computer Society Specialist Group on Artificial Intelligence.

This volume contains seventeen refereed papers which present the innovative application of a range of AI techniques in a number of subject domains. This year, the papers are divided into sections on *Data Mining and Bayesian Networks; Genetic Algorithms and Optimisation Techniques; Agents and Semantic Web; and Natural Language.*

This year's Rob Milne Memorial Award for the best refereed application paper was won by a paper entitled "Managing Restaurant Tables using Constraints". The authors are Alfio Vidotto and Kenneth N. Brown (University College Cork, Ireland) and J. Christopher Beck (University of Toronto, Canada). This award was instituted in 2005 in memory of the contribution that the late Rob Milne made to AI.

This is the fourteenth volume in the *Applications and Innovations* series. The Technical Stream papers are published as a companion volume under the title *Research and Development in Intelligent Systems XXIII.*

On behalf of the conference organising committee I should like to thank all those who contributed to the organisation of this year's application programme, in particular the programme committee members, the executive programme committee and our administrator Mark Firman.

Richard Ellis
Application Programme Chair, AI-2006

ACKNOWLEDGEMENTS

AI-2006 CONFERENCE COMMITTEE

Dr. Andrew Tuson, City University	(Conference Chair)
Dr. Tony Allen, Nottingham Trent University	(Past Conference Chair and Deputy Application Program Chair)
Dr. Alun Preece, University of Aberdeen	(Deputy Conference Chair, Electronic Services)
Dr Frans Coenen, University of Liverpool	(Deputy Conference Chair, Local Arrangements and Deputy Technical Programme Chair)
Prof. Adrian Hopgood, Nottingham Trent University	(Workshop Organiser)
Rosemary Gilligan, University of Hertfordshire	(Treasurer)
Dr Nirmalie Wiratunga, The Robert Gordon University, Aberdeen	(Poster Session Organiser)
Richard Ellis, Stratum Management Ltd	(Application Programme Chair)
Professor Max Bramer, University of Portsmouth	(Technical Programme Chair)
Alice Kerly, University of Birmingham	(Research Student Liaison)
Dr. Miltos Petridis, University of Greenwich	(UK CBR Organiser)
Mark Firman, City University	(Conference Administrator)

APPLICATION EXECUTIVE PROGRAMME COMMITTEE

Richard Ellis, Stratum Management Ltd (Chair)
Dr Tony Allen, Nottingham Trent University (Deputy Chair)
Rosemary Gilligan, University of Hertfordshire
Prof. Adrian Hopgood, Nottingham Trent University
Dr Miltos Petridis, University of Greenwich
Mr. Richard Wheeler, University of Edinburgh

APPLICATION PROGRAMME COMMITTEE

Tom Addis (University of Portsmouth)

Tony Allen (Nottingham Trent University)

Victor Alves (Universidade do Minho)

Ines Arana (Robert Gordon Unuversity)

Euan Davidson (University of Strathclyde)

Sarah Jane Delany (Dublin Institute of Technology)

Argiris Dentsoras (University of Patras)

Richard Ellis (Stratum)

Pablo Gervás (Universidad Complutense de Madrid)

Rosemary Gilligan (University of Hertfordshire)

John Gordon (AKRI Ltd)

Phil Hall (Elzware)

Hopgood, Adrian (Nottingham Trent University)

Tom Howley (NUI Galway)

Estevam Hruschka Jr. (Federal Universisty of Sao Carlos)

John Kingston (University of Edinburgh)

Paul Leng (University of Liverpool)

Shuliang Li (University of Westminster)

Ann Macintosh (Napier University)

Michael Madden (National University of Ireland)

Lars Nolle (Nottingham Trent University)

Giles Oatley (University of Sunderland)

Ehud Reiter (University of Aberdeen)

Miguel Salido (Universidad Politecnica de Valencia)

Gerald Schaefer (Nottingham Trent University)

Anoop Srivastava (Tata Institute of Fundamental Research)

Simon Thompson (BT)

Cornelius Weber (Johann Wolfgang Goethe University)

Wamberto Weber Vasconcelos (University of Aberdeen)

Richard Wheeler (University of Edinburgh)

CONTENTS

SESSION 3: AGENTS AND SEMANTIC WEB

SESSION 5: NATURAL LANGUAGE

SHORT PAPERS

BEST APPLICATION PAPER

Managing Restaurant Tables using Constraints

Alfio Vidotto[1], Kenneth N. Brown[1], J. Christopher Beck[2]

[1] Cork Constraint Computation Centre, Department of Computer Science, University College Cork, Ireland.
av1@student.cs.ucc.ie, k.brown@cs.ucc.ie

[2] Toronto Intelligent Decision Engineering Laboratory, Department of Mechanical and Industrial Engineering, University of Toronto, Canada.
jcb@mie.utoronto.ca

Abstract

Restaurant table management can have significant impact on both profitability and the customer experience. The core of the issue is a complex dynamic combinatorial problem. We show how to model the problem as constraint satisfaction, with extensions which generate flexible seating plans and which maintain stability when changes occur. We describe an implemented system which provides advice to users in real time. The system is currently being evaluated in a restaurant environment.

1. Introduction

Effective table management can be crucial to a restaurant's profitability – inefficient use of tables means that the restaurant is losing potential custom, but overbooking means that customers are delayed or feel cramped and pressured, and so are unlikely to return. In addition, customer behaviour is uncertain, and so seating plans should be flexible or quickly reconfigurable, to avoid delays. The restaurant manager is faced with a series of questions. Should a party of two be offered the last four-seater table? For how long should we keep a favourite table for a regular customer? Should a party of four be offered a table for 8 p.m.? If no table is available at 7 p.m., what other times should be offered? When a party takes longer than expected, can we re-assign all diners who have not yet been seated to avoid delays? When a party doesn't appear, can we re-assign all other diners to gain an extra seating? In Computer Science terms, table management is an online constrained combinatorial optimisation problem – the restaurant must manage reservations, and manage unexpected events in real-time, while maximising the use of its resources.

In this paper, we describe an implemented solution to the restaurant table management problem which helps managers answer the above questions. The solution is based on constraint programming, and handles both flexibility and stability. The system we describe is currently being evaluated in a restaurant. The remainder of the paper is organised as follows. Section 2 presents more details of the table management problem, and describes one particular restaurant. Section 3 reviews the necessary elements of constraint programming. Section 4 presents a basic constraint model and search algorithm. Section 5 extends the model to represent flexibility, and to search for flexible plans, while section 6 describes our approach to finding stable plans. Section 7 presents the user interface for our implemented system. Finally, section 8 describes conclusions and future work.

2. Restaurant Table Management

Eco [1] is a popular medium-size restaurant in Douglas, Cork City, with a high turnover seven days a week. It was a pioneer in computer and internet solutions, first offering email booking in 2000. The restaurant has 23 tables, ranging in size from 2 to 8 (Figure 1). Some of the table capacities depend on the state of other tables: for example, tables 2 and 15 can both seat 6, but when one is occupied by 5 or 6 diners, then the other can seat at most 4. The tables can also be reconfigured: for example, the 2-seater tables 21 and 22 can be joined to accommodate 3 to 5 diners. The maximum party size that can be seated at a conjoined table is 30. There are over 100 different possible restaurant configurations, and thus the restaurant capacity ranges from 85 to 94. An evening session in the restaurant begins at 4 p.m., and the last party should be seated by 10:30 p.m. As a guide, the restaurant aims to have between 190 and 210 covers (individual diners) each evening – fewer than that, and the tables are not being well utilised; more than that, and the kitchen will be stretched to provide the food on time. Table management in Eco, as in most restaurants, has two distinct phases: *booking* and *floor management*.

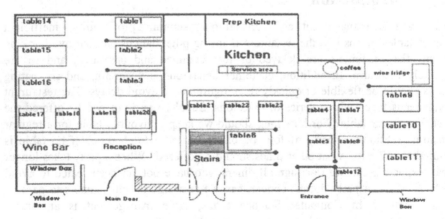

Figure 1: Layout of the restaurant *Eco*

In the booking phase, the booker must negotiate start times with customers to ensure that customers' requirements are satisfied, while maintaining a flexible table assignment that maximises the chances of being able to seat the desired number of covers. Typically, the booker will allocate specific tables to each booking request, and these rarely change; when a request cannot be accommodated on the current booking sheet, either the customer must be persuaded to accept another time, or the request must be declined. It is possible, however, that a reallocation of diners to tables would allow the new request to be accepted. In some cases, in order to maintain a balanced plan, a restaurant will decline a booking, or suggest a different time, even if a table is available. In addition, the booker must estimate the expected duration of the meal, based on the characteristics of the booking (including time, day of the week, and party size).

In floor management, the objectives are different. The evening starts with a partially completed booking sheet. The customers have been given definite times, and the aim is now to seat the customers with minimum delay, to modify the seating plan when changes happen, and to accept or decline "walk-ins" – customers arriving at the restaurant without a booking. The main challenge is that individual customers are unpredictable – they may arrive late, they may not arrive at all, they may take longer or shorter than expected, they may change the size of their party, and they may arrive believing a booking has been made when none has been recorded. The floor manager must make instant decisions, balancing current customer satisfaction with expectations for the rest of the evening.

The initial problem is to construct an interactive software tool, which assists restaurant staff in both the booking and floor management phases. As a research problem, our goal is to evaluate whether constraint programming techniques can provide support for the dynamic and uncertain aspects of the problem. If the research prototype is successful, a new tool will be developed, and incorporated into customer relationship management software.

3. Constraint Programming

A *Constraint Satisfaction Problem* (CSP) is defined by a set of decision variables, $\{X_1, X_2, ..., X_n\}$, with corresponding domains of values $\{D_1, D_2, ..., D_n\}$, and a set of constraints, $\{C_1, C_2, ..., C_m\}$. Each constraint is defined by a scope, i.e. a subset of the variables, and a relation which defines the allowed tuples of values for the scope. A state is an assignment of values to some or all of the variables, $\{X_i=v_i, X_j=v_j, ...\}$. A solution to a CSP is a complete and consistent assignment, i.e. an assignment of values to all of the variables, $\{X_1=v_1, X_2=v_2, ..., X_n=v_n\}$, that satisfies all the constraints. The standard methods for solving CSPs are based on backtracking search interleaved with constraint propagation. An introduction to constraint programming can be found in [2], while [3] surveys recent research.

For search, the order in which variables and values are tried has to be specified as part of the search algorithm, and has a significant effect on the size of the search tree. The standard variable ordering heuristic chooses the variable with the smallest current domain, or the smallest ratio of domain size to the number of constraints acting on the variable. For an instance of a CSP, a single run with a single ordering heuristic can get trapped in the wrong area of the search tree. To avoid this, randomized restarts have been proposed [4] – for a single heuristic, if no result has been found by a given time limit, the search is started again. Tie breaking and value ordering are done randomly, and so each restart explores a different path. Similarly, algorithm portfolios [5] interleave a set of randomized algorithms. In [6] search robustness is enhanced by combining multiple variable and value ordering heuristics with time-bounded restarts.

In constraint propagation, the domains of unassigned variables are reduced by removing values which cannot appear in any solution that extends the current state. For example, if we have the constraint $X < Y$, and X and Y's domains are $\{2,3,4,5\}$ and $\{1,2,3,4\}$ respectively, then the values 4 and 5 can be removed from X's domain, and 1 and 2 from Y's domain, since none of those values could possibly satisfy the constraint. Reducing the domains reduces the size of sub-tree that has to be explored. A large part of the success of constraint programming tools is due to efficient domain filtering algorithms for specialised constraints; e.g. [7].

Dynamic problems are problems that change as the solution is being executed – for example, in scheduling, a machine may break down, or a scheduled action may be delayed due to the late arrival of supplies. Dynamic CSPs [8] model changes to problems. The aim may be to minimise the effort to find new solutions, or to minimise the distance between successive solutions. Attention has recently turned to problems where we have some model of what the changes might be. Both [9] and [10] reason about the probability of future events: [9] searches and propagates constraints over a tree of possible futures; [10] samples possible futures, and then selects an action which minimises regret over the samples. [11] searches for optimally stable solutions. They start with the original solution and iteratively check whether reassigning one variable, two variables, etc., is sufficient to solve the new problem. [12] proposes special stability constraints. Some approaches aim to prevent instability by providing robust solutions. In [13] flexible solutions to scheduling problems are achieved by adding slack to activity durations. Super solutions [14] are solutions that guarantee a limited number of repairs in case of changes.

4. Modelling the static table management problem

As discussed in section 2, the restaurant problem is inherently dynamic, but we can view it a sequence of static problems, each linked by a set of changes. In this section, we describe our representation of the static problem as a CSP, and discuss our algorithm for solving it.

We model table management as a scheduling problem, viewing tables as resources, and parties as tasks. Each party has a fixed start and end time, and a size. Each party must then be allocated to a table (or set of tables), such that the table is large enough for the party, and such that no two parties that overlap in time are allocated to the same table. Each party must be seated without interruption on the table. The problem is to determine whether or not a set of parties can be seated, and to provide a feasible seating plan if there is one. Despite having fixed start and end times, the underlying scheduling problem is NP-complete [15]. Figure 2 shows a problem instance with five parties (left) and a possible allocation (right), where tables T_2 and T_3 have been joined for the first two time slots.

To represent this as a CSP, we model the parties as decision variables, and the tables as the values to be assigned. The detailed constraint model is generated automatically from a template and from details of the restaurant. Figure 3 shows the resulting model for the simple problem of Figure 2. The variables P_1, P_2, P_3, P_4, and

P_5 can take values from the domains D_1, D_2, D_3, D_4, and D_5 respectively. Since T_3 can be joined onto T_2 to give a capacity of 6, T_2 appears in D_2. Constraints C1 and C2 ensure that any parties overlapping in time use different tables. C3 ensures that if the extra capacity of T_2 is required, then T_3 cannot be assigned simultaneously (P_2 is the only party that could require the increased capacity). C4 is an extra constraint that ensures that T_3 and T_4 cannot both be fully occupied at the same time (which could only happen if they are assigned P_3 and P_2 respectively). C5 ensures that in timeslot 1, the number of usable tables is not less than the number of parties, where the number of usable tables is decremented each time two tables are joined. C6 and C7 similarly ensure that the number of seats is not less than the number of diners. For this example, C5, C6 and C7 are always true, but are shown here for illustration. Finally, C8 breaks a symmetry in the problem, and ensures that an ordering is forced between pairs of equivalent parties.

Party	Size	Start	End
P_1	2	0	2
P_2	4	0	2
P_3	3	1	3
P_4	2	2	4
P_5	2	2	4

Table[size]	0	1	2	3
$T_1[2]$		P1		P4
$T_2[3]$		P2		P5
$T_3[3]$				
$T_4[4]$			P3	

Figure 2: Problem instantiation at time 0 *(left)*; and a possible seating plan *(right)*

Variables: $\{P_1, P_2, P_3, P_4, P_5\}$
Domains: $D_1=\{T_1, T_2, T_3, T_4\}$, $D_2=\{T_2, T_4\}$, $D_3=\{T_2, T_3, T_4\}$, $D_4=\{T_1, T_2, T_3, T_4\}$, $D_5=\{T_1, T_2, T_3, T_4\}$
Constraints:

    C1.   alldifferent([P_1,P_2,P_3])
    C2.   alldifferent([P_3,P_4,P_5])
    C3. $(P_2{==}T_2) => (P_1 \neq T_3, P_3 \neq T_3)$
    C4. $(P_3 \neq T_3) \,\|\, (P_2 \neq T_4)$
    C5. $3 + (P_2{==}T_2) \leq 4$
    C6. $P_1.size + P_2.size + P_3.size \leq 12$
    C7. $P_3.size + P_4.size + P_5.size \leq 12$
    C8. $P_4 < P_5$

Figure 3: CSP Model for the problem of Figure 2

Restaurant table management is a real-time problem – neither the booker nor the floor manager can wait for an exhaustive search before replying to a customer. Therefore, we impose a time limit on each search, and if no seating plan is found within that limit, we report no solution. Even with the time limit, though, solvers can give widely varying results depending on the particular search heuristic used. Initial tests showed that search based on a single heuristic may solve some instances quickly, but can be too slow on others, exceeding the time limit. Different heuristics tried over the same set of instances showed different partitions between hard and easy instances. However, there were very few instances that none of the heuristics could solve.

Therefore, we devised a restart approach with multiple different ordering heuristics, and an increasing time limit for each set of restarts. This *multi-heuristic* algorithm (MH) was described in [6], where we demonstrated the benefit, in terms of efficiency and robustness, of the approach. The pseudocode for the algorithm is shown below.

```
while Solve(heuristic(i),limit) == false
    limit = Increase(i,limit)
    if  i == n then i = 1
    else  i == i + 1
```

Solve(.,.) takes heuristic *i* (composed of a variable and a value ordering), and applies standard search up to a time *limit*. If it finds a solution, or proves there is no solution, it returns *true*; otherwise it hits the time limit and returns *false*. *Increase(.,.)* is the time limit function and takes the form *Increase(i,limit)=limit*10 if i=n; limit otherwise*. MH thus tries each ordering in turn for a limited time, restarting the search after each one, and gradually increasing the time limit if no result was found. This is similar to the way iterative deepening [16] explores each branch to a certain depth, and then increases the depth limit, and is similar to randomized restarts, except we use different ordering heuristics. In total, we have 11 different variable ordering heuristics, including versions of min-size-domain and lexicographic, and including orders based on increasing and decreasing party size and start time. We have 3 different value orderings (increasing table size, decreasing table size, and lexicographic), giving a total of 33 different heuristic combinations.

Using this model configuration we are able to solve the static problem efficiently. Instances representing a full booking sheet of 200 covers can be solved in less than 0.5 seconds on average (examples will be shown in section 7). Note that the real problems are typically smaller than this, either because we build the plan incrementally, or when we react to changes, some diners have already started and cannot be moved.

5.   Flexibility and Optimisation

The previous section described a satisfaction problem: i.e. it does not consider optimisation, but simply returns the first allocation it finds, or reports failure. However, there are likely to be many possible seating plans, and some will be significantly better than others in terms of efficient use of the tables, and thus in their ability to accept future bookings. In this section we describe a measure to estimate the quality of a solution, and an algorithm which uses that measure to search for seating plans of increasing quality.

Ultimately, seating plans should be assessed by the final number of covers achieved. Therefore, whether we are in the booking phase or in the floor management phase, we should maintain a seating plan aimed at maximising the covers. Thus after each change, we should be searching for:

$$\text{argmax}_{\text{seating plan}} [current covers + expected future covers] \qquad (1)$$

0	1	2	3	4	5	6	7	8

$T_1[2]$	1		$P_1[3]$		4	3	2	1
$T_2[2]$	1				4	3	2	1
$T_3[3]$	8	7	6	5	4	3	2	1

(i)

0	1	2	3	4	5	6	7	8

$T_1[2]$	8	7	6	5	4	3	2	1
$T_2[2]$	8	7	6	5	4	3	2	1
$T_3[3]$	1		$P_1[3]$		4	3	2	1

(ii)

Figure 4: Flexibility maps for two possible allocations

As the number of *current covers* is known and constant, we focus on the *expected future covers*. We do not have well-founded distributions of the new requests we can expect, and so our measure of expected covers must be an approximation. Thus we introduce a heuristic measure, *flexibility*, and search for:

$$\text{argmax}_{\textit{seating plan}} \, [\textit{flexibility}] \qquad (2)$$

The flexibility measure is based on the number of usable start times for future requests. Let TB be the number of tables, and T be the time horizon discretised in 15-minute units. We superimpose a grid G of size TB×T over the seating plan. For each grid square (table, time-unit) in G that corresponds to an unoccupied slot we compute the number of time units available before the table becomes occupied again. Squares with numbers less then a standard dinner duration d are ignored, as they do not represent usable start times. We then compute flexibility as follows:

$$\textit{flexibility} = \Sigma_{\textit{tb} \in \textit{TB}, \, \textit{tu} \in T} \, (\, (G[\textit{tb},\textit{tu}] \geq d) \times \textit{size}(\textit{tb}) \,) \qquad (3)$$

The term $(G[\textit{tb},\textit{tu}] \geq d)$ takes value 1 when the pair $(\textit{tb},\textit{tu})$ represents a *usable start time*, and 0 otherwise, while $\textit{size}(\textit{tb})$ is the size of table $(\textit{tb})$.

As an illustration, consider Figure 4, which shows a restaurant with 3 tables: T_1 and T_2 have capacity 2, T_3 has capacity 3, and T_1 and T_2 can be joined to give a capacity of 4. The evening is divided into 8 time units. Party P_1 (size 3, start 1, end 4) has two possible allocations, shown in *(i)* and *(ii)*. The remaining grid cells show the number of time units available. If we assume the standard dinner duration is $d = 3$, then we count only squares with value at least 3, and we obtain: *flexibility(i)=(2x2)+(2x2)+(3x6)=26*, and *flexibility(ii)= (2x6)+(2x6)+(3x2)=30*, and thus plan (ii) would be preferred. Note that the values for T_3 are given a higher weight, since it can seat more customers.

For each problem instance, we then perform a branch-and-bound search, optimising for flexibility. Inside the search, we again apply the multi-heuristic approach. The benefit resulting from applying this optimisation criterion is illustrated in section 7 (Figures 9, 10, and 12).

6. Minimising Disruption

The constraint satisfaction and optimisation models described above do not consider the number of table reallocations from one plan to the next – their aim is to find any (improving) plan. During the floor management phase, however, too many changes cause confusion in the restaurant, making it difficult for staff to understand and evaluate each new solution. In particular, frequent changes in the table configurations will annoy both staff and customers. Therefore, the table management system should, when possible, try to maintain the stability of the plan, and should prefer new plans with few changes.

Therefore we extend the previous models, so that when changes occur, we search for new solutions in two phases: first, we search in the neighbourhood of the previous solution, placing a limit on the number of changes allowed; second, if no acceptable plan is found in the first phase, we allow all allocations to float, and we search for any new solution. The pseudocode is shown below.

```
solution = original
discrepancy = 0
while ( (timer < timeout_1) && (discrepancy < discrepancyMax) )
    if Solver.solve(CSP,MH,timeout_1,original,discrepancy) == true
        solution = getSolution()
        return solution
    else discrepancy += 1
if Solver.solve(CSP,MH,timeout_2,original,any) == true
    solution = getSolution()
return solution
```

The number of allowed changes from the *original* solution is represented by the variable *discrepancy*. The initial *discrepancy* limit is set to 0: i.e. we first check to see if the new event can be integrated into the original solution without any further changes. If not, the discrepancy limit is incremented until either a solution is found, or the limit reaches *discrepancyMax*. In the latter case, a final search is carried out for a new solution with no limit on the number of changes. The solve procedure is extended to include the discrepancy limit, which is posted as a constraint on the solution. A similar procedure is applied when searching for flexible solutions, which allows the user to trade-off stability for flexibility. Section 7 (Figure 12) will illustrate how this is performed.

7. The Integrated Table Management Adviser

The models and algorithms described in the previous three sections have been implemented using Ilog Solver 6.0. Access to the models is provided by a graphical user interface, which also presents other relevant information regarding the state of the restaurant or booking sheet, and allows the user (booker or floor manager) to

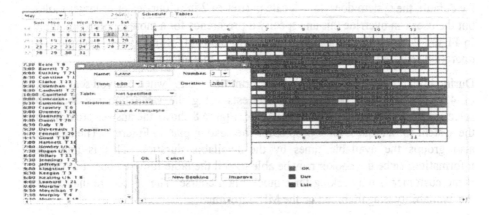

Figure 5: User interface, displaying a seating plan and a new booking request

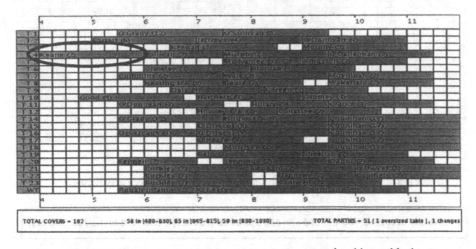

Figure 6: Seating plan with the new request accommodated into table 4

control the table allocation process, switching between manual operation, basic solving, optimising for flexibility, or maintaining stability.

A screen shot of the interface is shown in Figure 5, displaying one possible seating plan on one evening in May 2006. The list on the left side displays in alphabetical order the parties (with time, name and table) which are allocated on the plan. New booking requests are processed by editing a form, and selecting time, party size, and expected duration. The user has the option to specify or forbid a table for the new party; otherwise the system will use any suitable table.

Figure 6 represents the seating plan accommodating the new request (Keane). It also shows the total covers, the covers partitioned in 3 periods, the total parties, the number of parties seated at oversized tables, and the number of changes from the previous plan. Note that O'Grady at 5:30, Buckley at 6:00, O'Driscoll at 7:00 and Counihan at 9:30 are all seated at conjoined tables.

By default, the system does not allocate parties of 2 into four-seater or larger tables, but the user can override this and specify a preference for a more comfortable table. In Figure 7, party Keane has been moved to table 11, which is for 5 people. The operation required 3 changes from the previous table allocation.

During booking, availability requests are common – e.g. "when can you seat a party of 4?" The user can process such requests using the same booking form, by selecting "not specified" in the "Time" box. Figure 8 shows the answer provided by the system for a request for 4 people, for the seating plan in Figure 7. The message also groups the available times by the available duration. This is important information, since the booker may be able to sell the table for one hour at 7 o'clock if the customer is only asking for a quick main course. The procedure that checks the availability is again based on the MH algorithm.

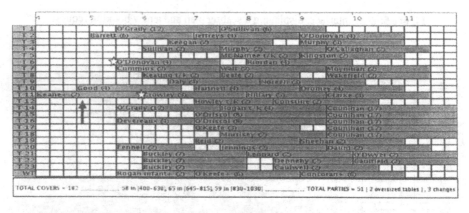

Figure 7: New seating plan after imposing a preference for party Keane

Availability over time: 400 430 500 530 600 930 1000 [200 hrs] — 630 [130 hrs] — 700 [100 hrs]

Figure 8: Message showing the availability for 4 people on the sheet of Figure 7

Figure 9 (top) shows a reallocation of the plan in Figure 7 that accommodates a new party Meane at 9:00 in table 8. Note that in this case the number of changes necessary to find a new plan is higher, i.e. the system performed a more complex operation. Figure 9 (bottom) represents a first step in a search for a more flexible allocation. The new plan has been obtained pressing the "Improve" button (Figure 5). Note that there has been only one change from the previous plan, with party Crowley (3 people at 6:00) moved from table 6 (6-seater) to table 9 (4-seater). The increase in the flexibility estimate is 16 (8 time units × 2 table size saved), which may allow an extra 2-hour dinner (8 time unit) for 2 people. The run time to obtain the change is 0.16 sec.

The user can repeat the improvement process to find more flexible seating plans. Figure 10 (top) shows the plan obtained after four iterations, and (bottom) the plan obtained unlocking party Keane from table 11 (and after three more iterations).

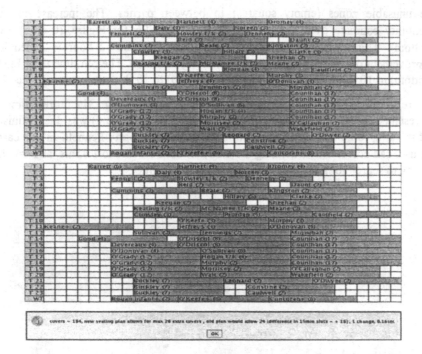

Figure 9: Adding party Meane *(top)*, first flexibility improvement *(bottom)*

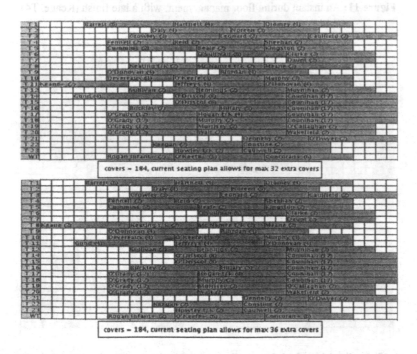

Figure 10: Improvement after several steps, with Keane fixed *(top)*, unfixed *(bottom)*

In both phases, we can observe the effect of our flexibility measure, which by increasing the number of usable start times makes better use of tables, and reduces

14

the unusable zones (empty squares) in between parties. The increase in the flexibility estimate over Figure 9 (top) is 68 and 96 for Figure 10 (top) and (bottom). This can be regarded as 3 and 5.5 times the (2 hour × 2 people) improvement obtained from the first step of Fig 9-bottom. The run time from Fig 9 (bottom) to 10 (top) was 8.1 sec, and from 10 (top) to 10 (bottom) was 1.01 sec.

Figure 11 shows an instant during the floor management phase. The current time is represented by the vertical line at 5.30pm. Party Keane (table 4) was due to finish, but is going to be late, creating a conflict with the next party Fennell. In this case, the user can edit Keane, extending the duration from 1.30hrs to 1.45hrs, and ask the system to search for a reallocation that avoids the conflict.

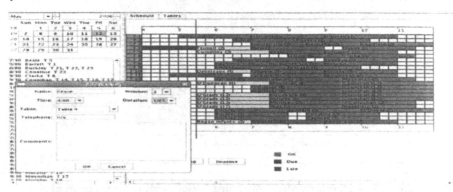

Figure 11: An instant during floor management, with a late finish (Keane, T4)

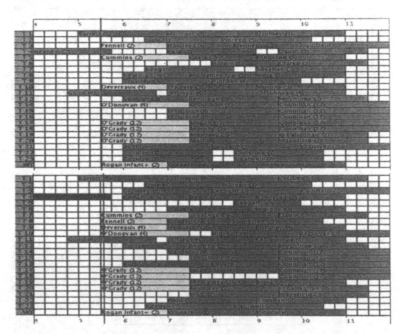

Figure 12: Reallocation after a late finish *(top)*, improvement after four iterations *(bottom)*

Figure 12 (top) represents a first reallocation, while on the bottom we see a seating plan after four improvement iterations. We can again observe the benefit of the improvement, with fewer unusable zones, and more possibilities to seat extra parties. The four iterations have improved the flexibility estimate by steps of 4, 5, 4, and 26, for a total of 39, or ~2.5 (2 hour × 2 people) dinners. The number of changes from the initial allocation was 2, 1, 3, and 36; the last iteration gave a large improvement but required a large change in the seating plan.

By default, the *timeout* for each improvement step is set to 10 seconds, partitioned in 7 seconds for search with limited discrepancy and 3 seconds for unlimited (or global) search. These limits are configurable by the user.

The research prototype software discussed above is currently being evaluated in the restaurant. The main aim of the evaluation is to determine whether constraint-based methods could support a practical restaurant management tool. Specifically, the evaluation will check that the software:

(i)   models the restaurant adequately;

(ii)   provides acceptable seating plans in reasonable time;

(iii)   can join and separate tables correctly;

(iv)   proposes flexible seating plans in reasonable time;

(v)   reports quickly whether or not a booking request can be accepted, and recommends sensible alternative times for a booking;

(vi)   provides useful advice when a seating plan has to be reconfigured.

If the evaluation is positive (and first indications are promising), then we will investigate commercial development.

8.   Conclusions and Future Work

In this paper we presented a constraint based solution for enhancing restaurant table management. We introduced the table management problem, describing the main issues concerning booking and floor management. We presented a basic constraint model, which can be used to solve the underlying static problem. We then described two enhancements, which (i) optimise a flexibility measure, and (ii) search for similar plans after a change occurs. The flexibility measure is based on a weighted count of the possible start times for new bookings, and is intended to allow more efficient use of resources. The search for similar solutions minimises the number of changes to the seating plan, and is intended to simplify floor management. We have described the integrated system, which allows a user to control table allocation, while receiving advice from the underlying models. The system has been implemented, and is currently undergoing trials in Eco restaurant.

Future work will focus on improving the flexibility measure, to take into account the expected distribution of demand. Monday evenings, for example, show a noticeably different pattern of dining from Friday evenings, and thus the system should tailor its advice accordingly. Our first approach will be to include weights in the flexibility measure, increasing the importance of availability at specific times. Should the current evaluation trial prove positive, we expect to begin a development phase. This will include redeveloping the constraint models to ensure they are suitable for the operating environment, and redeveloping the user-interface, based on the feedback from the evaluation.

Acknowledgements

This work is funded by Enterprise Ireland under grant number SC/2003/0081. We are grateful for the problem description, data and advice given by the Eco restaurant in Douglas, Cork. The user interface was developed by James Lupton, and supported by the Science Foundation Ireland Overhead Investment Plan, 2005-2006. Finally, we are grateful for the external liaison assistance of James Little at Cork Constraint Computation Centre.

References

1. www.eco.ie
2. Dechter, R. *Constraint Processing*, Morgan Kaufman, 2003.
3. Rossi, F., van Beek, P. and Walsh, T. (eds.), *Handbook of Constraint Programming*, Elsevier, (forthcoming) 2006
4. Gomes, C.P.; and Shmoys, D.B. "Approximations and Randomization to Boost CSP Techniques", *Annals of Operations Research*, 130:117-141, 2004
5. Gomes, C.P.; and Selman, B. "Algorithm portfolios", *Artificial Intelligence* 126(1-2):43-62, 2001
6. Vidotto, A.; Brown, K.N.; and Beck, J.C. "Robust Constraint Solving Using Multiple Heuristics", *Proceedings of the Sixteenth Irish Conference on Artificial Intelligence & Cognitive Science (AICS'05)*, 203-212, 2005
7. Régin, J.-C. "A Filtering Algorithm for Constraints of Difference in CSPs", *Proceedings AAAI-94*, pp 362–367, 1994.
8. Verfaillie, G.; and Schiex, T. "Solution Reuse in Dynamic Constraint Satisfaction Problems", *Proceedings AAAI-94*, pp307-312, 1994
9. Fowler, D.W.; and Brown, K.N. "Branching constraint satisfaction problems and Markov Decision Problems compared", *Annals of Operations Research*, 118(1-4):85-100, 2003
10. Bent, R.; and Van Hentenryck, P. "Regrets Only! Online Stochastic Optimization under Time Constraints", *Proceedings AAAI-04*, 2004
11. Ran, Y.; Roos, N.; and van den Herik, J. "Approaches to Find a Near-minimal Change Solution for Dynamic CSPs" *CPAIOR'02: Proceedings of the 4th International Workshop on Integration of AI and OR techniques in Constraint Programming for Combinatorial Optimisation Problems*, pp373-387, 2002
12. Petcu, A.; and Faltings, B. "Optimal solution stability in continuous-time optimization", *DCR-05: Proceedings of the 6th International Workshop on Distributed Constraint Reasoning*, pp207–221, 2005
13. Davenport, A.J.; Gefflot, C.; and Beck, J.C. "Slack-based Techniques for Robust Schedules", *Proceedings of the Sixth European Conference on Planning (ECP-2001)*, 2001
14. Hebrard, E.; Hnich, B.; and Walsh, T. "Robust Solutions for Constraint Satisfaction and Optimization", *Proceedings of the Sixteenth European Conference on Artificial Intelligence, ECAI-04*, 2004
15. Arkin, E.M.; and Silverberg, E.B. "Scheduling jobs with fixed start and end times", *Discrete Applied Mathematics*, 18:1-8, 1987
16. Korf, R. E. "Depth-first iterative deepening: an optimal admissible tree search", *Artificial Intelligence*, 27:97—109, 1985.

SESSION 1:

DATA MINING AND BAYESIAN NETWORKS

Use of Data Mining Techniques to Model Crime Scene Investigator Performance

Richard Adderley
Senior Partner
A E Solutions (BI)
11 Shireland Lane
Redditch
Worcestershire B97 6UB
RickAdderley@A-ESolutions.com

John Bond
Scientific Support Manager
Northamptonshire Police
Police Headquarters
Wootton Hall
Northampton NN4 0JQ
John.Bond@northants.pnn.police.uk

Michael Townsley
Senior Research Fellow
Jill Dando Institute
University Colege London
2nd Floor, Brook House
2 – 16 Torrington Place
London WC1E 7HN
M.Townsley@ucl.ac.uk

Abstract

This paper examines how data mining techniques can assist the monitoring of Crime Scene Investigator performance. The findings show that Investigators can be placed in one of four groups according to their ability to recover DNA and fingerprints from crime scenes. They also show that their ability to predict which crime scenes will yield the best opportunity of recovering forensic samples has no correlation to their actual ability to recover those samples.

1. Introduction

The importance of forensic intelligence (principally fingerprint or DNA identifications) as a standard forensic technique for the investigation and detection of a wide spectrum of crime types from volume crime (burglary dwelling, burglary of commercial buildings, theft of motor vehicles and theft from motor vehicles) to serious and major crime such as rape and murder is now well established. Some ten years ago an evaluation of the UK police service's use of forensic science revealed a lack of awareness by police officers of forensic science and there is a wide variation between forces in the number of Crime Scene Investigators (CSIs) relative to the numbers of police officers or the number of reported crimes [29]. In the same year, a joint report by the Association of Chief Police Officers and the UK Forensic Science Service [4] noted that, for most UK police forces with a limited number of CSIs, a 'selective attendance' policy is most appropriate. The report also noted that performance indicators for CSIs were almost exclusively activity based (i.e. the number of scenes visited) and not outcome based (i.e. did the scene visit assist in the detection of the crime). Despite this, little actual research has been carried out to examine the role played by the CSIs in the forensic process and how this resource can be best utilised.

Notwithstanding the need for proper control over CSI activity, there is still a wide variation amongst UK police forces in terms of the percentage of volume crime attended by a CSI. Only six of the forty-three UK police forces attend more than 95 percent of reported domestic burglaries and, for theft of motor vehicle offences, only nineteen forces attend more than half of the reported offences. One force attended less than three percent of reported theft of motor vehicle incidents [23] although tackling acquisitive crime is a high priority for both the UK Home Office and police forces [17].

More recent work [30] has considered the management of police forensic resources, CSIs, in the context of the relationship between management practice and service delivery and noted that *'a number of forces concede that current scientific support performance indicators need further development'*. He also recommended that police forces should consider the relationship between the workload and performance of individual CSIs and also the effect that this relationship has on overall performance. The introduction of computer based systems for tracking CSI activity was viewed as a step forward to better understanding this relationship.

In this paper we consider a novel approach to assessing CSI performance. The main aim of which was to ascertain whether CSI performance could be quantified in a systematic way using a computer based unsupervised learning algorithm. The secondary aim was to ascertain the feasibility of automating the process.

2. Current CSI Activity and Assessment

All Northamptonshire Police CSIs are deployed centrally which is unusual as many UK forces direct them from an Area base. This enables the most effective resource (in terms of location, skill etc.) to be deployed for the task in hand. Between the hours of 0800 and 1700 Monday to Friday personnel are deployed from staff within the CSI FHQ base but out of those hours, deployment is direct from the Incident Management Centre (IMC) at Force Headquarters (FHQ). A white board at FHQ gives a 'snapshot' of all CSI deployment, current and outstanding jobs at any point in time. Due to the process of central deployment, CSIs cannot choose to attend particular crimes which means that the data will not contain groups of crimes that have been attended by an individual due to his/her preferences.

Northamptonshire Police have three levels of CSI which are equivalent to: -

Level 1 - Basic Volume Crime Scene Examiner. This person has received sufficient training within the force to enable the proficient recovery of forensics at volume crime scenes such as burglary dwelling, burglary of commercial buildings, theft of motor vehicles and theft from motor vehicles.

Level 2 - Volume Crime Scene Examiner who, in addition to Level 1, has passed the national Foundation Course in Crime Scene Examination at the training centre in Durham.

Level 3 - CSI who, in addition to Level 2, has passed or is working towards the Diploma in Crime Examination Skills and has passed the conversion course for the crime scene examination of major crime at the training centre in Durham. Major crime can be considered as murder, rape, serious assaults etc.

All Levels described above receive on-going training which is delivered within the force by the Senior Training CSI and attend external courses.

Each time that an individual CSI attends a crime scene it is recorded as an "activity" on the Trak-X computer system and is allocated a unique reference number. Trak-X is a computer system that has been designed for use within Northamptonshire Police to record and monitor crime scene activities. There can be many activities associated to a single crime meaning that a single CSI can attend many times, several CSIs can attend the same scene or a combination of the two. An activity record comprises the following: -

- Time, day and date attended
- Time, day and date completed
- Forensic samples retrieved
- Results of forensic examination

On returning to their base the CSIs submit the recovered samples, which are grouped by 'type', for example, fingerprints, DNA and footwear marks, for analysis. Footwear and fingerprints are examined by force experts and DNA is submitted to the Forensic Science Department for profiling. The analysis results, when known, are entered onto Trak-X.

In Northamptonshire Police, CSIs are currently assessed using Trak-X data as a means to analyse their activity. They do not have to complete additional forms or paperwork as their performance data is derived as a consequence of them entering details of their activities onto the computer system. Each CSI has, on a monthly basis, a one-page sheet that shows in graphical form their performance for key evidence types (DNA, fingerprints and footwear) against the rest of the staff. This 'performance'; includes not only recovery but also success in terms of identifications and detections. It is possible to identify good practice where one individual is performing to a consistently high standard. All of this is achieved by conducting SQL type queries and manually comparing the results which is a time consuming process.

3. Methodology

Data mining encompasses a range of techniques each designed to interpret data to provide additional information to assist in its understanding. This reveals insights into a range of functions in an organisation which can assist in the areas of decision support, prediction, resource handling, forecasting and estimation. The techniques trawl systems which often contain voluminous amounts of data items which has limited value and difficult to examine in its original format, finding hidden information producing benefits to the organisation.

Data mining embraces a range of techniques such as neural networks, statistics, rule induction, data visualisation etc., examining data within current computer systems with a view to identifying operational issues by uncovering useful, previously unknown information. Today computers are pervasive in all areas of organisational activities which has enabled the recording of all workplace operations making it possible not only to deal with record keeping and information for performance management but also, via the analysis of those operations, to improve operational performance. This has led to the development of the area of computing known as Data Mining [3].

The majority of organisations record and store large amounts of data in a variety of databases and often there is restricted access to these data. In order to glean information, a user would ask a specific range of questions, for example; who is the most prolific offender? The ironic reality of the information age is that we are overwhelmed with information. Pertinent research questions are not articulated because the task of comprehending the full dimensions of an information system is too large to sensibly work through the myriad of possibilities. Data mining can provide methods to identify the questions to be asked in order to gain a greater understanding of the data and analytical processes [21].

By applying the techniques identified above, organisations have utilised their data relating to tasks such as identifying customers' purchasing behaviour, financial trends, anticipate aspects of demand, reduce and detect fraud etc. For example, by employing such techniques J Sainsbury [9] is said to have saved £500,000 a year by analysing patterns of shoplifting within its stores.

Although the practice of mining data has been performed for a number of years the term data mining has only recently received credibility within the business community. The Gartner Group analysts' [25] estimate that within targeted marketing, the number of companies using data mining will increase from the current level of five percent to eighty percent within 10 years. Currently, little use has been made of data mining techniques within policing, the majority of police computer systems do not utilise such technology. Early attempts to introduce data mining concentrated on visualisation techniques and expert systems [14, 18] with varying degrees of success but have never transferred into main stream policing. There is, however, great scope for these techniques to be used [20, 22].

3.1 CRISP-DM

The CRoss Industry Standard Process for Data Mining (CRISP-DM), Figure 1 below, has been the data mining cyclic methodology used within the Northamptonshire Police project as it was designed by a consortium of businesses to be used with any data mining tool and within all business areas [7]. It is also reported to be the most widely used methodology [12] and is recommended for use in crime prevention and detection [22].

This study was undertaken using the commercially available data mining workbench software tool, Insightful Miner. It is a tool that uses a graphical user interface to retrieve, manipulate, model and present data. Results are achieved by placing nodes onto a worksheet to build the required business process and passing the data through that process. Figure 2 below illustrates the Insightful Miner tool kit (www.insightful.com).

Initially, it is important to have a clear understanding of the business domain in order to understand the operational analytical processes [28], the problems that are to be surmounted, the opportunities that may be realised and to assess the availability of data. Exploring and preparing the data, although time consuming[26], is a crucial stage in the cycle. New fields may be derived from one or more existing fields, missing and boundary values identified and processed, relationships between fields and records identified form some of the pre-processing tasks that assist in cleaning the data prior to the mining process. Once data has been prepared for mining, the modelling stage can begin. Choosing and developing models involve domain knowledge [6, 8] the results of which are validated against known or expected results and either deployed or refined. This is an iterative process as the results produced by the techniques alone may not provide the desired business advantage.

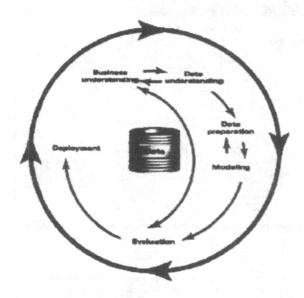

Figure 1. CRISP-DM modelling Cycle

4. Data Manipulation

Northamptonshire Police record all of their crime into an ORACLE based relational database which was written and developed in-house. The Scientific Support Department use the Trak-X computer system to record and manage all scientific support functions. Trak-X was designed in-house and developed by an external software supplier.

Crime and forensic data between 1st January 2000 and 19th July 2005 was used for this study. The data sets were merged to produce 47,730 individual activity records relating to volume crime scenes; burglary dwelling, burglary in commercial buildings, theft of and theft from motor vehicles. These four offence types were chosen for a number of reasons as they:

- Offer potential to examine a large number of crime scenes for forensic material.

- Are key offences for most police forces and also the UK Home Office [17]

- Are typically 'recidivist' offences.

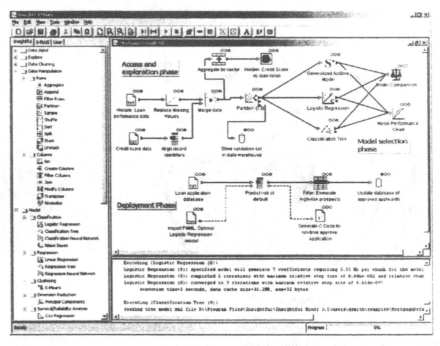

Figure 2. Insightful Miner Data Mining Workbench Tool

The data to analyse should comprise only of records that relate to crime scene investigation and not to administrative tasks or erroneous data. Having discussed the data with CSI supervisors it has been ascertained the following three activity sets should be removed: -

1. Activities that take in excess of five hundred minutes to complete. As the data set comprises volume crime, it was suggested that the long activity times are as a result of input error.

2. Activities that take less than 6 minutes to complete. This short amount of time at the scene is normally as a result of the victim not being present and the CSI completing a calling card. The card is left at the scene to await a telephone call from the victim to arrange for a suitable time to re-attend.

3. Activities that relate to CSIs who are no longer employed.

Having removed the three data sets described above, 31,470 records remained for analysis.

When fingerprints are recovered from the crime scene they are sent to the Fingerprint Bureau for examination. The experts classify the results into one of four groups: -

1. Insufficient: Either the quality of fingerprint is not good enough or there is not enough of the actual print to be classified.

2. Eliminated: Those fingerprints that can be attributed to people who have legitimate access to the crime scene.

3. Matched: Fingerprints that are matched to a person who is recorded in the national database, Ident1.

4. Outstanding: Fingerprints that are of sufficient quality to be classified but have not been matched to a person who is recorded in Ident1.

For the purpose of this study two new flag fields were created. One field identifying the fact that a fingerprint has been recovered by combining the four groups identified above and the other identifying the fact that the recovery has resulted in a match. Both fields contain a "1" meaning positive and a "0" meaning negative.

A similar process was undertaken regarding the recovery of DNA samples. They were classified into a group containing four categories each relating to its capability to identify an individual who is recorded on the National DNA Database.:-

1. Match: The sample uniquely identifies an individual person who is recorded on the database.

2. FullProfile: A good sample that has been profiled and stored on the database but does not currently match and individual person.

3. PartialProfile: The sample collected from the scene contains DNA from more than one person which cannot be separated.

4.   Insufficient: There is not enough of the sample to be classified.

A further two flag fields were created identifying the fact that DNA has been recovered and that it has matched an individual as discussed above.

Two fields were created that identified the mean number of DNA samples and fingerprints recovered per activity per CSI.

It was decided that, as time was a continuous variable, the time in minutes that a CSI spent at the crime scene would be placed in bands. The bands were established in consultation with the CSI supervisors and were 0-15, 16,30, 31-45, 46-60, 61-75 and Long (in excess of 76 minutes).

A K-Means unsupervised learning clustering algorithm [13] was used to model the data. Unsupervised learning is a method of machine learning where a model is fit to observations. It is distinguished from supervised learning by the fact that there is no *a priori* output. In unsupervised learning or clustering there is no explicit teacher, and the system forms clusters or natural groupings of the input patterns. Natural is always defined explicitly or implicitly in the clustering system itself. Unsupervised learning then typically treats input objects as a set of random variables 10,31].

5. Results

The time bands, described above, were used to analyse the amount of time that a CSI took at the crime scene to recover forensic samples (DNA and fingerprints).

Figure 3 below illustrates that, for the four volume crimes where a forensic sample was recovered, most of the scenes are completed within the first time band of 0-15 minutes. Figure 4 illustrates, where a forensic sample is not recovered, three of the four crime types are completed in the next time band of 16-30 minutes, with theft from motor vehicle offences remaining in the 0-15 minute band. This indicated that scenes where forensics are recovered are completed in a shorter time period. This appeared counter intuitive but a reason was suggested by the CSI supervisors. Where forensics are found early in the scene examination, possibly at the point of entry, the victim tends to leave the CSI to recover the sample(s) but where they are not so evident the CSI interacts with the victim not only in examining the scene but also performing a reassurance role.

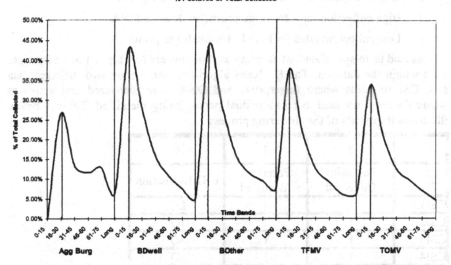

Figure 3. Time spent at the crime scene where forensic samples were recovered.

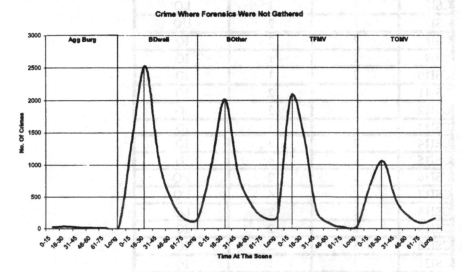

Figure 4. Time spent at the crime scene where forensic samples were not recovered.

The first analysis considered the collection rates of two types of forensic data (DNA and fingerprints). It was speculated that there could be four archetypal CSIs: -

1. High collection rates for both DNA and fingerprints

2.   High collection rates for DNA but not for fingerprints

3.   High collection rates for fingerprints, but low for DNA

4.   Low collection rates for both DNA and fingerprints

This lead us to speculate that as many as four clusters (or 'types') of CSIs might exist within the data set. The K-Means algorithm was run on two different data sets, CSI activities where fingerprints and DNA were recovered and activities where the recovery lead to an individual person being identified. Table 1 below illustrates the results of the clustering process.

1	2	3	4
CSI	Forensics Collected	Forensics Identified	CS1 Evaluation
CSI1	1	1	LQ
CSI2	1	2	IQ
CSI3	1	1	IQ
CSI4	1	1	IQ
CSI5	1	2	IQ
CSI6	1	1	LQ
CSI7	1	2	UQ
CSI8	2	2	IQ
CSI9	2	1	IQ
CSI10	2	1	IQ
CSI11	2	2	IQ
CSI12	2	2	IQ
CSI13	2	1	IQ
CSI14	2	3	IQ
CSI15	2	4	IQ
CSI16	2	2	UQ
CSI17	2	4	UQ
CSI18	2	2	LQ
CSI19	2	2	IQ
CSI20	3	2	IQ
CSI21	3	1	IQ
CSI22	3	3	IQ
CSI23	3	3	IQ
CSI24	4	3	IQ
CSI25	4	3	LQ
CSI26	4	3	UQ
CSI27	4	2	LQ
CSI28	4	3	LQ

CSI29	4	2	IQ
CSI30	4	3	IQ
CSI31	4	3	UQ
CSI32	4	4	IQ

Table 1. Results of k-means modelling and CSI personal predictions

Column 1 represents the individual CSI. Column 2 is the cluster relating to the activities where forensics have been recovered. Column 3 is the cluster where the recovered forensics has led to an individual person being identified. Column 4 is discussed below.

5.1 CSI Personal Predictions

Columns 2 and 3 of Table 1 above illustrate an individual CSI's capability to recover DNA and fingerprints from a crime scene together with their success at the sample resulting in a match. A question could be asked, "If CSIs are directed to a crime scene would they anticipate (predict) that they would recover a forensic sample, if so, would this influence the actual recovery?" To answer this question Every Northamptonshire Police CSI was given a list of 50 randomly selected crimes. The list contained the following variables:-

Sub Division, Beat, Sub Beat, Offence, Street, District and Town.

They were asked to use their experience to suggest whether a forensic sample would be recovered from the crime scene based on the above information. There was a ranking used; 1 to 10, 1 being uncertain and 10 being certain. All 1 to 5 responses were encoded as NO and 6 to 10 as YES. The results of actual recovery for each scene were known but not available to the CSIs.

The results of the questionnaires were averaged and the accuracy of human experts predicting forensic recovery was thirty-nine percent which rose to a maximum of forty-one percent when additional modus operandi (MO) fields were presented.

These results were placed into quartiles with a view to ascertaining whether those who were good at recovering samples and subsequent matches were also good at predicting whether a sample would be recovered. Column 4 of Table 1 illustrates the quartile ranges relating to their predictive capabilities, the upper quartile (UQ) being those whose predictive abilities were best, the lower quartile (LQ) were considered the worst and the remainder were categorised in the inter quartile (IQ) range. The table illustrates that there is no relationship between a CSI's predictive capability and their actual ability to recover forensic samples.

We explored, for all Northamptonshire CSIs, the volume of collections and matches for DNA and fingerprints. The ratio of these two amounts, at the individual level, can be thought of as a matching efficiency. If two CSIs produce the same volume of matches, yet have very different collection rates, the one with the lower collection rate is more efficient.

We found that the volume of DNA matches was proportional to the volume of DNA collections, i.e. the matching efficiency did not influence the number of matches. This implies that, all things being equal, it appears that encouraging higher DNA collection rates will not dilute the matching rates for DNA samples.

In terms of fingerprint performance, the results were equivocal. Overall, the relationship between the volume of fingerprints collected and those ultimately matched appears to be roughly consistent but not positively correlated. Like DNA performance, we would expect the range of collection rates to differ according to matching efficiency. It does not change, indicating that both collection-prolific and collection-adverse CSIs exist at all levels of matching efficiency.

6. Conclusion

The results of the clustering give a clear and objective rationale for staff development. The process seems relatively clear for DNA, but further work is required for applying the results for fingerprints. It would seem that CSIs would benefit from being supported to collect more DNA as matching rates do not appear to be effected by the volume collected (or in the least determine how certain CSIs manage to consistently collect more DNA than their colleagues). That is, there is no dilution impact associated with high collection rates.

Summarising the results for the fingerprint and DNA clusters, it appears that separate approaches to staff development may be required for DNA and fingerprints. The 'low DNA low fingerprint' CSIs are characterised by low collection rates for both types of forensic data. Their development could be tailored around joint deployment with a CSI in any other cluster, i.e. those with a high collection rate for at least one forensic data type. Those CSIs in a cluster typified by deficient collection of one forensic type would benefit from time spent with CSIs from clusters with high collection rates of that forensic type; and so on.

Speculatively we might say DNA and fingerprints differ in that the provenance of the former is usually obvious to the victim (for example, blood or saliva in an unusual location) whereas this is not the case with the latter. That is, CSIs do not have the capacity to say whether recovered fingerprints belong to someone with legitimate access (only an expert can do that) but they can easily find out whether (for example) the cigarette end is the victim's or alien to the scene.

It should be noted that CSIs in Northamptonshire have no discretion over which scenes they attend. This means that allocation to a 'good' cluster could not be the result of hand picking easy jobs. Also, the definition of 'high' and 'low' here is relative. We are far from certain whether a 'high' collection rate would be considered high nationally or indeed if a Northamptonshire low collection rate would be considered inferior if considered in the context of a larger sample of CSIs.

The aim of this study was to ascertain whether data mining techniques could be used to model crime scene investigator performance. This paper suggests that such CSI performance modelling is a viable option for managers.

References

1. Adderley, R. & Musgrove, P.B. (2002). Modus operandi modelling of group offending: a data mining case study. *The International Journal of Police Science and Management 5 (4)* (pp. 165-176)

2. Adderley, R. (2002). The use of data mining techniques in active crime fighting, Proceedings: International conference on computer, communication and control technologies and the 9th international conference on information systems analysis and synthesis, 1001, 11 July – 1 August 1001. (Orlando): CCCT and ISAS, (pp. 156-161).

3. Adriaans, P., & Zantinge, D. (1996). *Data Mining*, New York, Addison-Wesley.

4. Association of Chief Police Officers & Forensic Science Service. (1996) *Using Forensic Science Effectively*. London: ACPO.

5. Bishop, C. M., (1995). *Neural Networks for Pattern Recognition*, Oxford University Press, Oxford.

6. Brachman, R., J., Anand, T. (1996). 'The Process of Knowledge Discovery in Databases', In: Advances in Knowledge Discovery and Data Mining, Usama M. Fayyad, et al., *American* Association for Artificial Intelligence, AAAI Press, California.

7. Chapman, P., Clinton, J., Kerber, R., Khabaza, T., Reinhertz, T., Shearer, C., Wirth, R. (2000). CRISP-DM 1.0 Step-by-step data mining guide, USA: SPSS Inc. CRISPWP-0800.

8. Chen, H., Chung, W., Xu, J.J., Qin, G. W. Y., Chau, M. (1004). Crime data mining: a general framework and some examples. *COMPUTER, 17(4)* (pp. 50-56).

9. Computing (1996). *Mine, all Mine, Computing* 10th October 1996.

10. Duda, R.O., Hart, P.E. (1971). *Pattern Analysis and Scene Analysis*, New York; John Wiley.

11. Duda, R. O., Hart, P. E., Stork., D. G. (2000). *Pattern Classification*. John Wiley & Sons Inc, 1000.

12. Giraud-Carrier, C., Povel, O. (2001). Characterising data mining software. *Journal of Intelligent Data Analysis. 7(1)* (pp. 181-191).

13. Hartigan, J. A., Wong, M. A., (1979). A k-means clustering algorithm. *Appl. Stat.* 18, (pp. 100-108).

14. Haughton, E., (1991). Digging for Gold. *Computing*, 10th January 1994 (pp. 10-11).

15. Her Majesty's Inspectorate of Constabulary. (2000). *Under the Microscope*. London: ACPO.

16. Her Majesty's Inspectorate of Constabulary. (2002). *Under the Microscope Refocused*. London: ACPO.

17. Home Office (2004). *National Policing Plan 1005-1008*, Home Office, UK.

18. House, J. C. (1996). Towards a Practical Application of Offender Profiling: The RNC's *Criminal Suspect Prioritization System*, Investigative Psychology Conference, Liverpool University.

19. Langley, P., Sage, S. (1994). Induction of selective Bayesian classifiers, Proceedings *10th Conference on Uncertainty in Artificial Intelligence*, Seattle, WA; Morgan Kaufmann (pp. 119-406).

20. McCue, C., Stone, E. S., Gooch, T, P. (2001). Data mining and value-added analysis: more science, less fiction. Submitted to *FBI Law Enforcement Bulletin*.

21. Meltzer, M. (2004). Using data mining on the road to successful BI, Part 1, *Data Mining Direct Special Report* [on line], 11st September 2004. Available from: http://www.dmreview.com/editorial/newsletter_ more.cfm?nl=bireport. [Accessed 1nd May 2005].

22. Mena, J. (2002). Investigative data mining for security and criminal detection. Burlingto MA, Elsevier Science.

23. Police Standards Unit. (2005). *Forensic Performance Monitors*, London: Home Office.

24. Quinlan J, R,. (1996). Bagging, boosting, and C4.5 Proceedings *11th National Conference on Artificial Intelligence*, August 4 - 8. Portland USA.

25. SAS (2000), Data Mining Home Page, <http://www.sas.com/software/data_mining,>, (accessed on 5th June 2000)

26. Sherman, R. (2005). Data integration advisor: set the stage with data preparation, *DM Review*, February 1005.

27. Swingler, K. (1996). *Applying NeuralNnetworks; A Practical Guide*. San Francisco: Morgan Kaufman

28. Thomsen, E. (1998). Presentation: *Very Large Data Bases / Data Mining Summit*, Beverly Hills, California.

29. Tilley N, Ford A. (1996). Forensic science and criminal investigation. *Crime Detection and Prevention Paper 71*, London: Home Office.

30. Williams, S. R. (2004). The Management Of Crime Scene Examination In Relation To The Investigation Of Burglary And Vehicle Crime. Home Office: London.

31. Wikipedia (2006). *Definition of unsupervised learning*. http://en.wikipedia.org/wiki/Unsupervised_learning accessed 15th May 1006.

Analyzing Collaborative Problem Solving with Bayesian Networks

Rafael Duque, Crescencio Bravo, Carmen Lacave

Department of Information Systems and Technologies
School of Computer Engineering
University of Castilla – La Mancha
Paseo de la Universidad 4, 13071 Ciudad Real (Spain)
{Rafael.Duque, Crescencio.Bravo, Carmen.Lacave}@uclm.es

Abstract. Some learning theories emphasize the benefits of group work and shared knowledge acquisition in the learning processes. The Computer-Supported Collaborative Learning (CSCL) systems are used to support collaborative learning and knowledge building, making communication tools, shared workspaces, and automatic analysis tools available to users. In this article we describe a Bayesian network automatically built from a database of analysis indicators qualifying the individual work, the group work, and the solutions built in a CSCL environment that supports a problem solving approach. This network models the relationships between the indicators that represent both the collaborative work process and the problem solution.

Keywords. CSCL, Bayesian Networks, Machine Learning, Collaboration and Interaction Analysis, Solution Analysis

1 Introduction

The social dimension of learning has been studied since the 1920s, when Soviet psychologists [17] highlighted the benefits of the process of knowledge building in a group. According to this approach, a set of learners is expected to obtain common learning aims through a process of discussion that leads to knowledge building. The constructivist theories [9] state that it is the learner who must build new knowledge through experimentation, the search for new information, and the application of concepts and experiences already acquired, instead of being a passive receiver of knowledge from the teacher.

An approach of learning by problem solving nicely fits with these theories. However, the evaluation and study of these learning processes is not trivial. It is required to define and compute analysis indicators [7] that show the way in which the learners collaborate, that characterize the process of finding solutions to problems, and that measure the quality of these solutions. Moreover, in the context in which teaching traditionally occurs, it is necessary to take into account the difficulty of calculating such analysis indicators and of presenting them to the learners, since a totally customized support is needed for each learner and group.

In this situation the Computer-Supported Collaborative Learning (CSCL) systems are used to support collaborative learning and knowledge building, providing communication tools, shared workspaces where documents and artefacts can be manipulated, and tools to carry out analysis and automatic evaluation of the users (teachers, learners and evaluators). Sometimes, it is the teacher who measures the group performance; whilst at other times, an external person plays the role of evaluator and evaluates the group work. The CSCL systems allow the storage of the interactions between the learners and the system in structured repositories. The analysis of these data can facilitate an evaluation of the collaboration between the group members as well as of the problem solution, and a study about the influence of the collaboration process on the solution built by the learners.

This article approaches the analysis of the way in which a group of learners collaborate to solve design problems and how this collaboration influences the search for and the building of solutions. This problem solving process is studied taking a specific CSCL environment as a reference. This environment, called DomoSim-TPC [2], is used for the learning of Domotics. Domotics is also known as house automation or intelligent building design. The problems to be solved in Domotics consist of the design of automation services in a house or building. In order to model and analyze this process of collaboration and solution building a Bayesian network is used to follow a probabilistic approach. Bayesian networks are a very useful tool, because they do not only allow evaluators to obtain predictive models, but they also provide information about the relations between the analysis indicators. In so doing, evaluators (and/or teachers) get a better understanding of the collaborative problem solving.

In the next section, some studies that have used Bayesian networks to model the learner's knowledge in some subject matters and to represent the learner's behaviour in some intelligent tutoring systems are described. The DomoSim-TPC system and the variables used as analysis indicators of the group work, the individual work and the solution are briefly described in Section 3. Section 4 discusses the Bayesian network generated from a data set for the DomoSim-TPC analysis indicators. The results obtained are analyzed and interpreted in Section 5. Finally, some conclusions are drawn and some lines of future work are proposed (Section 6).

2 Bayesian networks in teaching and learning

Bayesian networks [13] are defined by an acyclic directed graph where the nodes represent random variables which take values that, a priori, are not known with certainty. The arcs define causal influences between these variables. The conditional probability of each variable (node) with respect to its parent nodes has to be specified in the arcs.

Nowadays, this way of dealing with uncertainty is applied with increasing interest in the field of education. Some works have used Bayesian networks to model the learner's knowledge, which is estimated by means of test answers [4, 11, 16]. By so doing, it is possible to adapt the tests to the learners according to their levels of knowledge.

Bayesian networks are also used to study the relationships between the variables that describe the learner's efficiency when using an intelligent tutoring system (correct answers, help needed, response time, etc.) and the variables that make reference to the perceptions or personal behaviour of the learner [1] obtained as a result of the carrying out of surveys. This way, the learner's behaviour can be inferred and characterized using the data registered during the work with the intelligent tutoring system.

Some authors propose the use of computational methods as useful techniques for the analysis of collaborative processes. It is not common to find Bayesian networks amongst these techniques in spite of their usefulness in the field of Education. Studies undertaken in order to analyze collaborative processes are usually based on the Hidden Markov Models [15], the Decision Trees [5], the Petri Nets [10] and the Plan Recognition [14].

Next, our approach to tackling the evaluation of design problem solutions in CSCL systems using Bayesian networks is presented. In order to solve them, these problems require the interactive building of a design according to the problem objectives, and are therefore more complex than the problems solved by means of a test. The resolution of these problems is carried out by means of group work, since it is a common situation in the professional sphere and of great interest in the area of education as was mentioned in Section 1. We will analyze how behaviours and attitudes of group work influence the solutions to the problems proposed.

3 Collaborative problem solving in DomoSim-TPC

In order to define a probabilistic graphical model that represents the process of collaborative problem solving and the characteristics of the solutions to the problems we took DomoSim-TPC [2] as a frame of reference. DomoSim-TPC is a CSCL environment that supports constructivist learning. With this environment the learners work in groups to solve design problems by using collaborative modelling and simulation tools. Fig. 1 shows an example of such solutions. A problem solution is made up of a set of interconnected objects that represent automation operators. This object model is built on the plan of a house. For each problem the teacher defines some requirements and constraints. The students are required to build a model combining a set of receivers, actuators and control systems (see Fig. 1) in order to build a design (solution) according to the problem specifications.

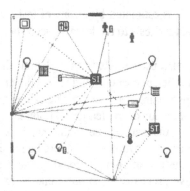

Fig. 1. An example of a domotical design (solution to a problem) with DomoSim-TPC.

DomoSim-TPC includes an analysis tool that allows the evaluators (and teachers) to calculate some analysis indicators. An analysis indicator gives information about the quality of the individual activity, the mode of collaboration or the quality of the collaborative product [7]. The analysis tool provides three sets of analysis indicators to qualify the work process and the solutions built [3]. The indicators are discrete variables that take value (in most of the cases) in the set {VL:Very low; L:Low; I:Intermediate; H:High; VH:Very high}. Fig. 2 shows the user interface of this tool. The evaluator can choose among different types of analyses (process or product, group or individual), types of variables (quantitative or qualitative), and representations (table or graph). The figure shows the values of some indicators in a bar diagram. This interface provides teachers and evaluators with an intuitive representation of the group and individual performance and of the solution indicators. Indicators are represented with different colours according to the information dimension they show.

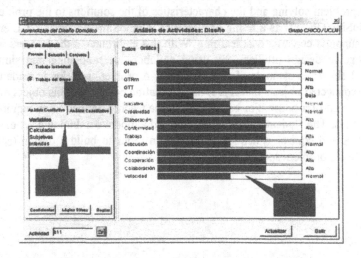

Fig. 2. The analysis tool of DomoSim-TPC (the user interface is in Spanish).

The analysis indicators considered in DomoSim-TPC belong to three dimensions [3]: group work, individual work and solution.

- Group work dimension: This represents the way in which the group worked in the problem solving. The indicators belonging to this dimension are the following:
    - *Communication*: This indicates the degree of discussion by means of message exchange between the group members.
    - *Work*: This refers to the amount of effort made by the group towards the resolution of the problem. It is measured counting the number of interactions of the group/user with the system.
    - *Velocity*: This is the speed of the group in developing its work.
    - *Willingness_Experimentation*: This evaluates the attitude of the group in the experimentation (simulation) tasks.
    - *Coordination*: This represents the degree of communication and interaction for the arrangement of the activities among the learners.
    - *Collaboration*: This gives an indication of the collaborative attitude of the group in the realization of the tasks.
- Individual work dimension: This dimension gives information about the work of the learners at individual level. The indicators identified are the following:
    - *Modelling*: This represents the degree of individual modelling work, i.e., the work specifically related to the building of the model (design) that solves the problem.
    - *Work_User*: This is the amount of effort made by the learner in the collaboration and the problem solving.
    - *Speed*: This is the speed of the learner in developing his/her work.
    - *Attitude*: This estimates the willingness of the learner as regards the successful achievement of the tasks, thus enhancing the group work.
    - *Discussion*: This is the importance given at individual level to the interchange of ideas and discussion.
    - *Participation*: This indicates the degree of participation in the development of the tasks.
- Solution dimension: This includes a set of indicators that characterize and qualify the solution built by the learners as a solution for the problem outlined to them. These indicators are the following:
    - *Experimentability*: This is an evaluation of the degree of experimentability of the model (number of hypotheses proposed, of simulation cases defined, etc.).
    - *Well_Formed*: This indicator measures whether the solution is built according to the building rules of the domain (syntax and semantics).
    - *Validity*: This variable represents the degree to which a solution verifies the problem constraints.
    - *Difficulty*: This is an indication of the solution difficulty, calculated using the complexity and size attributes of the problem.
    - *Cost*: This quantifies the cost of the design (solution); the greater number of objects in the solution, the higher cost the designed installation will have.

- *Accuracy*: This assesses whether the solution solves the problem, satisfying its objectives.
- *Quality*: This is a general indicator that gives an indication of the solution quality, agglutinating the rest of the indicators.

These variables are independent of a particular domain, so they can be applicable to other systems.

4 A Bayesian network to model collaborative work

The first objective of our work has been to derive a Bayesian network from a database containing a set of values for the indicators described in Section 3. This data was obtained during some problem solving activities. In these activities Secondary Education students from two different centres used DomoSim-TPC to solve five problems. These students were randomly organized in groups. The teacher proposed problems of increasing complexity. The problems required designs of automation services according to a set of specifications to be made. The analysis indicators were computed for all the activities by the analysis tool of DomoSim-TPC from the log of interactions.

The Elvira environment [8] was used to derive a Bayesian network from the data collected. This environment provides some automatic methods for building Bayesian networks from data. We chose the K2 search algorithm [6]. This algorithm considers the order of the input variables in order to search for a network. We chose an order that allowed us to study the effects of the variables that represent the collaboration and working process on the variables that characterize the solution.

The generated graph (Fig. 3) represents the network found by Elvira. Some interesting relationships between some variables can be seen. For example, all the nodes that lack parent nodes (*Communication* and *Coordination*) contain variables related to the group work. The remaining variables of group work (*Collaboration, Velocity, Willingnes_Experimentation* and *Work*) have variables of the same dimension (group process indicators) as parents. An opposite situation occurs with the nodes that contain solution variables, since in most cases they do not have descendants (*Cost, Quality, Validity* and *Experimentability*) and in the remaining cases their descendants are also solution indicators (*Well_Formed, Difficulty* and *Accuracy*).

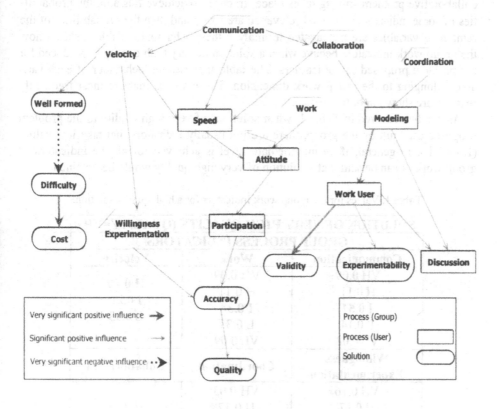

Fig. 3. Network found by Elvira.

It is also necessary to highlight that some of the relationships identified were expected, such as the relationship between the cost of a solution and the problem difficulty, the fact that the quality of the solution depends on its accuracy, or that the group collaboration level is closely related to the *Communication* indicator for instance. Some other interesting and surprising relationships are the following: the *Well_Formed* indicator is in direct relationship with the problem difficulty (this relationship is inversely proportional, also called negative), and the validity of a solution usually depends on the level of the individual work.

This network reveals relationships between variables that can allow the evaluators to draw conclusions about the influence of the group work process on the solutions obtained in this process.

5 Data analysis

In this section we carry out a study consisting of analyzing the behaviour of some variables of the Bayesian network when a situation of special interest in the process of collaborative problem solving takes place. In order to achieve this aim, the probabilities of some indicators of special relevance are fixed, and then the probabilities of the remaining variables are propagated to analyze their behaviours. Table 1 shows how the group work indicators behave when a solution of very high quality is produced for the problem proposed to the learners. The table specifies the behaviour of each variable belonging to the group work dimension. Those values that are most frequently reached are shown in bold typeface.

As can be observed in Table 1, when solutions of very high quality to the problem proposed are built by the group, there are not usually indicators that take low values (L or VL). In general, if an intermediate level is achieved for all the indicators of group work, it can be said that a solution of very high quality would be obtained.

Table 1. Values for the group work indicators for a high quality solution.

SOLUTION OF VERY HIGH QUALITY (QUALITY=VH)		
GROUP PROCESS INDICATORS		
Communication	Work	Velocity
VH 0.09 H 0.11 **I 0.57** L 0.14 VL 0.08	VH 0.09 H 0.11 **I 0.34** L 0.31 VL 0.09	**H 0.46** I 0.21 L 0.33
Willingness Experimentation	Coordination	Collaboration
VH 0.16 H 0.17 I 0.17 **L 0.33** VL 0.16	VH 0.03 H 0.12 **I 0.42** L 0.39 VL 0.03	H 0.13 **I 0.67** L 0.19

In Table 2 the behaviour of the remaining variables related to the solution are analyzed when the *Quality* variable takes a very high value. As Table 2 shows, no indicator had a value lower than the intermediate level (I) as the value with highest probability. The solutions of very high quality were obtained above all in problems of high difficulty and when these solutions presented high accuracy and high validity, were well formed, and had intermediate values of *Experimentability* and *Cost* variables. Therefore, it seems evident that a solution of very high quality generates high or very high values of *Accuracy*, *Validity* and *Well_Formed*. However, some results are interesting, such as, that the solutions of very high quality are usually obtained in difficult problems. This situation is explained by the fact that DomoSim-TPC proposes the problems to the learners from low to high complexity, which supports the hypothesis that the students learn throughout an increasing-complexity process and are therefore able to solve problems of great complexity at the final stages of their learning process.

Table 2. Values that the solution indicators take when the solution quality is very high.

SOLUTION OF VERY HIGH QUALITY (QUALITY=VH)		
SOLUTION INDICATORS		
Experimentability	Well-Formed	Validity
VH 0.24	VH 0.33	
H 0.24	**H 0.51**	**H 0.48**
I 0.24	I 0.12	I 0.38
L 0.16	L 0.02	L 0.15
VL 0.12	VL 0.01	
Accuracy	Difficulty	Cost
H 0.72	**H 0.58**	H 0.28
I 0.13	I 0.40	**I 0.61**
L 0.14	L 0.02	L 0.11

Table 3 puts together the main indicators of the three dimensions when a very high communication takes place. *Communication* is an indicator on which most of the group work indicators depend. According to Table 3, when this indicator reaches a very high value, high levels of *Collaboration*, *Velocity* and *Modelling*, intermediate values for *Discussion*, *Work_User*, *Experimentability* and *Accuracy*, and solutions that are well-formed and of quality in a high degree will most probably be obtained.

Table 3. Values of some indicators for a very high level of communication.

VERY HIGH LEVEL OF COMMUNICATION (COMMUNICATION=VH)			
GROUP PROCESS INDICATORS			
Collaboration		Velocity	
H 0.60		**H 0.60**	
I 0.20		I 0.20	
L 0.20		L 0.20	
USER PROCESS INDICATORS			
Discussion		Work_User	Modelling
VH 0.24		VH 0.02	VH 0.16
H 0.24		H 0.24	**H 0.26**
I 0.24		**I 0.31**	I 0.20
L 0.16		L 0.30	L 0.22
VL 0.12		VL 0.12	VL 0.17
SOLUTION INDICATORS			
Well_Formed	Accuracy	Quality	Experimentability
VH 0.38		VH 0.16	VH 0.24
H 0.49	H 0.27	**H 0.49**	H 0.23
I 0.11	**I 0.40**	I 0.24	**I 0.24**
L 0.01	L 0.33	L 0.23	L 0.16
VL 0.01		VL 0.12	VL 0.12

Consequently, it can be inferred from the data collected in Table 3 that the *Communication* indicator takes on special importance in the collaborative problem solving process, since very high levels of *Communication* usually imply very positive values for some other significant indicators.

6 Conclusions

The construction of a probabilistic model to represent dependences between the analysis indicators generated by a CSCL environment makes it possible to infer solution attributes from group and individual work. Taking into account the data analysis carried out in the previous section, we can state that there is a clear correlation between the collaboration and communication level among the group members and the quality of the solution to the problem. The analysis was made with the results (in the form of a database with analysis indicator values) of the learning activities in which students of different centres participated (see Section 4).

The existence of a Bayesian model aimed at identifying the way in which the collaboration between learners should be developed to reach good solutions opens the door to the use of real-time algorithms based on Bayesian networks in order to give advice to the learners during their learning tasks. This advice would allow the learner to correct situations in relation to the collaborative work that do not lead to good solutions.

Diverse works have approached the adaptation of tests proposed to the learners according to their level of knowledge, which is calculated using Bayesian networks. Our approach uses Bayesian networks to calculate the dependences between some analysis indicators from different dimensions (group work, individual work and solution). These indicators are calculated by means of an analysis tool available in a specific CSCL environment.

This approach is a starting point. When more data from learning activities is available, more significant conclusions will be obtained regarding influences between variables. In the future we will focus on extending this approach to a not so structured environment such as DomoSim-TPC, on creating probabilistic models that facilitate the formation of work groups according to the value of the analysis indicators, and on advice strategies for tutoring the learning using methods based on Bayesian networks that are calculated in real time during the carrying out of the learning tasks.

Acknowledgments

This work has been supported by the Comunidad Autónoma de Castilla-La Mancha (Spain) in the PBI-05-006 project.

References

1. Arroyo, I., Woolf, B.: Inferring learning and attitudes from a Bayesian Network of log file data. Proceedings of the 12th International Conference on Artificial Intelligence in Education. Amsterdam (2005)
2. Bravo, C., Redondo, M.A., Ortega, M. and Verdejo, M.F.: Collaborative environments for the learning of design: A model and a case study in Domotics. Computers and Education 46 (2), (2006) 152-173
3. Bravo, C.: A System to Support the Collaborative Learning of Domotical Design through Modelling and Simulation Tools'. Doctoral Dissertation, Departamento de Informática, Universidad de Castilla - La Mancha. ProQuest Information and Learning (Current Research). http://wwwlib.umi.com/cr/uclm/fullcit?p3081805 (2002)
4. Conati, C., Gertner, A., VanLehn, K. and Druzdzel, M.: On-line student modelling for coached problem solving using Bayesian networks. Proceedings of the 6th International Conference on User Modelling UM'97, Vienna, New York. Springer-Verlag, (1997) 231-242
5. Constantino-González, M.A., Suthers, D.D., Escamilla de los Santos, J.G.: Coaching web-based collaborative learning based on problem solution differences and participation. International Journal of Artificial Intelligence in Education 13, (2003) 263-299
6. Cooper, G.F., Herskovits, E.: A Bayesian method for the induction of probabilistic networks from data. Machine Learning, 9 (1992) 309-347
7. Dimitrakopoulou, A., et al: State of the Art on Interaction Analysis: Interaction Analysis Indicators. Kaleidoscope Network of Excelence. Interaction & Collaboration Analysis Supporting Teachers and Students' Self-Regulation. Jointly Executed Integrated Research Project. Deliverable D.26.1 (2004)
8. Elvira Consortium. Elvira: an environment for Probabilistic Graphical Models. In Gámez J. A., Salmerón A. (eds.): Proceedings of the First European Workshop on Probabilistic Graphical Models, Cuenca (2002) 222-230
9. Fishman, B.J., Honebein, P.C., Duffy, T.M.: Constructivism and the design of learning environments: Context and authentic activities for learning. NATO Advanced Workshop on the design of Constructivism Learning (1991)
10. McManus, M., Aiken, R. "Monitoring computer-based problem solving," Journal of Artificial Intelligence in Education, 6(4), (1995) 307-336
11. Millán, E., Pérez-de-la-Cruz, J.L.: A Bayesian Diagnostic Algorithm for Student Modeling and its Evaluation. User Modeling and User Adapted Interaction, 12, 2-3 (2002) 281-330
12. Muehlenbrock, M., Hoppe, U.: 'Computer supported interaction analysis of group problem solving'. Computer Support for Collaborative Learning (CSCL'1999). Palo alto, CA, USA, (1999) 398-405
13. Pearl, J.: Probabilistic reasoning in intelligent systems. Morgan-Kaufmann (San Mateo) (1988)
14. Redondo, M.A., Bravo, C.: DomoSim-TPC: Collaborative Problem Solving to Support the Learning of Domotical Design. Computer Applications in Engineering Education. Ed. John Wiley & Sons, vol. 4, N°1, (2006) 9-19
15. Soller A., Wiebe, J., Lesgold, A.: A Machine Learning Approach to Assessing Knowledge Sharing During Collaborative Learning Activities. Proceedings of Computer Support for Collaborative Learning, (2002)
16. Vomlel J.: Bayesian networks in educational testing. In Gámez J. A., Salmerón A. (eds.): Proceedings of the First European Workshop on Probabilistic Graphical Models, Cuenca (2002) 176-185.
17. Vygotsky, L.S. Mind in society: The development of higher psychological processes. Cambridge, MA: Harvard University Press (1978)

The Integration of Heterogeneous Biological Data using Bayesian Networks

Ken McGarry[1], Nick Morris[2], Alex Freitas[3]

[1] School of Computing and Technology, University of Sunderland
[2] Institute for Cell and Molecular Biosciences, University of Newcastle
[3] Computing Laboratory, University of Kent

Abstract. Bayesian networks can provide a suitable framework for the integration of highly heterogeneous experimental data and domain knowledge from experts and ontologies. In addition, they can produce interpretable and understandable models for knowledge discovery within complex domains by providing knowledge of casual and other relationships in the data. We have developed a system using Bayesian Networks that enables domain experts to express their knowledge and integrate it with a variety of other sources such as protein-protein relationships and to cross-reference this against new knowledge discovered by the proteomics experiments. The underlying Bayesian mechanism enables a form of hypothesis testing and evaluation.

1 Introduction

A growing worldwide health problem is the increased number of those suffering from diabetes. There is a strong link between obesity and type II diabetes and worldwide obesity is on the increase. This increase has typically arisen from changes in the diet and lifestyles of individuals, such as an increased calorific intake and reduced level of exercise, resulting in raised levels of white adipose tissue (WAT) in the body. These changes can be detrimental to the health of a person and will typically lead to diabetes (insulin resistance), heart disease and a range of other complications.

Our research is concerned with developing the computational tools necessary for discovering the effects of insulin in the stimulation of glucose transport in fat cells from experimental data. At present this biological process is not fully understood, obtaining a better understanding of this is very important to give us further insight into diabetes, a disease which is becoming a major health concern. A recent publication from the US Center for Disease Control and Prevention estimated there are around 20.8 million diabetics in the US (this represents 7% of the population - 14.6 million diagnosed, 6.2 million undiagnosed). In the UK recent government figures from 2005 show there are over 2 million diabetics in the UK, with potentially another 750,000 undiagnosed cases.

This article presents our technique of using bayesian networks as a principled framework to augment microarray and 2DE protein data by incorporating domain knowledge of pathway interactions from domain experts and from online ontologies such as BIND and KEGG. The objective of data and knowledge integration is to enable a biologist to test out a hypothesis using many sources of information from ontologies to databases and compare it with experimental data to see if it refutes or confirms it. Bayesian networks are a widely used graphical model for representing and managing the difficulties involved with missing, noisy and uncertain data. They can also incorporate subjective human beliefs that can be later refined and updated in the light of new evidence, aspects that are not available using a traditional frequentist approach to probabilities. For a general introduction to Bayesian networks see [3].

The bayesian network formalism described in this paper is a major component in a much larger larger system that we are developing for biological hypothesis formulation and exploration. It is appropriate here to discuss the use of bayesian networks in detail and only to briefly describe the full system.

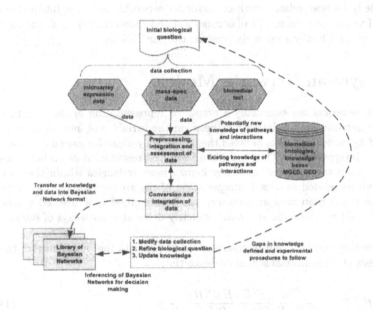

Fig. 1. The system block diagram showing the data sources and flow

Figure 4 shows the overall system operation, the flow of information starts with the formulation of the hypothesis to explore; this can be as simple as a pair of protein names or as complex as a pathway definition. This requires text composed in natural language supported by information provided to the GUI. The conversion of the experimental data from genomic and proteomic sources into the same Bayesian Network (BN) format as the higher level knowledge from ontologies and databases allows the integration of heterogeneous information. The BN will now be composed of low level experimental data integrated with higher level PPI and pathway information. Whenever possible, additional information extracted by text mining the literature will be integrated also, if deemed relevant and is not present in the repositories. The next phase involves inferencing and making predictions based on the available knowledge represented by the BN. The output will be candidate entities, such as genes, proteins or pathways and will be identified and ranked according to their similarity of form and function. This information will be used to guide the targets of the experimental process. When the results are available from the experimental process, they will be feed back into the system and the hypothesis modified accordingly.

The remainder of this paper is structured as follows: section two discusses the issues of Bayesian graphical models and how they are useful for this particular application area; section three outlines how we use Bayesian networks to integrate the heterogeneous data used by our project, here we also describe the data sources and the particular problems inherent in each type; section four briefly reviews related work on bayesian networks and data integration; section five presents the results of our method and shows the types of pathways discovered; and finally section six presents the conclusions.

2   Bayesian Networks Models

Bayesian networks are essentially a graphical representation of the structure i.e. the interconnection relationships between the variables of interest are represented by nodes and links between them, and they allow for causal discovery or causal interpretation. They provide a useful representation of probabilities which enables the exploitation of any known independencies within the data which can be related to causal interpretation of the arcs connecting the nodes (variables). Bayesian network structure can be described as a directed acyclic graph (DAG) in which the arcs have explicitly delineated pathways of interaction [7].

Bayes theorem is shown in equation 1 and presents the probability of the hypothesis (H) conditionalised on evidence (E).

$$P(H \mid E) = \frac{P(E \mid H)P(H)}{P(E \mid H)P(H) + P(E \mid \neg H)P(\neg H)} \tag{1}$$

Where: $P(H \mid E)$ defines the probability of a hypothesis conditioned on certain evidence, $P(E \mid H)$ is the likelihood, $P(H)$ is the probability of the hypothesis prior to obtaining any evidence, is the $P(E)$ evidence. Therefore, according to Bayesian theory we can update our beliefs regarding the hypothesis when provided with new evidence that is conditional upon using probabilities and is called *conditionalization*.

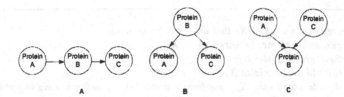

Fig. 2. Bayesian networks can be used to represent a number of relations: in (A) a causal chain is represented in the sense that protein A activates protein B which activates protein C. In (B) we demonstrate that protein A and C have a common cause which is protein B. In (C) protein B may be activated by either protein A or protein C.

The conditional probability distributions (CPD) are described by $P(X_i \mid U_i)$, where X_i represents node i and U_i are its parent nodes. We must specify the prior probabilities of the nodes and the conditional probabilities of the nodes given all the combinations of their ancestor nodes. The joint distribution of random variables is given by $X = \{X_1, ..., X_n\}$ and together with the CPD values is used to calculate the choice of X_i and is given by :

$$P(X_1, ..., X_n) = \prod_i P(X_i \mid U_i) \tag{2}$$

The CPD's values are easy enough to calculate and inference but require the number of parameters is dependent upon the number of parent nodes, they are usually represented in table format. The nodes are assumed to be discrete or categorical values, however, continuous values may be discretised [10].

$$P(X_1, ..., X_n) = \frac{1}{Z} \prod_j \pi_j [C_j] \tag{3}$$

The algorithm that actually constructs the network is described in figure 3:-

The task of inferring results or queries when new data is presented to the Bayesian Network is quite flexible for reasoning because any node or combinations of nodes may be used to pass data through and thus infer new information. Other, machine learning approaches typically require a fixed architecture of inputs and outputs.

When training Bayesian Networks from sparse biological data, we must be aware that the posterior probability over the models is diffuse and will result in a set potential networks that model the uncertainty in the data. We must therefore try to extract the key features of local and global properties of the Bayesian Network. The optimum network is the one that best represents the most probable parameters and structure given the available data and knowledge. For overcoming some of the computational complexity problems involved

1. *choose relevant variables X_i that describe the domain*
2. *choose an ordering for the variables, $< X_1...X_n >$*
3. *while there are variables left:*
   (a) *add next variable X_i to the network*
   (b) *add arcs to the X_i node from minimal set of nodes already in network parents (X_i), such that the following conditional independence property is satisfied:*
      $$P(X_i \mid X_1', ...X_m') = P(X_i \mid Parents(X_i))$$
   (c) *define the CPT for X_i.*

Fig. 3. Pearl's Bayesian Network Algorithm.

with estimating the posterior distributions, we use Markov chain Monte Carlo simulation (MCMC). The MCMC technique probabilistically selects a sequence of samples from the training set to form a Markov Chain. This means that the probability of discovering a particular model is dependent on the current model rather than the sampling history. A rapid convergence to the optimum structure can be obtained by using a *burn-in* period, before the samples are actually drawn. Equation 4 shows the Metropolis-Hastings acceptance criteria which defines how the sample networks are to be updated.

$$P_{MH} = min \left\{ 1, \frac{p(Y \mid D, I)q(X_t \mid Y)}{p(X_t \mid D, I)q(Y \mid X_t)} \right\} \tag{4}$$

Where: $p(X \mid D, I)$ is the posterior density of the model parameters and $q(Y \mid X_t)$ is the proposal distribution, which for Gaussian distributions would mean that the probability density decreases with distance away from the current sample.

2.1 Modification of Bayesian Network through Informative Prior Knowledge

The key to the successful application of Bayesian techniques is through the use of *prior knowledge* to improve the estimation of the posterior. If we have a prior belief about a situation then we can use this information to pre-structure our BN. For example a particular gene (IPA) is known to regulate several target genes (GDH, GL4, HK2), we would then assign this relationship within the BN by setting the edges between these two entities and setting the values in the conditional probability table to define the structural prior accordingly. This is a powerful strategy, but only when it makes sense to do so. The application of incorrect beliefs will produce unreliable estimates of the true posterior regardless of the abundance of the likelihood evidence. Equation 5 shows how we modify the BN with prior knowledge (causal intervention) from experts and from online protein databases [4].

$$P(X_{i,j} = z \mid par_M(x), M, \theta : X_{i,j} = Z, ...) = 1 \tag{5}$$

Where par_M are the parameters within the model, $X_{i,j}$ are the known effects of the parents of a given node, θ is the conditional probability conditionalized and represents the causal conditions. The biological knowledge are incorporated into the BN by specifying the probability for the existence of each potential connection (edge) between them. We assume independence between edges and the variables in the BN are also assumed to be discrete, this ensures that the calculations are computationally tractable.

2.2 Related Work on Bayesian Networks

The modeling of gene networks with bayesian networks using microarray data has seen considerable attention in recent years [14]. However, the initial work on integrating heterogeneous data within a bayesian network framework was led by Friedman and Segal [5, 16]. This work proved that Bayesian Networks could be trained on genomic data to reconstruct the relationships between genes. They were conscious of the limitations of their data and used the Expectation Maximization algorithm to infer the missing values. Troyanskaya *et al* developed the MAGIC system (Multi Association of Genes by Integration of Clusters) [18]. The MAGIC system integrated microarray expression data with protein-protein interactions derived from GRID for the purpose of accurately and efficiently predicting gene function annotations. The system was somewhat reliant on the functional notations defined by Gene Ontology (GO) to determine the relevance of gene groupings, and the authors correctly suspected that GO itself contained annotation errors but that the level of errors would not overly effect system accuracy.

Work by Chrisman et al, highlights the use of BN for knowledge incorporation [4]. In this respect our work resembles that of Chrisman *et al*, since higher level knowledge from experts knowledge incorporation. Although, Chrisman's work appears not to have been followed up, it presents some interesting results. Also, related to our work is that of Hartemink and Bernard, who have performed important work in genomic data integration [6, 1]. Similar work by Le *et al* considers the incorporation of gene sequence information [11].

The novelty and approach of our work lies in the principled integration of high level knowledge through the setting and clamping of inter-node relationships within the Bayesian Network.

3 Integrating Heterogenous Sources of Data

The information we are integrating consists of raw numeric data and knowledge in the form of rules and probability estimations. The stochastic characteristics of experimental data means that it is inherently noisy and incomplete (with potentially many missing values). These difficulties are accommodated by the probabilistic semantics of Bayesian networks, which makes this kind of network robust to noisy and incomplete data. In addition, Bayesian networks parallel the scientific reasoning undertaken by biologists when they formulate and revise hypotheses as current knowledge is extended. Most existing formalisms for representing this are monotonic and cannot deal with the problems encountered in biology or other domains with inherently incomplete knowledge. The Bayesian network approach enables the modeling of various facets not usually expressible in standard statistical models. Having outlined the Bayesian Network approach of defining conditional probabilities the next task is to define the domain knowledge relating the proteins and their interactions in the various pathways. The characteristics and encoding problems associated with each type of information will now be discussed.

- Biological data, in the form of microarray (genomic) data 2DE protein gels (proteomic data).
- Expert opinion, from biologists familiar with insulin-resistance and diabetes.
- Knowledge of pathways and transport mechanism, protein-protein interactions from ontologies.

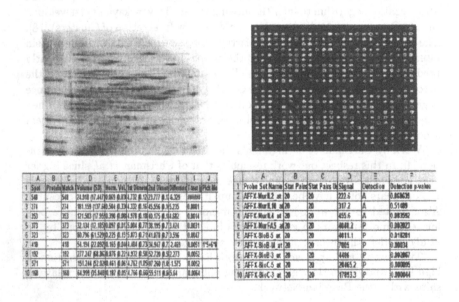

Fig. 4. Proteomic data and Genomic generation: the left-hand side shows the 2-Dimensional Electrophoresis gel (proteomic) and associated Excel file containing the digitised data. The right-hand side contains the microarray image (genomic) and associated Excel file.

3.1 Genomic Data (Microarray Data)

Microarrays are a recent technological breakthrough that has enabled the detailed analysis of cellular activity and condition [2]. Recent work has highlighted how components of metabolic pathways can be identified and how the protein targets of drug treatment can be determined using expression profiles [17]. A typical microarray data set will identify many thousands of active genes taken over a series of microarrays. The problem is not only dealing with large numbers of variables with few samples but of the almost complete lack of *gold standards* [8].

3.2 Proteomic data (2DE Gels)

The best technique for proteome analysis is 2-dimensional electrophoresis gels (2DE), they provide an indication of protein activity. Identifying those proteins that have changed mean in terms of diabetes. Our ultimate aim is to identify the point of dysfunction in insulin signalling cascade in diabetes. It depends on a number of factors, i.e. we pick the ones that show the biggest changes, also we pick the ones that change across multiple sets of conditions. Each gel typically show a large number of spots, which contain information regarding the features such as protein relative abundance, protein shape and appearance [9]. This information is usually digitised by image analysis software and presented to data mining mining algorithms for analysis [12, 13].

The data set shows the differences between protein levels in the plasma membrane of non-diabetic and diabetic cells that have been stimulated with insulin (we should get a loss of protein trafficking, i.e. no spot, in the diabetic cells). Transcriptome varies, as does protein. However, there is not a direct correlation between mRNA levels (and therefore microarrays) and protein levels and thus cell function. This is a counter-intuitive result, but mRNA can be made in large amounts and have a very short life span, and therefore produce relatively small amounts of protein. However, some mRNA could be produced in small amounts but have a long life span and therefore produce a lot of protein.

3.3 Expert opinion and diabetes domain knowledge

The knowledge from recent experiments into the potential causes of Insulin resistance led to the incorporation of glucose transport-4 (Glut4) discovered by Perera [15], see figure 5. Another pathway was described by Wang [19] and downloaded from KEGG.

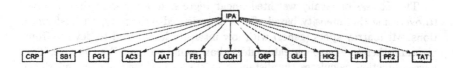

Fig. 5. The IPA pathway and components.

Here we take advantage of existing knowledge of known pathways and proteins responsible for insulin resistance in type II diabetes mellitus. In type II diabetes there is a failure of insulin to stimulate cellular responses. For example, there is a loss of the trafficking of the glucose transporter (GLUT4) to the plasma membrane (PM) and also a reduction in GLUT4 expression. At present we do not fully understand the mechanism by which insulin stimulates the trafficking of GLUT4, or how this process is impaired in diabetes. An understanding of the changes that occur in the cell at a protein (proteome) level may give further insight in to the dysfunction seen in diabetes.

4 Experimental Procedure

The system was implemented in Matlab and we used the Bayesian Network toolbox developed by Kevin Murphy and MCMC toolbox extension by Dirk Husmeier. The MCMC method requires that certain parameters for "burn-in" and sampling are to be set. We used a "burn-in" period of 10,000 before samples are taken and a sampling rate of 1,000 drawn after burn-in. Each sample is a Bayesian Network with a topology extracted from the posterior distribution.

Our methodology was to use the microarray (genomic) data sets to develop a model that would act as gold standard. This was on data we were reasonably sure contained pathways that have been identified in the literature, the task was then to train BN's on the microarray data to "rediscover" these pathways. The difficulty to overcome is the amount of microarray data required to ensure reliable results.

4.1 Data preprocessing

The genomic expression levels were compared against biologically related samples to see which genes are differentially expressed. This is a ratio between the sample and control genes, However, there are disadvantages to using only expression ratios for data analysis. The ratios can help determine important relationships between genes but they also remove information relating to the absolute gene-expression levels. The information pertaining as to wether a gene is up- or -down regulated appears differently when using ratios; i.e. a up- factor of 2 have a value of 2 while those genes that are down-regulated by 2 have a value of -0.5. Transforming the data using a Log2 base produces a more intuitive range of values.

The *Lowess* or locally weighted linear regression analysis method is able to overcome the intensity based effects experienced by log_2 type transformations. Microarray spots (genes) with low intensity levels tend to deviate from zero and therefore have a greater effect than would normally be the case. The lowess function calculates the distances in the ratio-intensity plot and those that are *far away* from each data point will be transformed to have a smaller contribution. Figure 6 shows the lowess function.

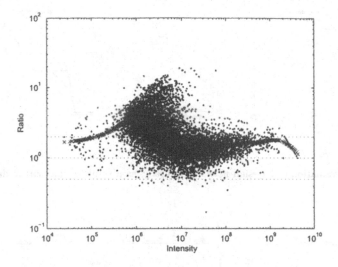

Fig. 6. Lowess based transformation

4.2 Results

Figure 7 shows the receiver operating characteristic curves for the insulin pathway which was trained using a variable number of microarray experiments. The reason for developing these particular models was to ascertain the minimum number of microarray experiments to construct reliable pathways. The results suggest that fewer than nine microarrays will produce pathways that are inferior and unlikely to model the biological reality. In each diagram, the green diagonal line running from bottom left to top right, is the expected ROC curve of a random classifier. Good classifiers tend to have a large area under the ROC curve, which in figure 7 gets worse as the number of samples decreases.

In order to evaluate the BN accuracy, we need to calculate the sensitivity and specificity. These measures are calculated from the false positives and true positives, where a false positive defines an relationship between genes that does not exist, whereas a true positive is where the BN has correctly identified a relationship (edge) between two genes.

The sensitivity and specificity are calculated by: $sensitivity = TP/(TP + FN)$, $specificity = FP/(TN + FP)$, where: TP=true positives, FP= false positives, TN= true negatives and FN= false negatives. The ROC curves generated by our Bayesian Networks confirms previous work by Zak et al, which concluded that constructing genetic networks only from microarray data alone was highly unreliable [20]. These results motivate the need to incorporate additional information from other sources.

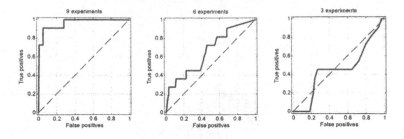

Fig. 7. Evaluation of bayesian network accuracy, as a result of microarray data set size.

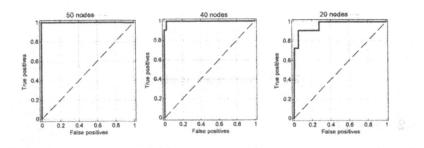

Fig. 8. Incorporating prior knowledge into the bayesian network accuracy

In figure 8 the results of incorporating domain knowledge within the model in addition to the microarray data. The number of nodes refers to the amount of domain knowledge that is incorporated. In table 1 we show the breakdown of "rediscoveries" made using the various combinations of data and knowledge. The act of minimising the amount of false positives, makes the overall effects of prior knowledge a worthwhile endeavor, as even a small positive predictive value can be of enormous value to a biologist.

The graphical properties of one of the Bayesian Networks (BN) is shown in figure 9. In this BN we are interested in the discovery of the causal arrangements i.e. the interconnection relationships between the variables of interest and they allow for causal discovery or causal interpretation. The relationships between the insulin resistance problem and how it is affected by the proteins ACE and GLUT4 and the effects of insulin resistance upon other proteins such as GLUT1 and ADRB3. The CPD tables highlight the child/parent relationship between the nodes, giving the numeric values of the conditional probability tables for each possible outcome. This particular BN was trained on classified microarray

Table 1. Increasing the amount of knowledge increases the probability of making a valid discovery

Data Source	Pathways	Genes	TP	TN	FP	FN
microarray	14	23	14	220	34	20
microarray + 2DE	34	55	75	296	27	23
microarray + 2DE + Path	34	87	70	300	29	9
microarray + 2DE + Knowledge	78	155	92	310	100	15

data, where many of the genes involved in insulin resistance (IR) have been identified.

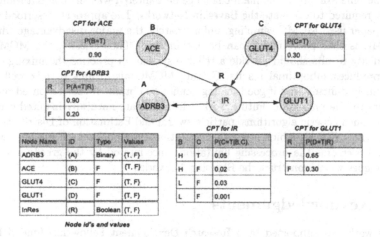

Fig. 9. Relationships identified by the Bayesian Network.

The BN enables a limited form of hypothesis exploration, in the sense that the inferencing mechanism has several possibilities. We use the diagnostic reasoning approach which enables the relationships between symptoms to causes to be evaluated, thus when given some evidence regarding the presence of *Glut4* we can update our beliefs about the likelihood of IR being present. When using predictive reasoning we can derive new information about effects given some new information regarding the causes. Using intercausal reasoning, we can infer the mutual causes of a particular effect by explaining away the variables relationships which are initially independent but when knowledge of one possibility is known the other is less likely to have been the cause. The bayesian network approach is very flexible and this is represented by the combined reasoning diagram. Here we are able to simultaneously combine diagnostic and predictive reasoning, in fact any combination of node-to-node reasoning is possible.

5 Conclusions

In this paper we have presented our preliminary results of a novel probabilistic framework for integrating several types of heterogeneous information in a principled way. The use of prior knowledge in the form of expert rules and known pathways from the literature can under certain conditions overcome the difficulties of the noisy data that typical characterises microarray (genomic) data. There is now evidence from this work and the work of others to conclude that microarray data alone is not sufficient to accurately build models that describe the true biological pathways and their components. The data we have used is necessarily incomplete but as the project continues more data and knowledge will become available. The main challenge encountered was the computational effort required to calculate the Bayesian Networks. The approach described in this paper used MCMC sampling, unfortunately, the major disadvantage with MCMC is that poor mixing can be encountered. Theoretically, the MCMC ergodicity results should provide a reliable system, in practice the mixing often produces suboptimal results. Getting MCMC algorithms to mix well is extremely difficult, and if good mixing cannot be obtained, the computed posteriors will be unreliable. Future work will investigate naturally inspired computing such genetic algorithms, particle swarm and Estimation of Distribution Algorithms (EDA), which is another evolutionary, global search method and should overcome the processing limitations encountered by the greedy search techniques which construct the Bayesian Networks.

6 Acknowledgements

This work was supported by a Research Development Fellowship funded by HEFCE. We are also grateful to Dirk Husmeier and Lonnie Chrisman for helpful discussions regarding Bayesian Networks. The BNT toolbox of Kevin Murphy was used in these experiments.

References

1. A. Bernard and A. Hartemink. Informative structure priors: joint learning of dynamic regulatory networks from multiple types of data. In *Pacific Symposium on Biocomputing*, pages 459–470, 2005.
2. V. Brown, A. Ossadtchi, A. Khan, S. Yee, G. Lacan, W. Melega, S. Cherry, R. Leahy, and D. Smith. Multiplex three-dimensional brain gene expression in a mouse model of parkinson's disease. *Genome Research*, 12:868–884, 2002.
3. E. Charniak. Bayesian networks without tears. *AI Magazine*, 12(4):50–63, 1991.
4. L. Chrisman, P. Langley, S. Bray, and A. Pohorille. Incorporating biological knowledge into evaluation of causal regulatory hypothesis. In *Proceedings of the Pacific Symposium on Biocomputing*, pages 128–139, Kauai, Hawaii., 2003.

5. N. Friedman, M. Linial, I. Nachman, and D. Pe'er. Using bayesian networks to analyze expression data. *Journal of Computational Biology*, 7(3-4):601–620, 2000.

6. A. Hartemink, D. Clifford, T. Jaakkola, and R. Young. Combining location and expression data for principled discovery of genetic regulatory network models. In *Pacific Symposium on Biocomputing*, pages 437–449, 2002.

7. D. Heckerman, D. Geiger, and D. Chickering. Learning bayesian networks: The combination of knowledge and statistical data. *Machine Learning*, 20:197–243, 1995.

8. D. Husmeier. Sensitivity and specificity of inferring genetic regulatory interactions from microarray experiments with dynamic bayesian networks. *Bioinformatics*, 19(17):2271–2282, 2003.

9. R. Jenkins and S. Pennington. Novel approaches to protein expression analysis. In S. Pennington and M. Dunn, editors, *Proteomics from protein sequences to function*, pages 207–224. BIOS Scientific Publishers Ltd, 2001.

10. K. Korb and A. Nicholson. *Bayesian Artificial Intelligence*. Chapman and Hall/CRC, 2004.

11. P. Le, A. Bahl, and L. Ungar. Using prior knowledge to improve genetic network reconstruction from microarray data. *In Silico Biology*, 4(3):335–353, 2004.

12. J. Malone, K. McGarry, and C. Bowerman. Intelligent hybrid spatio-temporal mining for knowledge discovery on proteomics data. In *Symposium on Knowledge Representation for Bioinformatics*, Helsinki, 2005.

13. J. Malone, K. McGarry, and C. Bowerman. Automated trend analysis of proteomics data using intelligent data mining architecture. *Expert Systems with Applications Journal*, 30(1):24–33, 2006.

14. I. Ong, J. Glasner, and D. Page. Modelling regulatory pathways in E. coli from time series expression profiles. *Bioinformatics*, 18(1):241–248, 2002.

15. H. Perera, M. Clarke, N. Morris, W. Hong, L. Chamberlain, and G. Gould. Syntaxin 6 regulates glut4 trafficking in 3t3-l1 adipocytes. *Molecular Biology of the Cell*, 14.

16. E. Segal, B. Tasker, A. Gasch, N. Friedman, and D. Koller. Rich probabilistic models for gene expression. *Bioinformatics*, 17(1):243–252, 2001.

17. L. Soinov, M. Krestyaninova, and A. Brazma. Towards reconstruction of gene networks from expression data by supervised learning. *Genome Biology*, 4(1):1–10, 2003.

18. G. Troyanskaya, K. Dolsinki, A. Owen, R. Altman, and D. Botstein. A bayesian framework for combining hetergeneous data sources for gene function prediction (in saccharomyces cerevisiae). *Proceedings National Academy of Science*, 100(14):8348–8353, 2003.

19. Y. Wang, A. Xu, J. Ye, E. Kraegen, C. Tse, and G. Cooper. Alteration in phosphorylation of p20 is associated with insulin resistance. *Diabetes*, 50:1821–1827, 2001.

20. D. Zak, F. Doyle, G. Gonye, and J. Schwaber. Local identifibility: when can genetic networks be identified from microarray data? In *Proceedings of the Third International Conference on Systems Biology*, pages 236–237, 2002.

Automatic Species Identification of Live Moths

Michael Mayo[1] and Anna T. Watson[2]
[1]Dept. of Computer Science
The University of Waikato
Hamilton, New Zealand
[1]mmayo@cs.waikato.ac.nz
[2]kisalsera@yahoo.co.uk

Abstract. A collection consisting of the images of 774 live moth individuals, each moth belonging to one of 35 different UK species, was analysed to determine if data mining techniques could be used effectively for automatic species identification. Feature vectors were extracted from each of the moth images and the machine learning toolkit WEKA was used to classify the moths by species using the feature vectors. Whereas a previous analysis of this image dataset reported in the literature [1] required that each moth's least worn wing region be highlighted manually for each image, WEKA was able to achieve a greater level of accuracy (85%) using support vector machines without manual specification of a region of interest at all. This paper describes the features that were extracted from the images, and the various experiments using different classifiers and datasets that were performed. The results show that data mining can be usefully applied to the problem of automatic species identification of live specimens in the field.

1. Introduction

The demand for computer-based systems that can automatically identify the species of live plants, insects or animals from digital images or recordings is only likely to increase in the future. Worldwide, there is a growing need for biodiversity monitoring, while at the same time the number of trained taxonomists declines [2]. Accurate species identification is also of critical importance in many practical areas, such as agriculture and border control, where pests and invaders must be identified swiftly and eradicated before becoming established as unwanted visitors in a country or agricultural region.

Can data mining techniques be applied to build useful, practical species recognition systems with the express purpose of assisting non-taxonomists in taxonomic tasks? Two significant challenges that data mining practitioners must face if they are to take up this challenge are firstly the need to handle a very high number of classes, perhaps in the order of 1000-2000 classes for a typical, practical working system. And secondly, a species identification system must also be able to distinguish correctly between an individual from a species that the system has been trained on, and an individual belonging to a species that the system has not been trained on. In other words, the presence of novel species must be accurately recognized.

Traditional machine learning datasets, on the other hand, usually only have a small handful of classes. Furthermore, traditional classifiers do not usually need to detect novelty: they simply return the best matching class, even if the probability of a match is very low.

In this paper, the first of these challenges is addressed: to evaluate data mining techniques when applied to a species dataset with a high number of classes. Although 35 classes is not high relative to the ultimate goal (in which the number of classes can be counted in the thousands), it does represent a significant increase in the number of classes compared to traditional data mining domains and is therefore a good test-bed for study.

The results presented here show that data mining techniques can be effective for species identification tasks. In particular, the best classifier (a support vector machine) in a jackknife test achieved approximately 85% accuracy when no manual preprocessing of the images was performed. In contrast, the original analysis of these images used a neural network-based system to achieve approximately 83% accuracy in a jackknife test [1]. However, in that study, the best wing in each image was manually outlined and mirrored so that that best wings in all the images were in the same orientation, and could be cleanly segmented from the background. In the study presented here, we classified the raw images with no manual human intervention required.

In the following section, an overview of the automatic species identification field is briefly given. The live moth image dataset is then discussed in more detail in Section 3. Section 4 describes the features that were extracted from the moth images for this study, and Section 5 contains the results of the experiments. Section 6 is the conclusion.

2. Recent Work on Automatic Species Identification

Researchers from a variety of different backgrounds have in recent times attempted to build accurate species identification systems. Most systems to date have a particular and focused domain, although the "grand challenge" in this area is to design a generic species identification system that can identify any organism on the planet from visual and any other type of available data – quite a lofty challenge.

One interesting aspect of this field is that data need not necessarily be limited to images. Animals may, for example, be recognized by the sounds they make, which is the basis for much research into bird species recognition (see, e.g., [3,4]). Furthermore, there is no reason why a human in the field who is trying to identify the species of an organism could not provide auxiliary information for the classification process in the form of answers to questions (e.g. "was this creature found in a hole in the ground?"). However most research to date is currently focused on image analysis and classification.

Three main image-based systems have appeared in the literature. The first is DAISY (Digital Automated Identification System) [1,2], the second is SPIDA [5], and the third is ABIS [6]. The first two systems use a neural network for the core classification task. DAISY is generic and can be used for any type of image classification, and the system has in the past been used for classifying fish, pollen, and plants of different types, although the main focus appears to be moths. SPIDA, on the other hand, is specifically designed to distinguish between 121 species of Australian spider (it has also recently been tested on bumblebee wings with limited success). An interesting feature of SPIDA is that it is currently available on the Internet, and users can submit their own images of spiders for classification, although some expertise and equipment is required to obtain optimal images. Aside from providing a useful service to people, this is also a novel method of obtaining more training data. The third system, ABIS, is used to recognize bee species from the pattern on a bee's wings. It is based on support vector machines, and has achieved over 95% accuracy.

In general, all three of these systems have been trained on images taken from dead specimens. In a lab, dead specimens can be carefully positioned and photographed under consistent and ideal lighting conditions. In addition, details such as anatomical cross sections can also be provided as inputs to the system.

In the field, however, specimens are more often alive and moving than dead. Live specimens may not adopt the ideal pose required, they may move when the image is being captured, and the lighting conditions outside the lab may be poor and change unpredictably as a series of images of a group of images is taken. This tends to make the recognition task much more difficult. Furthermore, if the background is not guaranteed to be uniform (e.g. a moth is photographed when it lands on a tree branch), then the classification task becomes even harder because the system must distinguish the object of interest from the background. To our best knowledge, the Macrolepidoptera dataset used in this research is the only collection of images of live specimens taken in the field that is currently described in the literature.

Other systems have also been used for species identification. For example, Moyo et al. [7] discuss recognition of mammalian species in forensics from patterns occurring on a single hair when examined under a microscope, and Yuan et al. [8] report on the recognition of rat species from images of their tracks (which is paramount for determining the presence of invasive rat species that can cause the extinction of other species).

Researchers have also focused on the automatic identification of plant species, such as Samul et al. [9] who report on a method of recognizing the species of a tree given textural features, and Sogaard [10], who describes recent work on classifying weed plants from non-weed plants in order to minimize the wastage of herbicides in agriculture.

3. The Macrolepidoptera Image Collection

The dataset used in this study is a library of live moth images created by the second author [1] over a period of nearly a year. A moth trap was set up in Treborth Botanical Garden, Gwynedd, UK, and cleared every morning. Captured live moths were photographed then released.

Figure 1 gives examples of two images in the dataset. Figure 1(a) is most typical of images in the dataset, in which a moth has been photographed against a nearly uniform background (although the lighting is not uniform from left to right). Figure 2(b) is an example of an image taken against a non-uniform background, in which the colour of the moth is actually quite similar to the colour of the background, making this image difficult to segment. Due to the practical nature of the task (photographing live moths) it is not surprising that all of the images do not have clean, uniform backgrounds. In practice, it would be desirable for a classifier to automatically learn the difference between a moth and the background, and for this reason images such as Figure 1(b) were retained in the dataset.

Figure 1. Images of (a) *Agrotis exclamationis* (uniform background) and (b) *Laothoe populi* (poorer background).

Each photographic image is 1024 x 960 pixels in resolution, and is a full 24-bit RGB image. In actuality, the complete image dataset contains examples of over 224 species of moth, but of those, only 70 species contain images of twenty or more individuals. Furthermore, because in the original analysis [1] the region in the image where the wing occurs was manually outlined in order to be separated cleanly from the background, and because this manual highlighting was extremely time consuming, only the best quality 35 classes, or a total of 774 images, were actually used. In this paper, we focus on only those 35 classes in order to compare our results with the results of the original analysis, and leave to future work a consideration of the expanded dataset with 70, or even all 224 classes.

4. Extracting Features from the Images

The open source image processing toolkit ImageJ [11] was used to analyse the images in the Macrolepidoptera collection and extract from each one a feature vector containing 11,300 numeric features. Feature extraction was automated using ImageJ's macro language facility, which enables any of ImageJ's GUI features to be invoked programmatically. The feature vectors were then written to a file in ARFF format, ready for further processing by WEKA [12].

To illustrate the feature extraction process, consider the image of an individual moth from the species *Polia nebulosa*, depicted in Figure 2. This image is interesting because the subject is off-centre to the right, which is typical for many of the images in the dataset. There is also some additional noise in the image, namely some distortions in the upper right-hand corner, and the moth has quite a distinct shadow due to the outside (uncontrolled) lighting conditions when the photograph was taken.

Figure 2. Image of *Polia nebulosa*.

Figure 3 depicts the automatic processing and feature extraction pipeline, using Figure 2 as an example input. Features were extracted from the image at multiple points during processing, with 11,300 numeric features per image ultimately being generated. The features were a mixture of global image statistics (taken at various points in the processing of the image) and also local image statistics, generated by breaking the image up into "patches" and taking individual statistics such as the mean pixel values from each patch, in an attempt to account for different moth shapes and wing patterns.

The first step in feature extraction was to smooth the image six times. Each smoothing operating replaces each pixel in the image with the average intensity of its 3x3 neighbourhood of pixels, and this is repeated in the red, blue and green planes. Figure 3(a) depicts the results of this smoothing when applied to the image of *P. nebulosa* in Figure 2. The image was then transformed from RGB colour into an 8-bit greyscale image, and the edges were detected using the Sobel edge detector, as shown in Figure 3(b).

The next step was to apply an automatic binary thresholding scheme to each edge-detected image to produce a binary image such as the image depicted in Figure 3(c). The actual value of the threshold used was, for each image, set automatically using the iterative Isodata algorithm [13].

With the original RGB colour image now transformed into a binary image, a number of features were calculated. The features consisted of the number of white (foreground) pixels, the number of black (background) pixels, the ratio of the above two statistics (giving an overall indication of the moth's size), as well some features related to the shape of the binarized moth such as the interior density, the standard deviation of pixel positions in the image, the skew, and the kurtosis.

To account for the fact that in many of the images, the moth is off-centre, the centroid of the binary image was also calculated. The centroid for the example image in Figure 3 (c) is (734, 465), and when the centroid is labelled on the image in Figure 3(d), it clearly gives a good estimate of where the centre of the moth is in relation to the image.

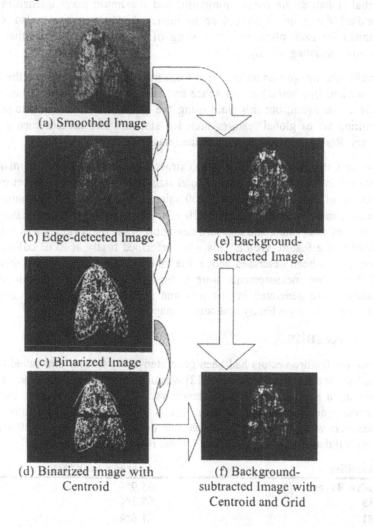

(a) Smoothed Image

(b) Edge-detected Image

(c) Binarized Image

(d) Binarized Image with Centroid

(e) Background-subtracted Image

(f) Background-subtracted Image with Centroid and Grid

Figure 3. The image processing and feature extraction process.

Once the centroid was calculated and the binary features extracted, the binarized version of the image was discarded (but the features calculated from it were retained) and all the further processing was performed on the original smoothed RGB colour version of the image in Fig. 3(a).

Processing of the smooth colour version of the image proceeded as following: first of all, the background was removed from the image using Sternberg's rolling ball algorithm [14]. The result is shown in Fig. 3(e). Next, global colour features were measured. Because Fig. 3(e) is a 24-bit colour image, separate measurements were taken for each of the red, green and blue planes of the image.

The measurements for each plane included the same measurements as taken from the binary version of the image (such as the skew and kurtosis), and also various global statistics: the mean, minimum, and maximum pixel intensities, and their standard deviation. Two colour frequency histograms were also encoded as features for each plane, one consisting of all 256 bins, and another condensed version consisting of only 16 bins.

Finally, the image was transformed from the RGB colour space to the HSB (Hue, Saturation, Brightness) colour space and all of the measurements described above were taken again, but this time using the HSB version of the image. Thus, the resulting set of global features included statistics and measurements taken from binary, RGB, and HSB versions of the image.

The next step in processing was to extract local features from the images. This is depicted in Figure 3(f). A grid of total size 600 x 600 pixels was centred over the centroid of the moth. The 600 x 600 square was then subdivided into 400 square patches, each patch approximately 30 x 30 pixels in size. For each patch, the mean, minimum, maximum, and standard deviation of the pixel values was calculated and added to the feature vector. This was performed firstly in RGB colour space, and then, as has been described above, the pixels in the region were transformed into HSB and the measurements were taken again. Thus an additional 9,600 local features were generated in this way and added to the global features generated previously from the binary and colour images.

5. Results

Once the feature vectors had been generated using ImageJ and saved to a file, the machine learning toolkit WEKA [12] was used to perform further analysis. WEKA contains a number of different classifiers including naïve Bayes, instance-based learning, decision trees, random forests and support vector machines. Each classifiers was applied to the dataset with default parameters in a stratified 10-fold cross validation experiment. Table 1 gives results by classifier.

Classifier	Average Accuracy
Naïve Bayes	65.9%
J48	58.3%
IB1	71.6%
IB5	65.36%
Random Forests (n=200)	83.2%
SMO	85.0%

Table 1. Average prediction accuracy by classifier for Moth species classification.

Table 1 clearly shows that SMO, an implementation of support vector machines that builds a linear separating hyperplane, gives the best overall accuracy. Random forests with 200 randomly generated trees comes a close second, while Naïve Bayes, the decision tree learner J48, and instance-based learning with two different neighbourhood sizes (1 and 5 respectively) both perform poorly in comparison.

The next step was to perform a jackknife test (also known as leave-one-out-cross-validation) on the data using SMO. Jackknife tests give better estimates of how good a classifier is on a dataset, but it is only feasible to perform a jackknife test if the classifier runs relatively efficiently. A jackknife test with SMO in this case yielded a prediction accuracy of 84.8%, quite similar to the 10-fold cross validation result.

Overall, the SMO and random forest results compare favourably to the original analysis of this dataset in [1] in which DAISY achieved a classification accuracy of 83%, albeit with manual pre-processing of each image.

The next issue to consider was the number of attributes in the dataset, which is quite high at 11,300 features. Can the same performance be achieved but with a reduced number of features, thus incurring a smaller cost?

During informal testing before the experiments described here were carried out, it was observed that accuracy tended to increase as the number of cells from which local features were measured increased. That is, the present dataset generated by dividing the 600 x 600 grid over the centroid into 400 patches (that being 20 x 20 patches) gave better accuracy than when the same grid was divided into only 225 patches (being 15 x 15 patches). This is perhaps unsurprising, as a finer grid better captures the textures and patterns on a moth's wings, but at the cost of adding more features.

Experiments in which the local features were deleted completely leaving only global features such as the colour histograms, on the other hand, resulted in about 75% accuracy using SMO: a reasonably high contribution to performance from a relatively small proportion of the total number of attributes.

Another reason that the total number of attributes is quite high is that the same measurements were taken from both RGB and HSB versions of the moth images. It is not at all clear whether both colour spaces are needed for effective moth species classification, and if they are both not needed, it is not clear which colour space is the best. RGB and HSB were both used because transformations between them are straightforward.

With this question in mind, two new datasets that were subsets of the original dataset were generated. The first dataset contained all of the features derived from the binarized and RGB images only, and the second dataset contained all of the features derived from the binarized and HSB images only. A 10-fold cross validation experiment was performed using SMO, the best classifier as indicated in Table 1.

The results were 83.3% and 84.2% respectively: hardly a difference at all, and very close to the 85% accuracy achieved when all of the attributes were included. This result seems to indicate that duplicating measurements in more than one colour space is only likely to improve accuracy by a very small amount, and that the HSB measurements give slightly better quality predictions than the RGB measurements.

The next and more important question to investigate was which of the 35 classes in the dataset were the main contributors to the classification error rate. Statistics per class were recorded during the SMO jackknife test and they are presented in Table 2.

Class	TP Rate	FP Rate
Agrotis exclamationis	0.909	0
Alcis repandata	0.958	0
Anaplectoides prasina	0.864	0.001
Apamea monoglypha	0.917	0.005
Biston betularia	1	0
Cabera pusaria	0.875	0.012
Campaea margaritata	1	0.008
Charanyca trigrammica	0.952	0.001
Chloroclysta truncata	0.769	0.011
Cosmia trapezina	0.857	0.007
Crocallis elinguaria	0.923	0
Diarsia brunnea	0.818	0.003
Herminia tarsipennalis	0.7	0.009
Hydriomena furcata	0.792	0.005
Hylaea fasciaria	0.773	0.008
Hypena grisealis	0.571	0.016
Hypena proboscidalis	0.714	0.009
Idaea aversata	0.87	0.007
Lacanobia oleracea	0.905	0.003
Laothe populi	1	0
Lomospilis marginata	0.81	0.001
Noctua comes	0.85	0.007
Noctua janthe	0.81	0.007
Ochropleura plecta	0.9	0.001
Opistograptis luteolata	0.857	0.003
Orthosia gothica	1	0
Orthosia munda	1	0
Ourapteryx sambucaria	0.826	0.001
Polia nebulosa	0.857	0.001
Rivula sericealis	0.5	0.009
Sphrageidus similis	0.8	0.005
Xanthorhoe designata	0.85	0.005
Xanthorhoe ferrugata	0.682	0.001
Xanthorhoe montanata	0.762	0.009
Xestia triangulum	0.952	0

Table 2. True Positive (TP) and False Positive (FP) rates per class.

Looking at the true positive rates in Table 2, it is clear that some species such as *Biston betularia* and *Orthosia munda*, both with true positive rates of 1.0, are very easily recognised. Other species such as *Hypena grisealis* and *Rivula sericealis* however have unacceptably low true positive rates – 0.57 and 0.5 respectively in these cases.

There are two possible explanations for this: either the poorly recognized species themselves are physically very similar to one or more other species, in which case, individual misclassifications would be most frequently to those very similar other species, or the examples of the poorly recognized species in the dataset are of generally poor quality, in which case the misclassifications would be expected to be more or less uniformly distributed over the other species.

The confusion matrix produced by WEKA during the jackknife experiment with SMO was examined. The confusion matrix for this experiment is a 35 x 35 matrix showing how often instances of one class are either classified correctly, or if they are misclassified, it gives the frequency with which they are misclassified as another class. Although it is too large to reproduce the entire matrix here, some interesting observations can be made.

Consider first of all the two most poorly recognized species from Table 2, *H. grisealis* and *R. sericealis*. When *H. grisealis* is misclassified, the misclassifications (nine in total) are spread nearly uniformly over seven other species. Two examples of *H. grisealis* are classified as *R. sericealis*.

For *R. sericealis*, however, the misclassifications (ten) are highly skewed, with four of the erroneous misclassifications of *R. sericealis* images being to *H. grisealis*. It is not at all obvious from an examination of the misclassified images why they were misclassified. Figure 4 shows four images from the *H. grisealis* and *R. sericealis* classes. There are two images from each class, and one of the images in each case is classified correctly by WEKA while the other is misclassified.

Why were these two classes frequently confused, and why is the source of the confusion not apparent to the human eye? It appears that both *H. grisealis* and *R. sericealis* have quite distinct wing markings, which should easily distinguish them.

There are two possible explanations for this. Firstly, both species have very similar wing colourings, even if the pattern is different. It could be that the global colour histograms of both classes are very similar as a result, which would certainly hinder accurate classification.

Secondly, and perhaps more importantly, the moths were not all photographed at the same uniform distance. Rather, the "best shot" was taken of each moth, so some moths may appear larger relative to others than they actually are. Figures 1(a), 1(b), and 2 are all examples of images in which the moth size is fairly representative of the size of most of the moths in the collection's images. Clearly, however, if a moth photograph is taken from a further distance, then the moth will occupy less of the fixed size 600 x 600 grid of local features, which would hinder classification. Therefore it is much more likely that the spatial distribution of the moth's distinctive wing markings would become harder to recognize or "blurred" to the system in comparison to representations of the wing patterns in moths photographed at a closer distance.

H. grisealis classified as:

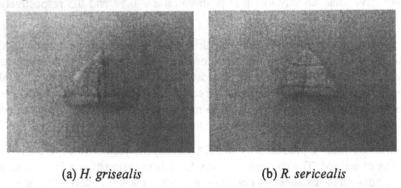

(a) *H. grisealis*   (b) *R. sericealis*

R. sericealis classified as:

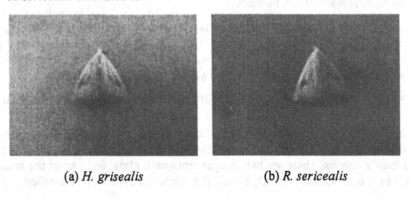

(a) *H. grisealis*   (b) *R. sericealis*

Figure 4. Correctly and incorrectly classified examples of *H. grisealis* and *R. sericealis*.

With this in mind, a refinement of the feature extraction process to consider in the future is size normalization. The size of the moth (actually a count of the number of foreground pixels in the binarized version of the image) was already recorded for each image during feature extraction; this value could be used to regulate the size of the grid from which the local features are extracted, so that the grid effectively becomes smaller for smaller species of moth, and larger for larger moths.

Examples of other frequently misclassifications are given in Figure 5. Out of seven misclassifications of *Xanthorhoe ferrugata*, four images were incorrectly classified as *Xanthorhoe montanata*. Again, this could be explained by the fact that the *X. ferrugata* appears slightly smaller in the images than the other moths, and therefore there is less information in the non-global features extracted for this class. Interestingly, none of the *X. montanata* images, which is of the usual size in the images, were misclassified as *X. ferrugata*.

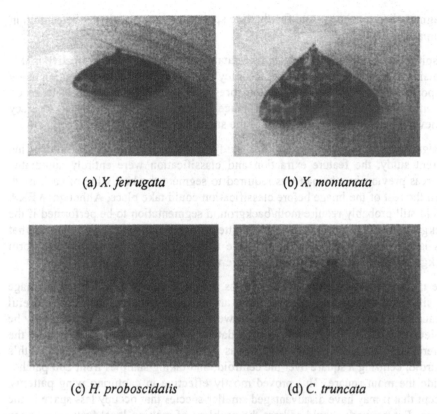

(a) *X. ferrugata* (b) *X. montanata*

(c) *H. proboscidalis* (d) *C. truncata*

Figure 5. Further examples of incorrect classifications of (a) *X. ferrugata* as (b) *X. montanata* and (c) *H. proboscidalis* as (d) *C. truncata*.

Finally, another common confusion was between *Hypena proboscidalis* and *Chloroclysta truncata*, with four misclassifications of former as the latter and two misclassifications in the opposite direction. There is no clear explanation as to why this happened.

6. Conclusion

In summary, this paper has reported on an investigation of a Macrolepidoptera image dataset using the ImageJ image processing toolkit [11] for feature extraction and the WEKA machine learning workbench [12] for classification. The purpose of the investigation was to determine whether data mining techniques could be effective for species classification, where the number of classes is higher than usual (in this case, there were 35 moth species).

This dataset is interesting because the images are of live moths. Whereas dead specimens can be carefully laid out, pinned to a board and imaged in a uniform way under lab conditions, there is much more variability and "messiness" in images taken from live samples. For example, live moths can easily move one of their wings as a photograph is being taken, resulting in a blurred image. Necessity may also dictate that a perfectly uniform background cannot always be used when imaging a live specimen. And finally, live specimens may not always be centred in an image.

Despite this, the results do indicate that data mining techniques are effective in this domain. A jackknife test achieved accuracy of 85% on the image collection using support vector machines, with random forests coming a close second in terms on classification accuracy. This performance exceeds the classification accuracy achieved in a previous investigation of the same dataset [1].

A significant difference between this study and the previous one is that in the current study, the feature extraction and classification were entirely automatic, whereas previously a human was required to segment the best wing of each moth from the rest of the image before classification could take place. Although WEKA would still probably require moth/background segmentation to be performed if the background of the images are highly cluttered, what has been shown here is that this is not necessary if an effort is made to image the moths against a uniform background, even if lighting conditions are variable.

The most important factor in the success of any machine learning-based image classification system is the features that are extracted. Global features are useful because they are invariant to rotation. However, further accuracy gains can only be achieved by adding local features to the dataset, which is necessary to capture the patterns on the moth's wings. This was achieved by calculating each moth's centroid, centring a square over the centroid, and taking samples from 200 patches inside the main square. This proved mostly effective in capturing wing patterns, except that it may have disadvantaged smaller species that occupy less space in the image. Future work should address the problem of making local feature selection invariant to the size of a moth.

Another interesting avenue for future research is the colour space used to encode image features. In this research, it was found that extracting image features in both RGB and HSB colour spaces, as opposed to just one colour space, boosted accuracy by a small amount. Most images are encoded in RGB colour simply because it is the most commonly used and accessible colour space. However, other colour spaces may be much more suitable for the task of species identification. A more thorough investigation of this possibility needs to be carried out.

Finally, future research must also address the scalability of applying machine learning methods to species recognition. Can support vector machines, the best classifier identified in this study, scale to thousands of classes and still remain efficient and accurate? The main impediment is that support vector machines are two-class classifiers, and therefore many of them must be trained in order to solve multi-class problems. This scalability question needs to be explored.

In summary, we are excited about the application and success to date of data mining techniques in the area of automatic species identification. We plan to continue investigations in this area into the future, using both the Macrolepidoptera dataset described here as well as datasets containing images of other types of species.

Acknowledgements

Thanks to Eibe Frank, University of Waikato, as well as the AI-2006 reviewers, for kindly giving valuable feedback on earlier versions of this paper.

References

1. Watson A., O'Neill M & Kitching I. 2004. Automated identification of live moths (Macrolepidoptera) using Digital Automated Identification System (DAISY). *Systematics and Biodiversity* 1(3): 287-300.
2. Gaston K. & Oneill M. 2004. Automated Species Identification: why not? *Phil. Trans. R. Soc. Lond.* **B** 259:655-667.
3. Chesmore D. 2004. Automated bioacoustic identification of species. *An. Acad. Bras. Cience.* 76(2): 435-440.
4. Somervu P. & Harma A. 2004. Bird song recognition based on syllable pair histograms. *IEEE International Conference on Acoustics, Speech, and Signal Processing (ICASSP'04)* Montreal, Canada.
5. Russell K., Do M., Huff J., & Platnick N. 2005. *Introducing SPIDA-web: wavelets, neural networks and Internet accessibility in an image-based automated identification system.* Draft yet to be published.
6. Arbuckle B., Schroeder S., Steinhage V. & Wittmann D. 2001. Biodiversity Informatics in Action: Identification and Monitoring of Bee Species using ABIS. In *Proc. 15th International Symposium for Environmental Protection*, Zurich, pp. 425-430.
7. Moyo T., Bangay S., & Foster G. The identification of mammalian species through the classification of hair patterns using image pattern recognition. In *Proc. AFRIGRAPH 2006*, Cape Town, South Africa, pp 177-181.
8. Yuan G., Russell J, Klette R., Rosenhahn B., & Stones-Havas S. Understanding Tracks of Different Species of Rats. In B. McCane (Ed.) *Proc. Int. Conf. Image and Vision Computing 2005* (IVCNZ), pp. 493-499.
9. Samul A., Brandle J. & Zhang D. 2006. Texture as the basis for individual tree identification. *Information Sciences* 176: 565-576.
10. Sogaard H. 2005. Weed Classification by Active Shape Models. *Biosystems Engineering* 91(3): 271-281.
11. ImageJ: Image Processing and Analysis in Java. http://rsb.info.nih.gov/ij/
12. Witten I. & Frank E. 2005. *Data Mining: Practical Machine Learning Tools and Techniques* (2nd Ed.). Morgan Kaufmann.
13. T.W. Ridler & S. Calvard. 1978. Picture thresholding using an iterative selection method. *IEEE Transactions on Systems, Man and Cybernetics*, 8:630–632.
14. Sternberg S. 1983. Biomedical Image Processing, *IEEE Computer* 16(1):22-33.

SESSION 2:

GENETIC ALGORITHMS AND OPTIMISATION TECHNIQUES

Estimating Photometric Redshifts
Using Genetic Algorithms

Nicholas Miles
Computer Science Dept
University of Kent,
Canterbury, Kent,
CT2 7NF, UK
nick@terado.co.uk

Alex Freitas
Computer Science Dept
University of Kent,
Canterbury, Kent,
CT2 7NF, UK
A.A.Freitas@kent.ac.uk

Stephen Serjeant
Physical Sciences
Open University,
Milton Keynes,
Bucks,
MK7 6AA, UK
s.serjeant@open.ac.uk

Abstract

Photometry is used as a cheap and easy way to estimate redshifts of galaxies, which would otherwise require considerable amounts of expensive telescope time. However, the analysis of photometric redshift datasets is a task where it is sometimes difficult to achieve a high classification accuracy. This work presents a custom Genetic Algorithm (GA) for mining the Hubble Deep Field North (HDF-N) datasets to achieve accurate IF-THEN classification rules. This kind of knowledge representation has the advantage of being intuitively comprehensible to the user, facilitating astronomers' interpretation of discovered knowledge. The GA is tested against the state of the art decision tree algorithm C5.0 [Rulequest, 2005] in two datasets, achieving better classification accuracy and simpler rule sets in both datasets.

1. INTRODUCTION

1.1 Spectroscopy & Photometry

Astronomers today face the challenge of needing large amounts of spectroscopic telescope time in extremely deep field surveys, to identify high redshift objects (where *redshift* is a shift in frequency of the light towards red; see section 2.1). Spectroscopy can prove too time costly to be worthwhile [Gwyn, 1996]. Photometry provides a practical and cost-effective method to obtain comparable results. Photometry is the measurement of fluxes through broad filters of astronomical objects, and from these measurements redshifts can be estimated.

Current methods for estimating redshift using photometry are unfortunately not perfect. By improving on the accuracy of this one can allow astronomers to take more reliable measurements without the cost and time spent on the telescopes.

1.2 Contribution

This paper proposes an Evolutionary Algorithm (EA) for discovering classification rules – supervised learning problem in machine language terminology. This problem is an interesting candidate for Evolutionary Algorithms (EA) because the data is inherently noisy and EAs in general are robust to noise. This work intends to explore how EAs can be used effectively to predict the correct classes, identified by spectroscopy, with greater accuracy than previously used methods. In addition, this produces comprehensible rules that astronomers can use to gain more insight about the data and the application domain. The discovered rules are expressed in a simple IF-THEN structure, as will be described later in section 4, and so they provide knowledge that is intuitively interpretable by astronomers, unlike, for instance, the output of black box classification algorithms such as standard artificial neural networks.

2. Extragalactic Astronomy

2.1 What is redshift?

Redshift is the decrease in frequency (towards the red end of the spectrum) of the light from when it was emitted. This is commonly a result of the emitting and receiving locations moving apart from one another, causing the light rays to stretch (conceptually similar to the Doppler shift, also a commonly observed effect with sound waves). Redshift (z) is formally defined as:

$$1 + z = \frac{\lambda_{observed}}{\lambda_{emitted}}$$

where $\lambda_{observed}$ is the observed wavelength of the light, and $\lambda_{emitted}$ is the wavelength emitted at the source.

When observing distant galaxies, the observed shift is not caused by the movement of galaxies away from us. The distance is simply too great to be able to discern such changes. Instead, it is the effect of universal expansion being observed, which in turn is causing the distance from other galaxies to increase. The expansion of the universe results in a stretching of space, including of the light rays from when they were emitted at their source to when they arrive to us. This stretching means the light has a longer, redder wavelength. The further away the observed astronomical objects are, the larger this effect is, as the light travels a greater distance and therefore undergoes more prolonged stretching.

Because of this effect, there is a relationship between distance and the amount of redshift; therefore, redshift is often used as a measure of distance to galaxies.

2.2 Finding high-redshift objects

Distant objects are very faint and small. Finding these against the many closer small and faint objects is often difficult, involving taking spectra to directly observe the redshift of these. Therefore it can be hard to reliably find and catalogue a large number of high-redshift objects. Inevitably with enough spectra, one will find some of the high-redshift objects. Deep field imaging will therefore find many more faint, distant objects than it is practicable to obtain spectra for.

2.3 Photometric Redshift

Redshifts of extragalactic objects can be measured via spectroscopy. Emission and absorption lines are identified and wavelengths measured, then compared to known rest wavelengths to determine redshift.

Broadband photometry looks at far wider wavelength intervals, typically 1000Å wide, therefore requiring a much shorter exposure time. Comparisons can then be made with predictions from galaxy Spectral Energy Distributions (SED) to determine the photometric redshift (Figure 1). Rather than observing narrow spectral features of galaxy spectra, the photometric redshift technique concentrates on broad features, such as the 4000Å break and the overall shape of a spectrum [Gwyn, 1996].

One method used takes a training set of measured spectroscopic redshifts and derives an empirical relation between these measured redshift and observed magnitudes [Connolly et al., 1995]. Another version of this method derives redshifts by way of a linear function of colours [Wang et al., 1998].

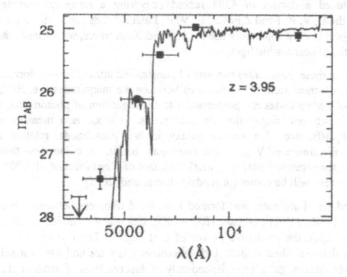

Figure 1: An example of photometric redshift determination for a faint galaxy in the HDF-S NIC3 field. The filled points are the fluxes measured in the five colours observed with the VLT Test Camera (U, B, V, R and I) and in the infrared H spectral band with the NICMOS instrument on the HST. The curves constitute the best fit to the points obtained from a library of more than 400,000 synthetic spectra of galaxies at various redshifts. [ESO, 1998]

2.4 Deep Field Surveys

Deep field surveys are becoming more common: examples include the HDF (Hubble Deep Field) North and HDF South, the NTT Deep Field, and the FORS Deep Field. These were all chosen for the sparseness of highly luminous foreground objects [ESO, 1999].

One of the major motivations currently in deep field surveys is the measurement of colours for all observed galaxies in the field so that photometric redshifts can be inferred.

3. Preparation of the data to be mined

Data was collected from several sources covering the HDF-N including Team Keck Treasury Redshift Survey (TKRS) [Wirth et al., 2004], Hubble's Advanced Camera for Surveys (ACS) Great Observatories Origins Deep Survey (GOODS) [Cowie et al., 2004] and Fernandez-Soto spectroscopic data set [Fernandez-Soto et al., 1999]. Merging these catalogues was done based upon the position on the sky. To prevent misclassifications of nearby objects the magnitudes are also compared. IDL (Interactive Data Language) was used to cross reference and match the entries, which was then used to combine the data into one dataset with just the necessary parameters for the application.

This produced a dataset of 4398 records covering a range of wavelengths, including the B, V, R, I and Z bands. B, V, R, I and Z bands (also referred to as the UBVRI system) are a commonly used set of wideband filters, with a large range in wavelengths of near visible light.

Finally, from these magnitudes two sets of constructed attributes were formed. The first set was formed from the differences between the magnitudes (i.e. B-V, V-R, R-I and I-Z). Magnitudes are proportional to the logarithm of photon flux, so the differences between magnitudes are flux ratios. Colour is a measure of the magnitude difference of a star or galaxy in two pass bands, relative to the magnitude difference of Vega in the same pass bands. A colour less than zero indicates a temperature hotter (or bluer) than that of Vega (around 10,000K), and higher than zero will be cooler (or redder) [Richmond, 2005].

The second set of attributes was formed from the differences between the colours (i.e. (B-V)-(V-R), (V-R)-(R-I) and (R-I)-(I-Z)), this was then added to the colours to improve upon the predictive power of that dataset. The differences between colours is also described as BzK. BzK photometry is a method used for selecting actively star forming galaxies, independently of dust reddening [Daddi et al., 2004; Daddi et al., 2005]. Star formation rate (SFR) of galaxies is a challenging area within astronomy due to dust absorption and re-radiation which increases the wavelength (reddening). Nevertheless, it is an important task for accurately observing the processes and mechanisms involved in galaxy formation and evolution.

As a result of data preparation, the constructed data sets have a class attribute representing the discretized value of redshift, and continuous real valued predictor attributes, these were defined as follows:

3 classes: C_1 ($z < 0.8$), C_2 ($0.8 \le z < 2.2$), C_3 ($z \ge 2.2$)

Colour attributes: B-V, V-R, R-I, I-Z. We shall refer to these as BVmag, VRmag, RImag, IZmag respectively.

BzK atrributes: (B-V)-(V-R), (V-R)-(R-I), (R-I)-(I-Z)

The discretized class values are the same for all datasets. The discretization was performed considering the Lyman Break Method [Steidel, Hamilton, 1992; Steidel et al, 1995], based upon broad spectral features that can be easily identified. These include the Lyman Alpha Break and the Lyman Limits. We observe features at wavelengths of 912Å, 1216Å and 4000Å. These are then subtracted from the central regions in the photometric magnitude regions used in the Hubble surveys. These can be used with photometry to help identify photometric redshift.

The datasets shall be known as Dataset 1 and Dataset 2 from this point on and are defined as:

Dataset 1: [BVmag, VRmag, RImag, IZmag, Class]

Dataset 2: [BVmag, VRmag, RImag, IZmag, BVmag-VRmag, VRmag-RImag, RImag-IZmag, Class]

4. A Genetic Algorithm for estimating redshifts

4.1 Individual Representation

Each individual in the proposed genetic algorithm represents a single classification rule. A rule has the form IF (conditions) THEN (class), a commonly used construct in data mining. The antecedent (IF part) is a conjunction of conditions, where each condition refers to lower and upper bounds for a predictor attribute.

Recall, in section 3, that the predictor attributes given to the system are colours (from the difference in magnitudes B-V, V-R, R-I and I-Z).

Each rule condition is internally encoded into the individual as a gene. Each gene consists of a sextuplet of elements, defined as <LowerValue, Operator, Attribute, Operator, UpperValue, Active Flag>. The Attribute element is the name of one of the attributes of the data being mined, in particular a colour attribute in Dataset 1 and a colour or BzK attribute in Dataset 2. In the current version of the GA the two Operator elements are both the relational operator less than or equal to "≤". LowerValue and UpperValue are thresholds representing the lower and upper values of the attribute. The rule condition encoded by a gene is satisfied by an example if and only if the value of the corresponding attribute for that example is between the LowerValue and UpperValue thresholds. Finally, Active Flag switches on or off this condition of the rule. The operators are fixed in this version of the algorithm but are included into the individual encoding as we intend to explore other values for a future version of the algorithm. The individual encoding contains one gene for each attribute of the data being mined. However, only the genes with Active Flag set to 1 ("on") are actually present in the rule decoded from the individual. An example of an individual encoding for the target dataset is as follows (showing one gene per line to facilitate interpretation):

```
0.1200 ≤ BVmag ≤ 0.3000 [1]
0.1100 ≤ VRmag ≤ 0.2800 [0]
0.1800 ≤ RImag ≤ 0.3200 [0]
0.0700 ≤ IZmag ≤ 0.3800 [1]
```

In this example individual, only the conditions referring to the BVmag and IZmag attributes would be present in the decoded rule, so that the decoded rule antecedent would be:

IF $0.1200 \leq BVmag \leq 0.3000$ AND $0.0700 \leq IZmag \leq 0.3800$

The decoded conditions are connected by an AND operator to produce an antecedent consisting of a conjunction of conditions.

Note that the class predicted by the rule (in its THEN part) does not need to be encoded in the genome of the individual, since it is fixed throughout the run of the GA, as will be explained in section 4.2.

The values of the genes for each individual are randomly generated when creating the initial population. In that initialisation phase, as well as during the entire run of the GA, the values of the gene elements LowerValue and UpperValue are subject to the restriction that they cannot be smaller than / greater than the minimum / maximum value observed for the corresponding attribute in the training set. This restriction ensures that all rules generated by the GA are sensible and useful to be applied to the test data.

4.2   Sequential Covering

Each run of the GA discovers a single rule, so many runs of the GA will be required to discover a set of rules covering all training examples. In order to discover a set of classification rules, we use the sequential covering approach. Sequential Covering is a technique often used in machine learning and data mining to discover all of the rules required to cover the training example set [Witten, Frank, 2000]. Each value in the set of discretized classes to be predicted is taken in turn as the positive class, the rest collectively become the negative class. The GA then iteratively discovers a rule covering as many positive examples as possible, then removes these examples before repeating the process until all positive examples are covered.

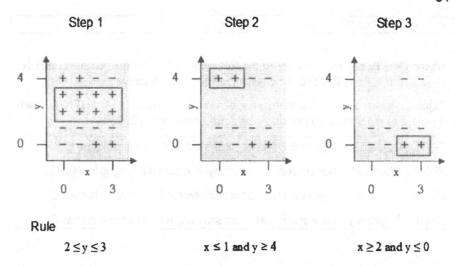

Rule

$$2 \leq y \leq 3 \qquad x \leq 1 \text{ and } y \geq 4 \qquad x \geq 2 \text{ and } y \leq 0$$

Figure 2: Sequential Covering. This shows 3 steps in the process, where the best positive class is identified from the population of rules and the positive examples covered by that rule are then removed from the data and the GA is run again. This process iteratively builds up a set of rules covering all of the positive examples (which identify just one class to be predicted).

Once all of the positive examples have been classified, and a set of rules has been created, the entire process is then repeated using the next class value. This iterative process is summarized in Figure 2.

Once a set of rules exists covering all of the training examples, they are ordered by the classification accuracy of those rules (i.e. their fitness). In order to classify examples that are not covered by any rule, the system enables a last "default rule", predicting the class covering most training examples.

When using these rules on the test set, for each test example, all rules covering that example are initially identified. If all rules covering the example predict the same class, the example is simply assigned that class. If multiple rules covering the example predict different classes, the rule with the highest fitness is chosen (i.e. the highest rule in the ordered set of rules). Finally, if no rules cover the example, the default rule is chosen, predicting the class which has the most examples in the training set.

4.3   Fitness Function

The fitness function in the GA measures the predictive accuracy of each individual (candidate classification rule). It first builds a confusion matrix based on the predictive accuracy of the rules against the examples in the training set. Then the confidence (also known in the astronomical community as reliability) and completeness (or true positive rate) are calculated as shown below, the product of these derives the fitness for each rule.

```
Confidence = TP/(TP+FP)
Completeness = TP/(TP+FN)
```

```
Fitness = Confidence * Completeness
```

where TP, FP, TN and FN refer to the following entries of the confusion matrix: True Positive, False Positive, True Negative and False Negative.

Table 1 shows a confusion matrix for a rule of the form IF A THEN C, each quadrant of the matrix has the following definition [Freitas, 2002]:

TP (True Positives)	Number of instances satisfying A and belonging to class C
FP (False Positives)	Number of instances satisfying A but not belonging to class C
FN (False Negatives)	Number of instances not satisfying A but belonging to class C
TN (True Negatives)	Number of instances not satisfying A nor belonging to class C

Table 1: Confusion Matrix

		Actual Class	
		C	not C
Predicted Class	C	TP	FP
	not C	FN	TN

4.4 Genetic Operators (Crossover and Mutation)

4.4.1 Crossover

The crossover operator is used to evolve the current generation of individuals into a new set of individuals with parents selected from the current population. The crossover method used in our GA is uniform crossover. This works by taking each gene (or rule condition) in turn and randomly choosing the value of that gene (the sextuplet) in one of the parents for one child and the value of that gene in the other parent for the other child. Therefore the two children will be made up from parts of the two parents. The crossover probability used here was 70%.

Uniform crossover was chosen as there is no positional bias as can be experienced using n-point crossover methods [Falkenauer, 1999; Syswerda, 1989]. In the application domain of the proposed GA, as well as in the classification task of data mining in general, the set of attributes has to be treated as a set in the mathematical sense of the term, where there is no ordering between the attributes. Therefore, the lack of positional bias associated with uniform crossover is appropriate for this application domain.

4.4.2 Mutation

Mutation in a GA maintains diversity in the candidate solutions and therefore allows greater exploration of the data space. In our GA, each individual's gene elements probabilistically undergo mutation. The elements of each gene that are affected include the upper threshold, the lower threshold and the active flag with a mutation probability on each of 0.01%. Mutation is applied to the upper and lower thresholds by increasing or decreasing the attribute values by up to 0.5, and to the active flag by flipping it to set whether this particular gene will be active, and therefore have that attribute included in the rule. Hence, the mutation of the active flag can effectively add or remove any condition within the current candidate rule, contributing to maintain a set of candidate rules with diverse lengths in the population.

4.5 Selection Method

Selection is the method used to pick parents that will undergo genetic operators such as crossover and mutation, in order to generate offspring in the next generation. In the proposed GA tournament selection is used, where five individuals are chosen at random and then pitted against each other in a virtual tournament. The best (highest fitness) survives and goes through for mating with another individual winner from another tournament.

5. Computational Results

In order to evaluate the proposed GA, we compared its performance against the performance of C5.0 [RuleQuest, 2005]. C5.0 is an industrial strength state of the art commercial decision tree and rule induction product from RuleQuest Research, developed by Ross Quinlan as the successor to his very successful and widely used ID3 and C4.5 systems. We used the C5.0 implementation available as a built in resource within the well-known Clementine data mining tool.

C5.0 can generate a classification model expressed either as a decision tree or as a set of rules. In order to make a direct comparison with the classification rules discovered by the GA, we used the rule set mode of C5.0. Both the GA and C5.0 were evaluated by running a 10-fold cross-validation procedure [Witten, Frank, 2000], as usual in machine learning and data mining. We used the default parameters of C5.0 and of the GA – i.e., we did not try to optimise the parameters of the GA, in order to make the comparison with C5.0 as fair as possible. In all runs of the GA, the population size was 100 individuals, and the number of generations was 10. Although this is a small number of generations, by comparison with values typically used in the GA literature, even with this value we found a set of rules representing a significant improvement over the set of rules discovered by C5.0, as discussed below. The class values used were the same for both datasets and were based upon spectral features as described in section 3. The probabilities of application of genetic operators were as mentioned in section 4. The results reported here are the average classification accuracy rate over the test set (unseen during training) across the 10 iterations of the cross-validation procedure. In that procedure, the same partition of the data into 10 folds was used by both the GA and C5.0, again to make the comparison between the two systems as fair as possible.

For each of the iterations of the cross validation procedure, the GA was run 10 times with different random seeds, whilst C5.0 was run just once, since it is a deterministic algorithm. The average classification accuracies across the 100 runs of the GA and the 10 runs of C5.0 are shown in Table 2:

Table 2: Classification accuracies for the runs of the GA and C5.0

Algorithm	Dataset 1	Dataset 2
GA	(93.16 +/- 0.46)%	(90.4 +/- 3.04)%
C5.0	(90.73 +/- 0.63)%	(89.852 +/- 2.23)%

The results upon Dataset 1 have >99% confidence that they are statistically significantly different and not by chance, as measured by a Student t-test. However, the difference in the accuracies of the GA and C5 in Dataset 2 are not statistically significant as measured by a Student t-test.

A measure of simplicity was taken of the rules, this is the number of discovered rules and the total number of terms, or conditions, for all discovered rules, as usual in the data mining literature. The measure of simplicity suggests that the rules generated by the GA are considerably simpler, and therefore more easily interpretable, than the rules generated by C5.0. The full simplicity results are shown in Table 3:

Table 3: Simplicity of rules generated by the GA and C5.0

Algorithm	Dataset 1		Dataset 2	
	Rules	Terms	Rules	Terms
GA	8.43 (+/- 1.64)	10.01 (+/- 2.66)	8.8 (+/- 1.66)	15.1 (+/- 4.39)
C5.0	16.5 (+/- 2.58)	41.8 (+/- 5.69)	19.1 (+/- 3.73)	57.9 (+/- 15.61)

The measurements of the number of rules and total number of terms in all rules upon Dataset 1 and Dataset 2 have >99% confidence that they are statistically significantly different and not by chance, as measured by a Student t-test.

Work is ongoing to interpret the classification rules discovered by the GA in the context of prior astronomical knowledge, such as the passage of known redshifted spectral features through the filter passbands.

6. Conclusion and Future Research

The first results of the new GA compared to C5.0 show an improvement in the accuracy with the GA performing with an accuracy over 2.4 percentage points higher than C5.0 for Dataset 1, a statistically significant difference. This can be considered a very good result, considering that C5.0 is the product of several decades of research in decision tree and rule induction, whilst the GA proposed here is still in its first version.

Results using BzK conditions showed a decrease in accuracy for both the GA and C5.0. This was surprising because of the relationship between redshift and SFR in galaxies shown in [Daddi et al., 2004]. In our future work we will continue BzK tests when we have additional data from other surveys.

The only attributes used in these runs were the constructed colour and BzK attributes. One research direction will be to introduce further attributes, including morphological parameters, by building up a more comprehensive catalogue. Another research direction will be to use relational conditions in the attribute space (e.g. B-V < R-I), which will extend upon our use of BzK relationships. Relational conditions are used in astronomy, for example in finding star forming galaxies [Daddi et al., 2004]. A third research direction is to perform template matching using HYPER-Z [Bolnzella et al. 2000] and to compare the results with the GA.

One of the main problems with using a χ^2 solution, such as HYPER-Z, is that it can sometimes confuse spectral features, such as the Balmer and Lyman breaks, therefore misclassifying. With further attributes we intend to build more sophisticated rules with the GA which will aim to prevent such misclassifications, or identify them as misclassified and correct them.

7. References

[Appenzeller, 2005] Appenzeller, I. FORS consortium; The FORS Deep Field (FDF) [http://www.lsw.uni-heidelberg.de/users/jheidt/fdf/fdf.html], Visited October 2005

[Bolnzella et al., 2000] Bolnzella, M. et al. Photometric redshifts based on standard SED fitting procedures, Astron. Astrophys. 363, 476–492, 2000

[Bowman et al., 1993] Bowman, B. et al. Reasoning about naming systems. ACM Trans. Program. Lang. Syst., 15, 5 (Nov. 1993), 795-825, 1993.

[Collister, Lahav, 2003] Collister, A. A., Lahav, O. ANNz: estimating photometric redshifts using artificial neural networks, astro-ph, 0311058, 2003

[Connolly et al., 1995] Connolly, A.J. et al. Slicing Through Multicolor Space: Galaxy Redshifts from Broadband Photometry, astro-ph/9508100, 1995

[Cowie et al., 2004] Cowie L.L. et al. A large sample of spectroscopic redshifts in the ACS-GOODS region of the HDF-N, astro-ph/0401354, 2004

[D'Odorico et al., 2005] D'Odorico et al. European Space Agency; The NTT SUSI Deep Field [http://www.eso.org/science/ndf/], Visited October 2005

[Daddi et al., 2004] Daddi et al., The Population of BzK Selected ULIRGs at z ~ 2, astro-ph/0507504v1, 2005

[Daddi et al., 2005] Daddi et al., Star-forming and Passive Galaxies, ApJ, 617, 746, 2004

[Ding, Marchionini, 1997] Ding, W., Marchionini, G. A Study on Video Browsing Strategies. Technical Report UMIACS-TR-97-40, University of Maryland, College Park, MD, 1997.

[ESO, 1998] ESO Education & Public Relations Department. Deep Galaxy Counts and Photometric Redshifts in the HDF-S NIC3 Field [http://www.eso.org/outreach/press-rel/pr-1998/pr-20-98.html], 1998, Visited on 15 August 2004

[ESO, 1999] ESO Education & Public Relations Department. The FORS/ISAAC Cluster Deep Field [http://www.eso.org/outreach/press-rel/pr-1999/phot-09-99.html], 1999, Visited on 15 August 2004

[Falkenauer, 1999] Falkenauer E., The Worth of the Uniform, CEC-99, 1999

[Fayyad, 1996] Fayyad U. M., Chapter 19: Automating the Analysis and Cataloging of Sky Surveys, Advances in Knowledge Discovery and Data Mining, AAAI Press / The MIT Press, 1996

[Ferguson, 2005] Ferguson H., Space Telescope Science Institute. The Hubble Deep Field [http://www.stsci.edu/ftp/science/hdf/hdf.html], Visited October 2005

[Fernandez-Soto et al., 1999] Fernandez-Soto A. et al. A new catalog of photometric redshifts in the Hubble Deep Field, Astrophys. J., 513, 34-50, 1999

[Freitas, 2002] Freitas A. Data Mining and Knowledge Discovery with Evolutionary Algorithms, Springer, 2002

[Giavalisco et al., 1997] Giavalisco M. et al. The Hubble Deep Field: Number Counts, Color-Magnitude and Color-Color Diagrams, 1997

[Gwyn, 1996] Gwyn, S., The Redshift Distribution and Luminosity Functions, astro-ph/9603149, 1996

[Kwedlo, Kretowski, 2000] Kwedlo W., Kretowski M. An Evolutionary Algorithm Using Multivariate Discretization for Decision Rule Induction, Proceedings of Evolutionary Computations on Principles of Data Mining and Knowledge Discovery (PKDD'00), Springer LNCS 1910, 2000

[Kwedlo, Kretowski, 1998] Kwedlo W., Kretowski M. Discovery of decision rules from databases: an evolutionary approach. Principles of Data Mining and Knowledge Discovery, PKDD'98. Nantes, France. Springer LNCS 1510, 1998

[Lahav et al., 1996] Lahav O. et al. Neural Computation as a tool for galaxy classification: methods and examples, MNRAS, 283, 207L, 1996

[Peacock, 1999] Peacock J. A. Cosmological Physics, Cambridge University Press, 1999

[Rengelink, 1998] Rengelink R. AXAF Field: Deep Optical-Infrared Observations, Data Reduction and Photometry, ESO Imaging Survey, 1998

[Rulequest Research, 2005] Rulequest Research. Data Mining Tools See5 and C5.0 [http://www.rulequest.com/see5-info.html], 2005, Visited on October 2005

[Richmond, 2005] Richmond, M., Photometric Systems and Colors [http://spiff.rit.edu/classes/phys445/lectures/colors/colors.html], Visited on October 2005

[Stanway et al., 2003] Stanway E. R. et al. Lyman Break Galaxies and the Star
Formation Rate of the Universe at z ~ 6, 2003

[Staneck, 1999] Stanek, R., Photometry
[http://astrwww.astr.cwru.edu/nassau/reference/photometry.html], CWRU
Astronomy Dept, 1999, Visited on October 2005

[Steidel, Hamilton, 1992] Steidel C. C., Hamilton D. Deep imaging of high
redshift QSO fields below the Lyman limit. I - The field of Q0000-263 and
galaxies at Z = 3.4, AJ, 104, 941-949, 1992

[Steidel et al, 1995] Steidel C. C. et al. Lyman Imaging of High-Redshift
Galaxies.III.New Observations of Four QSO Fields, AJ, 110, 2519, 1995

[Steidel et al., 1996] Steidel C. C. et al. Spectroscopic Confirmation of a
Population of Normal Star-forming Galaxies at redshifts z>3, AJ, 462, L17–
L21, 1996

[Syswerda, 1989] Syswerda G., Uniform Crossover in Genetic Algorithms, ICGA-
89, 1989

[Wang et al., 1998] Wang et al. A Catalog of Color-based Redshift Estimates for Z
<~ 4 Galaxies in the Hubble Deep Field, AJ 116, 2081, 1998

[Williams et al., 1997] Williams R. et al. The Hubble Deep Field: Images, 1997

[Wirth et al., 2004] Wirth G. et al. The Team Keck Treasury Redshift Survey of
the GOODS-North Field, astro-ph/0401353, 2004

[Witten, Frank, 2000] Witten I. H., Frank E. Data Mining – Practical Machine
Learning Tools and Techniques with Java Implementations, Morgan
Kaufmann, 2000

Non-linear Total Energy Optimisation of a Fleet of Power Plants

Lars Nolle[♣], Friedrich Biegler-König[♠] and Peter Deeskow[♦]

[♣]School of Computing and Informatics
Nottingham Trent University
Clifton campus, Clifton Lane
Nottingham, NG11 8NS, UK
E-mail: lars.nolle@ntu.ac.uk

[♠]Fachbereich Mathematik und Technik
Fachhochschule Bielefeld
33604 Bielefeld, Germany
E-mail: friedrich.biegler-koenig@fh-bielefeld.de

[♦]STEAG KETEK IT GmbH
Centroallee 261
46047 OberhausenGermany
E-mail: peter.deeskow@steag-ketek.de

Abstract

In order to optimise the energy production in a fleet of power plants, it is necessary to solve a mixed integer optimisation problem. Traditionally, the continuous parts of the problem are linearized and a Simplex scheme is applied. Alternatively, heuristic "bionic" optimisation methods can be used without having to linearize the problem. We are going to demonstrate this approach by modelling power plant blocks with fast Neural Networks and optimising the operation of multi-block power plants over one day with Simulated Annealing.

1. Introduction

Increasing prices for fossil fuels and the introduction of CO_2 credits to European markets have intensified the attempts to ensure energy efficient operation of power plants.

One of the well-known optimisation issues where mathematical modelling has proven to be indispensable is the unit commitment in power generation planning. It deals with the scheduling of start-up/shut-down decisions and operation levels for a fleet of power generation units such that variable costs are minimal or revenues are maximal. In this optimisation temporal constraints such as time dependency of power prices at the power exchange, limited availability of certain plants, costs for start-up or shut-down, limits for total emission or fuel consumption within a given period of time should be taken into account. Therefore the optimisation has to be carried out within a certain time window with sufficient time resolution.

Because of the involvement of decision variables (power plant on or off), and the fact that every unit has a lower limit of power that can be generated, the above-defined problem involves mixed integer programming. The well understood approach to this problem is to use the methods of mixed integer linear programming [1] in this context. It is widely used and allows for optimisation with complex temporal constraints with reasonable CPU time consumption.

A recent study [2, 3] has shown that a non-linear approach has the advantage of easily taking into account the current state of each of the plant components and thus opens additional potential for optimisation. It overcomes the usually high CPU time consumption of non-linear modelling based on closed analytical models by meta-modelling the power plant using neural networks. However, this approach was restricted to momentary optimisation only.

In this contribution the approach presented in [2] is extended to consider a model, which is discrete in time with complex constraints.

2. Approaches to Mixed Integer Optimisation

The common approach to optimisation in unit commitment uses a linear model of power generation and applies the simplex method of linear programming together with a Branch-and-Bound approach to solve the integer linear program.

The simplex method is an iterative method to solve linear programs with constraints. Within a finite number of steps it reaches the solution or proves infeasibility of the problem. The algorithm cannot be applied if some of the variables are restricted to integers. In that case methods are available which apply to a more or less general class of problems.

One of these methods is Branch-and-Bound which consists of three phases. In the branching phase the feasible region is partitioned, in the bounding phase linear simplex is used to find upper and lower bounds of the optimal objective values and in the coordination phase rules are applied for eliminating parts of the feasible region from further consideration (see e.g. [1]).

Unfortunately, the convenience of using the well-known mathematics of mixed integer linear programming comes to the expense of loosing details in the modelling. This may impact on the potential for optimisation.

An alternative approach is the application of so-called "Bionic Methods", i.e. methods that emulate the optimisation behaviour of biological or physical systems. Well-known among these are Genetic Algorithms, Simulated Annealing (SA), or Ant Algorithms (see e.g. [4]).

All these algorithms are iterative, based on heuristics, and have the advantage that they can easily deal with continuous variables as well as with discrete ones.

The number of iterations needed to produce good optimal states of the system is usually high. In most cases, however, it is impossible to prove that a found state is optimal.

The next section gives an introduction to the simulation approach for power plant blocks, before Simulated Annealing is applied to a problem of the described type in section 4.

3. Fast Simulation of Power Plants

In this study, a fleet of power plants with four blocks, which are identical in construction (a simple case), are considered. Each block can generate power in the range of 108 MW to 360 MW. A block cannot produce less than 108 MW. If a block is switched off, there are considerable costs to start it up again.

A detailed model of a power plant block was built using Ebsilon, a programme developed by Sofbid (http://www.sofbid.com/ebsilon/, see [5] and [6]) in Zwingenberg, Germany. Ebsilon is a simulator specialized in power generating facilities. Ebsilon models can be very complex (see Figure 1 for a section of a model of a power station block). After the model has been constructed, Ebsilon needs about 5 to 20 seconds on a PC to simulate a given situation for one block. This was far to slow for the problem at hand, since many thousands of model evaluations are usually required for heuristic optimisation algorithms like SA. Hence, in this research, a neural network was used as a meta-model of the power plant.

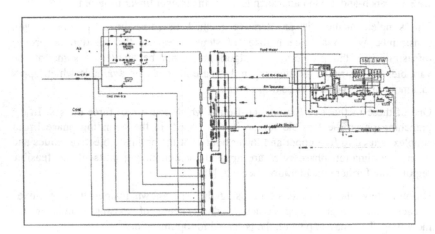

Figure 1 Section of Ebsilon Power Station Model

As described in [2], it is possible to replace the simulator Ebsilon by a much faster meta-model based on Neural Networks. The state of a power plant block is determined by only a few input parameters. The most important parameters are the amount of energy that the block is producing per hour. Other parameters describe the external conditions and settings by the operational staff:

- Temperature of cooling water (between 0 and 30 °C).
- Air ratio in combustion chamber (between 1.1 and 1.4).
- Live steam temperature (between 510 and 540 °C)
- Hot reheat temperature (between 510 and 540 °C)
- Flue gas re-circulation (between 0 and 50 kg/s).
- 8 more parameters specifying the degree of heat surface fouling.

Based on these input vectors, Ebsilon is calculating the amount of coal needed, which in turn determines the total costs involved.

For the experiments, 15,000 random input data vectors were produced, each containing 14 randomly determined values for the input parameters described above. Each vector describes a specific state of a power plant block. The associated required amount of coal for each input vector was then calculated using Ebsilon.

The resulting data set, containing 15,000 vectors with 14 input values and one associated output value, was then divided into a learning set (10,000 training vectors) and a validation set (5,000 test vectors). A standard feed-forward neural network with one hidden layer and 60 hidden neurones was trained and an MSE of 0.00009 and an EKK of 0.99901 was achieved after a few hundred iterations. The network is able to predict the required amount of coal for a given input with an average error of 1.2%. This error has the same order of magnitude as the simulation error of an Ebsilon calculations. The main advantage of the neural network is its response time; it is more than 5,000 times faster than Ebsilon, i.e. the response time on a standard PC is less than 0.001 seconds.

4. Simulated Annealing

Simulated Annealing (SA) is a robust general optimisation method that was first introduced by Kirkpatrick et. al. [7], based on the work of Metropolis et. al. [8]. It simulates the annealing of a metal, in which the metal is heated-up to a temperature near its melting point and then slowly cooled to allow the particles to move towards an optimum energy state. This results in a more uniform crystalline structure and so the process allows some control over the microstructure. SA has been demonstrated to be robust and capable of dealing with noisy and incomplete real-world data [9]. This makes SA suitable for engineering applications.

Simulated annealing is a variation of the hill-climbing algorithm. Both start off from a randomly selected point within the search space. Unlike in hill-climbing, if the fitness of a new candidate solution is less than the fitness of the current solution, the new candidate solution is not automatically rejected. Instead, it becomes the current solution with a certain transition probability $p(T)$. This transition probability depends on the difference in fitness ΔE between the current solution and the candidate solution, and the temperature T. Here, 'temperature' is an abstract control parameter for the algorithm rather than a real physical measure. The algorithm starts with a high temperature, which is subsequently reduced slowly, usually in steps. At each step, the temperature must be held constant for an appropriate period of time (i.e. number of iterations) in order to allow the algorithm to settle in a 'thermal equilibrium', i.e. in a balanced state. If this time is too short, the algorithm is likely to converge to a local minimum. The combination of temperature steps and cooling times is known as the annealing schedule, which is usually selected empirically. The behaviour of the algorithm at the beginning of the search is similar to a random walk, while towards the end it performs like ordinary hill climbing. Simulated Annealing may also work on a population of particles, i.e. solutions, rather than on just one particle.

5.   Power Plant Optimisation: A Case Study

We will now use Simulated Annealing to optimise the operation of our fleet of four power plant blocks in one day.

We assume that every hour a different amount of energy has to be produced and that these 24 values are given a day ahead (in reality, these estimates have a high accuracy).

For each time t_i, $i = 1, ..., 24$ the production of our power plant with 4 blocks is described by the vector

$$x(t_i) = (E_1, E_2, E_3, E_4, b_1, b_2, b_3, b_4)^T.$$

b_1, b_2, b_3 und b_4 are binary values and denote whether or not a block is switched off. E_1, E_2, E_3, E_4 are the production rates of the blocks. In every hour of the day they must add up to the given total production. We also have to consider the restrictions of minimal and maximal production rates: $108MW \leq E_i \leq 360MW$.

The objective function we want to minimize is the cost of energy production accumulated over the day. Since, for every hour in a day, we have a vector of eight variables, the total number of variables in our problem is 24x8 = 192. In our simple model the total costs consist of the costs for coal and the start-up costs for blocks going on-line. Thus the aim is not only to minimize the production costs in every single hour, but also to keep the number of switch-on-processes of power plant blocks low.

In order to apply the described algorithm we still have to define the elementary steps. Basically, two kinds of steps can be identified:

1.   Change of production rate E_k for block no. k without altering the configuration of the power plant. These steps try to optimize a given configuration. This corresponds to solving the continuous part of the problem. In the beginning a maximal step size S_{max} is defined. S_{max} is multiplied by a random number between −1 and 1. This yields the current step size. The block number k is also chosen randomly among the running blocks.
Afterwards the restrictions are checked (minimal and maximal production rates, total energy production). If it is not possible to satisfy all boundary conditions, another elementary step must be chosen.
This type of elementary step is applied with a probability of 95%.

2. Change of power plant configuration. In this case the binary valued variables are changed. Let n be the number of running blocks. Possible changes of configuration are: Starting up an additional block (4-n alternatives), shutting down a running block (n alternatives), interchanging a running and a pausing block (m alternatives with m=3 if n=1 or n=3, m=4 if n=2, otherwise m=0).

This type of elementary step is applied with a probability of 5%. Among these 5% the steps are chosen according to the number of alternatives.

After interchanging two blocks, it is not necessary to adjust the production rates, since in our case all blocks have the same limitations. Starting up or shutting down a block makes it necessary to readjust the production rates in order to satisfy the restrictions. If this is not possible, another elementary step must be chosen.

In addition to the elementary steps the following control parameter settings have been used for SA:

- $T_0 = 1000$.

- $T_E = 0.001$.

- $\alpha = 0.999$.

- Maximal number of iterations: $it_{max} = 10000$.

With this choice of parameters a very good value for the total costs over a day could be found, although it cannot be verified that the found solution represents the global optimum.

Example:

For our example we have used the described 4-block power plant of Elbistan (Turkey), a coal price of 30 Euros for a ton and a start-up price of 10,000 Euros for each block. For each hour of the day a required energy production rate is given. Additionally, the values for heat surface fouling and cooling temperature for block 1 have been changed for the worse, the corresponding values of block 3 have been changed for the better. A starting configuration has been chosen randomly which satisfies all constraints. Obviously, the starting configuration is pretty bad, since it contains a lot of start-up processes and uses all 4 blocks equally.

Figure 2 shows the production rates (vertical axis) in 24 hours (horizontal axis) of all four blocks before the optimisation, whereas Figure 3 presents the production rates after optimisation.

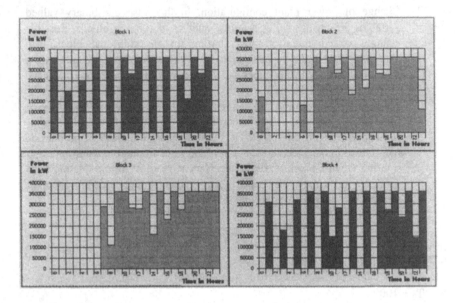

Figure 2 Power production of four blocks during one day before optimisation

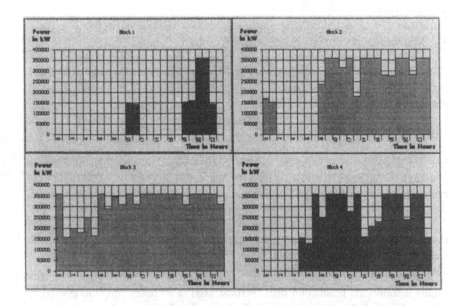

Figure 3 Power productions of four blocks during one day after optimisation with SA

As it can be seen, after the optimisation less start-up processes take place and there is a clear bias towards block 3. Block 1 is only used in peak times. The total daily production costs dropped from 1.8 million Euros to 1.3 million Euros a day.1000 Iteration with Simulated Annealing were performed to reach this result. That took less than a minute on a normal PC. The method is easily expandable to more power generating units.

6. Conclusion

This paper has discussed a concept for online optimisation in power plant technology, which combines different numeric "state-of-the-art" processes to form a method customized for power-engineering requirements.

Neural Networks can be trained with high accuracy to reproduce the results of the computational-intensive thermodynamic simulation programs on the basis of physical fundamentals. As such, non-linear detailed models of the individual power plant units can be generated, whose response time lies within the range of milliseconds.

Simulated Annealing is a heuristic optimisation algorithm, which appears to be suitable for solving the mixed-integer optimisation problems arising in power plants and which, together with fast neural network models, allows an online solution for the non-linear optimisation problems.

In an earlier study this concept was successfully applied to a momentary optimisation. The present study demonstrates that a suitable extension of the objective function allows for optimisation of a model, which is discrete in time and considers constraints linking different time intervals. Thus it is clearly shown that the described methods enable non-linear mixed integer optimisation of unit commitment in a fleet of power plants.

Because of the completely non-linear nature of the models, such approaches would be able to solve problems in future, which nowadays either cannot be solved at all or else only with difficulty using a classical optimisation on the basis of a linear modelling. Examples here are the consideration of the non-linear boundary conditions (temperatures in the steam piping) or a common optimisation of the load distribution to multiple units and, at the same time, the mode of operation of the individual units.

The next step of the development will be to define an algorithm that automatically generates the elementary steps for a general class of constraints. This is crucial for an easy application of the method to more complex cases. Once this extension is available it will be possible to apply the approach to more complex problems in order to compare its performance with the performance of the classical integer linear programming approach.

96

References

1. Schultz, R. Integer Programming Applied to Power Systems' Generation and Operation Planning, Gerhard-Mercator-Universität Duisburg, 2003.
2. Biegler-König, F., Deeskow, P. Fast Simulation and Optimisation with Neural Networks, Proc. 19th European Conference on Modelling and Simulation, Riga, 2005.
3. Deeskow, P., Biegler-König, F., Nolle, L. Schnelle Optimierung von Kraftwerksparks mit Neuronalen Netzen, Proc. 6. VDI-Fachtagung Optimierung in der Energiewirtschaft, Stuttgart, 2005.
4. Gerdes, I., Klawonn, F., Kruse, R. Evolutionäre Algorithmen, Vieweg Verlag, Wiesbaden, 2004.
5. Brinkmann, K., Pawellek, R. Ebsilon - Examples for the easier design and better operation of power plants. Proc. Conf. Energy Forum 2003, Konstantin Varna, 2003.
6. Brinkmann, K., Pawellek, R. Optimierte Prozessführung von Kraftwerksblöcken mit Online-Werkzeugen: Betriebserfahrungen. Proc. VDI Tagung Wissensbasiertes Betriebsmanagement senkt Kosten, Frimmersdorf, 2004.1.
7. Kirkpatrick, S., Gelatt Jr, C. D., Vecchi, M. P. Optimization by Simulated Annealing, Science, 13 May 1983, Vol. 220, No. 4598, pp 671-680
8. Metropolis, A., Rosenbluth, W., Rosenbluth, M. N., Teller, H., Teller, E. Equation of State Calculations by Fast Computing Machines, The Journal of Chemical Physics, Vol. 21, No. 6, June 1953, pp 1087-1092
9. Nolle, L., Goodyear, A., Hopgood, A., Picton, P., Braithwaite, N. On Step Width Adaptation in Simulated Annealing for Continuous Parameter Optimisation. Proc. 7th Fuzzy Days, Dortmund, 2001.

Optimal Transceivers Placement in an Optical Communication Broadband Network Using Genetic Algorithms

R. Báez de Aguilar-Barcala, F. Ríos, R. Fernández-Ramos, J. Romero-Sánchez,
J.F. Martín-Canales, A.I. Molina-Conde, and F.J. Marín
fjmarin@uma.es

Abstract. A genetic algorithm-based procedure for solving the optimal transceiver placement problem in an optical communication broadband network is presented. It determines the minimal number and type of transceivers and their geographic distribution in an optical network in order to guarantee the broadband demanded by the end user. The proposed method has been validated for standards networks of 10, 15 and 20 nodes, and compared with classical techniques of discrete location theory. Then, the genetic algorithm has been used on a real network (70 nodes) for the West area of Malaga city (Spain).

1. Introduction

Great investments are necessary to provide the hardware support to communication services and data networks. Currently, end users need even more bandwidth, because they want to use the new services that provide higher quality and efficiency in their data communications. At the same time, the facilities must be implanted by using low cost procedures that allow improving the profits and competitiveness without end user has to pay even more. It is for that reason why it should be researched new methods and procedures that allow carrying out wide band links for end users with speeds, reasonable investments and short run times.

Free space optical communications by non-guided laser beams is a feasible solution for fast implementation and low cost yield [1]. Currently, the state of art of both developments, electronic technology in solid state power laser and electro-optical converters including high frequency switching devices, allow us to implement non-guided laser link (transceiver) in a metropolitan area of several kilometres, with an availability of 99.9 %, and wide band links for end users with speeds between 1 and 10 Gbits/s, as high as fibre links [2]. An optical implementation demands for best results to minimize the number of transceiver and to distribute them well (transceiver placement) in order to obtain the maximum reliability (broadband and speed required) at minimum cost.

The transceiver placement is still a major problem in multicast networks, gateway placements, locate disaster recovery centres, optimal phasor measurement unit placement in energy management system [3], etc. In this work, we face the problem of finding, using genetic algorithms (GAs) [4], the minimal number and the type of transceivers in an optical network in order to guarantee the maximum reliability. Our method has been tested on 3 standards (10, 15 and 20 nodes) networks and the fitting of the parameters of the GA has been performed using discrete location theory (DLT). With optimum results therefore, we applied it on a real network (70 nodes) in the West of Malaga city (Spain).

2. Problem Description

From now on, let's call "potential nodes" to those city buildings where we could put transceivers, and "demand nodes" to those buildings which demand bandwidth.

Let us the index set $J = \{1, 2, \ldots, n\}$ the potential nodes denoted by c_j, $j \in J$. Index set $I = \{1, 2, \ldots, m\}$ will be associated with the demand nodes denoted by d_j, $i \in I$. As there is an underlying network in the problem scenario the c_j and d_j may be referred to as nodes in such a network. If all nodes are potential nodes as well as demand nodes then $m = n$.

The decision variables in the formulation are defined by:

$$X_i = \begin{cases} 1, \text{ if a facility is established at } c_j \\ 0, \text{ otherwise} \end{cases} \quad (1)$$

Thus, the placement problem can be mathematically expressed as follows [5]:

$$\min \sum_{j=1}^{n} c_j \Bigg/ \quad c_j = s_j + \sum_{i=1}^{m} p_i x_i \quad \text{subject to} \quad \sum_{j=1}^{n} a_{ij} x_j d_j \geq d_i \quad \forall x_i \in \{0,1\} \quad (2)$$

where, s_j is the cost of establish the transceivers needed to satisfy the demand of node j, p_i is the cost of establish the transceivers needed to supply bandwidth to node i, a_{ij} is the net zero-one adjacency matrix, and di, dj are the bandwidth demanded by nodes i, j, respectively. Costs s_j and p_i are interrelated, and they are directly proportional to the type of transceivers used. There are six types of transceivers, combining a 500, 1000 or 2000 meters range, and a 100 Mb/s or 1 Gb/s bandwidth. Therefore, the setup cost is given by the type of transceivers needed to satisfy the required bandwidth, and the transportation cost is given by the type of transceiver needed to send the signal through a distance the same or greater than the one existing between both nodes. The total cost is calculated by adding both costs, in order to get the highest network reliability.

3. Method Proposed

The placement problem is a NP-complete problem, with a solution space of 2^N possible combinations. This combinatorial optimization problem is difficult to solve due to the discrete nature of the search space with multiple local minima. So, we propose to use GAs to resolve it. The GA's encoding should be as follow: set the net bandwidth distribution tree (total cost), that is, the number and the type of transceivers that we have to place in the nodes. The codification scheme should be able then to distinguish between the node or nodes through which the needed bandwidth is supplied to the network (source node), the distribution tree nodes that don't supply any bandwidth to any other node (leaf nodes), and the nodes that get and supply bandwidth [6]. A heuristic method can be used to achieve this installation strategy. In order to calculate the fitness function we use the following rules:

1. Fix a low threshold that none of the possible solution will reach if it cannot solve the problem. This threshold is used to get a border between solutions that can solve the problem and solution that cannot.
2. Calculate the individual cost by adding the cost of the transceivers assigned to each node of the network.
3. Calculate an upper threshold, which represents the worst possible solution to the problem.
4. Subtract the value of the low cost level obtained in 2 from the value of the upper level obtained in 3.

Eventually, the fitness value will be the value calculated by rule 1 for the individuals that cannot solve the problem, or the value calculated by rule 4 for the individuals that can solve the problem. Using these rules, the GA works as a maximization method. Because of that, the most favoured individuals will be the ones worthy to solve the problem, and any individual is not able to do so (not valid solution) will have a low fitness (low threshold).

Example:

Given two random individuals that can solve the problem, which cost are 300 and 150 respectively. In the analysis of the problem, we have estimated the low threshold that none individual is not going to reach if it cannot solve the problem, to be 100, and the upper threshold that represents the most expensive solution to be 1000. The individual fitness is calculated as it is shown:

$$Fitness(1) = 100 + (1000 - 300) = 800$$
$$Fitness(2) = 100 + (1000 - 150) = 950$$

Therefore, we have achieved the less cost individual to be favoured for its fitness. The low threshold is created to have a region where we could store those individuals that cannot solve the problem. So, for instance, an individual that don't have any transceiver wouldn't be a solution of the problem, but its cost would be zero. If we hadn't created the former region, we would have obtained this individual to be the suitable when we had minimized the upper threshold, what it is incorrect.

4. Description of the Genetic Algorithm.

The first point to deal with is how we represent the information. We have chosen bit string representation, where each element of the string would be one of the network nodes. In our problem, the solution of the problem is given by a set of transceivers of different kind set up in the net nodes. The number and kind of transceivers to set up is calculated by the bandwidth that a certain node need to supply, and by the distance with the nodes it have to communicate with. To find this set of transceivers is trivial and it has only one solution (from a cost point of view) once we have the net bandwidth distribution tree. Therefore, an obvious solution would be that any gene of the chromosome represent the node that supply bandwidth to a certain node, that is, the source node of that node. So, an individual of our population could be as it is shown in figure 1.

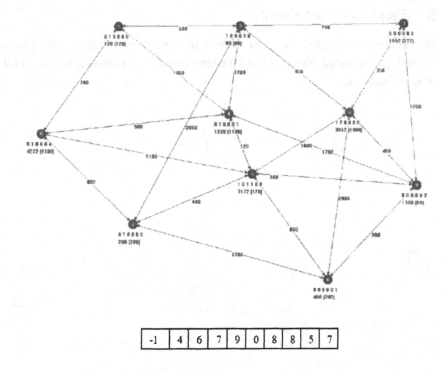

-1	4	6	7	9	0	8	8	5	7

Figure 1. Representation of a solution individual of a population generated for a 10 nodes network.

The value "-1" shows that this node is not supplied bandwidth by any node, that is, that this node is the network source node, which receive the total bandwidth that the network needs and that have to distribute it to its adjacent nodes (node 0). Every node which index does not appear in the chromosome is a network leave node, that is, a node that doesn't supply any bandwidth to any other node. So, for instance, in figure 1 we can notice how gene "1" have the value "4", what it means that its source is node "4".

Other points to study are the selection, crossover and mutation method used in this work. To get the best results, the first tests were made by using proportional or Whitley methods [7]; 1 or 2 crossover points; crossover probability between 0.6 and 0.8; normal, adaptive and selective mutation; and mutation probability between 0.005 and 0.01. Finally, and after study the results, the last tests (those where the network have a higher number of nodes) were made using normal selection operator, two crossover points, crossover probability of 0.7 and normal mutation operator. To improve the algorithm, we used Steepest Ascent Hill Climbing method, to accelerate the convergence of the solution of the problem.

5. Simulations and Results

The parameters adjustment has been made in small networks of 10, 15 and 20 nodes, low or high connected. Figure 2 shows the representation of a solution individual for a 10 nodes network.

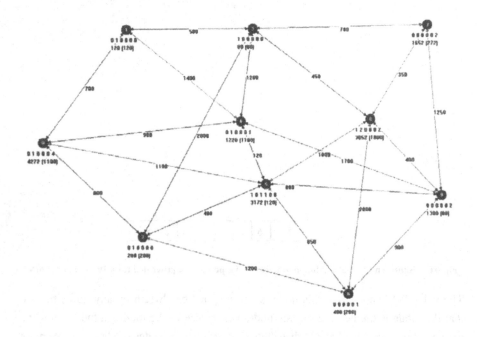

Figure 2. Individual solution for a 10 nodes network.

The results showed are the best values after running ten times each configuration with the following parameters: population of 100, 200 and 300 individuals; proportional selection method or *De Whithley* selection method [7]; one or two crossover points; crossover probability from 0.6 to 0.8; mutation fix by bit; adaptive mutation, changing the value each 5 generation, and one mutation method we proposed, the selective mutation, which use beforehand information about the solution characteristics. Table 1 shows the best values obtained with GAs. With the GAs, we have always obtained optimal solutions, as with the DLT classic method. There are barely any differences between the results obtained by the selection and by the mutation methods tested.

Table 1. Optimal solution with GA in 10, 15 and 20 nodes validation networks

Network Nodes	Population	Cross Prob.	Cross Points	Mutation Prob.	Number of Transceivers	Cost €	Time (minutes)
10	200	0'7	2	0'005	16	69.415	4'
15	200	0'7	2	0'005	25	136.727	160'
20	200	0'7	2	0'005	43	204.340	420'

Table 2 shows the results obtained by DLT method, where (*) means that is the best result got after running the simulation more than two week, and obtaining hereby a higher number of transceivers than the number obtained with the GA. The results obtained with smaller networks of 10 and 15 nodes, are the same that the results obtained with the GA, but the first one have a higher computational cost. It can be noticed that although the GA needs more time to find the first solution than the DLT, the improvement obtained with the former method is noteworthy: it reaches the best DLT-solution after 5 hours; a little later the GA surpasses the DLT-solution; and hardly half and hour later the GA reaches a value that DLT method isn't capable to reach even after two weeks running.

Table 2. Results obtained by DLT

Number of Nodes	Execution Time	Number of Transceivers	Cost
10	15h 10m 0s	16	69.415 €
15	70h 35m 57s	25	136.727 €
20	+2 weeks	--	215.198 €*

After this validation of our GA, we used it in a 70 nodes real network. Figure 3 shows the 70 nodes network corresponding to the West of Malaga City. The GA's evolution is shown in figure 4. In the upper graphic there are three waves, representing the evolution of the best individual (top wave), the population average (intermediate wave), and the worst individual (down wave). To bring out the correct evolution of the GA, we have incremented the scale in the lower graphic in order to highlight the best individual of the population. Here, we can observe the evolution of the GA through 500 generations. An elitist strategy has been used, where the best individual of the population is kept from one generation to the next one.

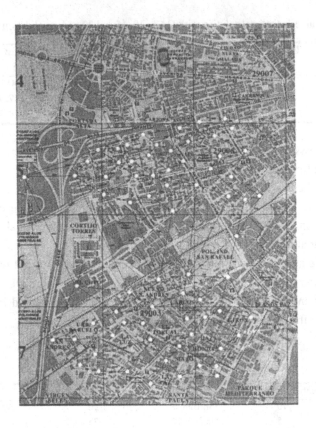

Figure 3. Real network of 70 nodes. West area of Malaga city.

5. Conclusions

This paper presents a real application for genetic algorithms. The results suggest that this approach to optical communication broadband network optimization offers a practical method of providing a flexible network design tool. When you have to deal with a high number of nodes, methods based in graph solution research, as those given by Discrete Location Theory, can't be achieved, although they supply the best solution to the problem, they become intractable. Even in small networks, execution time is high. Genetic algorithms are a good choice in this kind of problems, because they give the possibility of getting good results in acceptable times. Other than by DLT, the more connected the network is, the quicker a solution is supplied: this makes it more suitable for the problem we are facing.

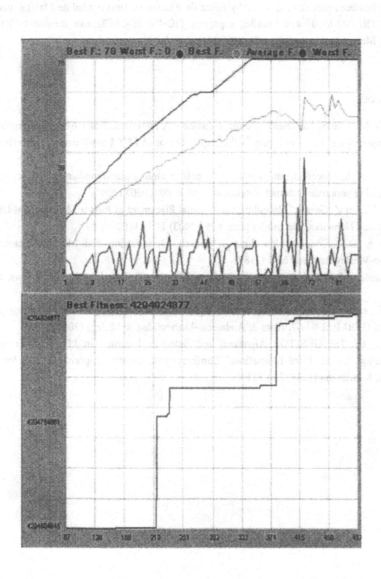

Figure 4. Evolution of the genetic algorithm for a 70-nodes network.

Acknowledgment

This work has been partially supported by Junta de Andalucía, Universidad de Malaga, under contract OTRI-PAI-03-07 and Excellence project TIC-486-06-08. Thanks are due to Town Council of Malaga and to Andalusia Statistical Institute for supplying data.

References

1. Britz, D. M. Free Space Optical Communication - A New Broadband Access Technology with Implications for Laser Safety in the Public Sector. AT&T Labs-Shannon Laboratories (2002)
2. Ríos, F., et al., Procedimiento y aparato de enlace punto a punto mediante haz láser en el espacio libre para redes ethernet. Patente, no. sol. P200400305 (2004)
3. Marin, F.J., et al. Genetic Algorithms for Optimal Placement of Phasor Measurement Units in Electrical Networks, Electronics Letters **39** (2003) 1403-1405
4. Goldberg, D.E. Genetic Algorithms in Search, Optimization and Machine Learning. Addison-Wesley Reading, MA. (1989)
5. Mirchandani, P.B. and R.L. Francis. Discrete Location Theory. John Wiley & Sons, Inc. (1990)
6. Ríos, F., et al., Desarrollo de un Sistema Comercializable de Comunicación Óptico para Internet. OTRI-PAI-03-07. Junta de Andalucía-Universidad de Málaga (2004)
7. Whitley, D., The GENITOR Algorithm and Selection Pressure. In J.D. Schaffer (ed.), Proceedings of the Third International Conference on Genetic Algorithms. San Mateo, Morgan Kauffmann (1989) 116-121

SASS APPLIED TO OPTIMUM WORK ROLL PROFILE SELECTION IN THE HOT ROLLING OF WIDE STEEL

Lars Nolle
School of Computing and Informatics
Nottingham Trent University
Clifton Lane
Nottingham
NG11 8NS,UK
lars.nolle@ntu.ac.uk

Abstract

The quality of steel strip produced in a wide strip rolling mill depends heavily on the careful selection of initial ground work roll profiles for each of the mill stands in the finishing train. In the past, these profiles were determined by human experts, based on their knowledge and experience. In previous work, the profiles were successfully optimised using a self-organising migration algorithm (SOMA). In this research, SASS, a novel heuristic optimisation algorithm that has only one control parameter, has been used to find the optimum profiles for a simulated rolling mill. The resulting strip quality produced using the profiles found by SASS is compared with results from previous work and the quality produced using the original profile specifications. The best set of profiles found by SASS clearly outperformed the original set and performed equally well as SOMA without the need of finding a suitable set of control parameters.

1. Introduction

Many scientific and engineering problems can be viewed as search or optimisation problems, where an optimum input parameter vector for a given system has to be found in order to maximize or to minimize the system response to that input vector. Often, auxiliary information about the system, like its transfer function and derivatives, etc., is not known and the measures might be incomplete and distorted by noise. This makes such problems difficult to be solved by traditional mathematical methods. Here, heuristic optimisation algorithms, like Genetic Algorithms (GA) [1] or Simulated Annealing (SA) [2], can offer a solution. But because of the lack of a standard methodology for matching a problem with a suitable algorithm, and for setting the control parameters for the algorithm, practitioners often seem not to consider heuristic optimisation. The main reason for this is that a practitioner, who wants to apply an algorithm to a specific problem, and who has no experience with heuristic search algorithms, would need to become an expert in optimisation algorithms before being able to choose a suitable algorithm for the problem at hand. Also, finding suitable control parameter settings would require carrying out a large number of experiments. This might not be an option for a scientist or engineer, who simply wants to use heuristic search as a problem-solving tool. In this research, Self-Adaptive Stepsize Search (SASS), a novel optimisation heuristic that has only on control parameter, has been applied to the problem of finding the optimum profiles for a wide strip steel mill.

Producers of steel need to offer a high quality product at a competitive price in order to retain existing customers and win new ones. Producers are under pressure to improve their productivity by automating as many tasks as possible and by optimising process parameters to maximise efficiency and quality. One of the most critical processes is the hot rolling of the steel strip [3], which is explained in more detail in the following section.

2.   Hot Rolling of Wide Strip

In a rolling mill a steel slab is reduced in thickness by rolling between two driven work rolls in a mill stand (Figure 1). To a first approximation, the mass flow and the width can be treated as constant. The velocity of the outgoing strip depends on the amount of reduction. A typical hot rolling mill finishing train might have as many as 7 or 8 close-coupled stands.

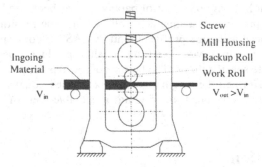

Figure 1 – *Layout of a 4-high rolling stand.*

2.1   Mill Train

A hot-rolling mill train transforms steel slabs into flat strip by reducing the thickness, from some 200 millimetres to some two millimetres. Figure 2 shows a typical hot strip mill train, consisting of a roughing mill (stands R1-R2) and finishing stands (F1-F7).

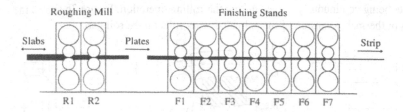

Figure 2 –*Typical hot strip mill train.*

The roughing mill usually comprises one or more stands which may operate in some plants as a reversing mill, i.e. the slabs are reduced in thickness in several passes by going through the stand(s) in both directions. When the slab or plate has reached the desired thickness of approximately 35 mm it is rolled by the "close-coupled" finishing stands in one pass. Strip dimensions, metallurgical composition, and the number of slabs to be rolled, together with other process dependent variables, are known as a *rolling program* or *rolling schedule*.

Within a rolling program, the width of the strip changes from wide at the beginning to narrow towards the end, because the edges of the strip damage the rolls. These damaged areas must not be in contact with the strip and therefore, only strip with a reduced width can be rolled at that point.

2.2 Strip Quality

The main discriminator for steel strip from different manufacturers is quality, which has two aspects: *strip profile* and *strip flatness*.

Strip profile is defined as variation in thickness across the width of the strip. It is usually quantified by a single value, the *crown*, defined as the difference in thickness between the centre line and a line at least 40 mm away from the edge of the strip (European Standard EN 10 051). Positive values represent convex strip profiles and negative values concave profiles. For satisfactory tracking during subsequent cold rolling a convex strip camber of about 0.5% - 2.5% of the final strip thickness is required [4]. Flatness - or the degree of planarity - is quantified in *I-Units*, smaller values of I-Units representing better flatness.

Modern steelmaking techniques and the subsequent working and heat treatment of the rolled strip usually afford close control of the mechanical properties and geometrical dimensions. In selecting a supplier, customers rank profile and flatness as major quality discriminators. Tolerances on dimensions and profile of continuous hot-rolled un-coated steel plate, sheet and strip are also defined in European Standard EN 10 051.

Both the flatness and profile of outgoing strip depend crucially on the geometry of the loaded gap between top and bottom work rolls. As a consequence of the high forces employed, the work rolls bend during the rolling process, despite being supported by larger diameter back-up rolls [5]. Figure 3a shows a pair of cylindrical work rolls. In Figure 3b the effects of the loading can be seen. Due to contact with the strip at temperatures between 800°C and 1200°C the rolls expand,

110

despite being continuously cooled during the rolling operation. Figure 3c shows the effect of thermal expansion of the unloaded work rolls on the roll gap.

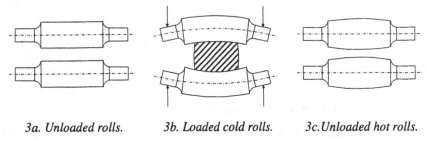

3a. Unloaded rolls.   3b. Loaded cold rolls.   3c. Unloaded hot rolls.

Figure 3 – *Roll gap geometry.*

If the geometry of the roll gap does not match that of the in-going strip, the extra material has to flow towards the sides (Figure 4). If the thickness becomes less then about 8mm, this flow across the width cannot take place any longer and will result in partial extra strip length, and therewith in a wavy surface (Figure 5).

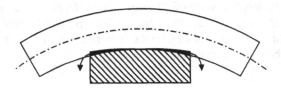

Figure 4 –*Mismatch between roll gap and strip geometry.*

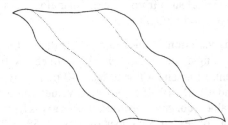

Figure 5 –*Wavy strip surface.*

The effects of bending and thermal expansion on the roll gaps, and the strip tension between adjacent mill stands, results in a non-uniform distribution of the internal stress over the width of the strip. This can produce either latent or manifest bad shape, depending on the magnitude of the applied tension and the strip thickness [6]. Bad shape, latent or manifest, is unacceptable to customers, because it can cause problems in further manufacturing processes.

2.3 Initially Ground Work Roll Profiles

To compensate for the predicted bending and thermal expansion, work rolls are ground to a convex or concave camber, which is usually sinusoidal in shape (Figure 6).

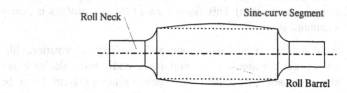

Roll Neck   Sine-curve Segment

Roll Barrel

Figure 6 – *Cambered work roll.*

Figure 7 shows how the initially ground camber can compensate for the combined effects of bending and expansion.

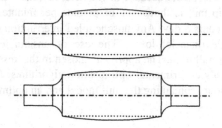

7a. Unloaded rolls

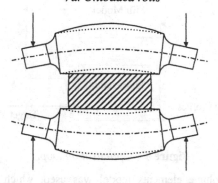

7b. Loaded, hot rolls

Figure 7 –*Compensating combined effects.*

Due to the abrasive nature of the oxide scale on the strip, the rolls also wear significantly. Due to this roll wear, the rolls need to be periodically reground after a specified duty cycle (normally about four hours), to re-establish the specified profile.

2.4   Roll Profile Specification

The challenge is to find suitable work roll profiles - for each rolling program - capable of producing strip flatness and profile to specified tolerances. In a new mill, these profiles are initially specified individually for every single roll program. These are often later changed, e.g. by the rolling mill technical personnel in an effort to establish optimum profiles! This fine-tuning of the roll profiles is nearly always carried out empirically.

Due to the lack of accurate model equations and auxiliary information, like derivatives of the transfer function of the mill train, traditional calculus-based optimisation methods cannot be applied. If a new rolling program is to be introduced, it is a far from straightforward task to select the optimum work roll profiles for each of the stands involved.

3.   Optimisation of profiles

The seemingly obvious solution of experimenting with different profiles in an empirical way is not acceptable because of financial reasons - the earning capacity of a modern hot strip mill is thousands of pounds per minute, and the mills are usually operated 24 hours a day. Any unscheduled interruption of strip production leads to considerable financial loss.   The use of unsuitable roll profiles can seriously damage the mill train. The approach chosen in this research is to simulate the mill and then apply experimental optimisation algorithms. Figure 8 shows the closed optimisation loop, containing the mill model and an optimisation algorithm.

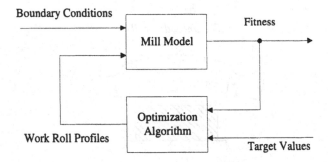

Figure 8 – *Optimisation loop.*

A finite constant volume elements model was used, which was developed in previous research. The accuracy of the model was increased by using real world data to train an Artificial Neural Network to compensate for the model error [7,8].

3.1 The Fitness Function

In the past, a number of optimisation algorithms were used to find optimum profiles for a single steel slab [7]. However, in the real world, a sequence of different slabs is rolled with the same set of profiles (see 2.1). Therefore, the profiles need to be suitable for each of the different slabs in the same rolling program. This has been taken into consideration in this research by adjusting the fitness function used to measure the fitness of a set of profiles.

The fitness (objective function) has been calculated by a combination of crown and flatness values of the centre-line, the edge, and the quarter-line (Equation 1). To avoid a division by zero, one been added to the denominator. The theoretical maximum value of this objective function is 1.0.

$$f(x,\alpha) = \frac{1}{n} \sum_{s=1}^{n} \frac{1}{1 + \frac{1}{\alpha} \sum_{i=1}^{3} I_i(x) + |c_{aim} - c(x)|} \tag{1}$$

where:

n: number of different slabs in rolling program

$f(x)$: fitness of solution x,
$I_i(x)$: I-Units at line i for solution x,
c_{aim}: target crown,
$c(x)$: achieved crown for solution x,
α constant to select the relative contribution of flatness and camber, chosen to be 5000 for the experiments.

As it can be seen from Equation 1, the fitness for the rolling program is the average fitness for each of the different slabs rolled during the program.

3.2 Self-Adaptive Stepsize Search

For heuristic search algorithms, like Hill-Climbing (HC), it was previously shown that the definition of the neighbourhood, and in particular the chosen step size, is crucial to the success of the algorithm [9], not only for continuous parameter search, but also for discrete parameters, when the search space is too large to consider direct neighbours of a candidate solution for performance reasons. It was shown that selection schemes with random step sizes with an upper limit (maximum step size s_{max}) outperform neighbourhood selection schemes with a constant step length. It was also demonstrated that using a scaling function for reducing s_{max} over time could again increase the performance of Hill-Climbing algorithms.

However, it would clearly be of benefit if the maximum step length would be more adaptive to the search progress itself. Therefore, a new population-based adaptation scheme with a self-adaptive step size, referred to as Self-Adaptive Step-size Search (SASS) has been developed for HC [10], where the temporary neighbourhood of a particle p_i is determined by the distance between itself and a randomly selected sample particle s_i of the population during each iteration.

At the beginning of a search this distance is likely to be large, because the initial population is uniformly distributed over the search space and the chances are high that s_i is drawn from a different region within the input space. When the search is progressing, each particle is attracted by a local optimum and hence the population is clustered around a number of optima. If both, p_i and s_i are located in different clusters, p_i has the chance to escape its local optimum if it samples from a region with a higher fitness, i.e. lower costs. Towards the end of the search, most particles have reached the region of the global optimum and hence their mean distance is much smaller than in the initial population. As a result, the maximum step size s_{max} is sufficiently small to yield the global optimum. Figure 9 shows pseudo code of the algorithm. The main advantage of SASS is, that it only has one control parameter that has to be chosen in advance, which is the number of particles n in the population. The processing time is proportional to the number of particles and hence the complexity of the algorithm is $O(n)$.

```
Procedure selfAdaptiveStepSizeSearch
Begin
   initialise population of n particles
   While stopping criterion not met
   Begin
     For every particle p in population
     Begin
       select random particle s ≠ p
       For every component pᵢ in particle p
       Begin
         s_max ← | pᵢ - sᵢ |
         generate random value r ∈ [-s_max; +s_max]
         p'ᵢ ← pᵢ + r
       End
       If f(p') better than f(p) then p ← p'
     End
   End
   Return best result
End
```

Figure 9 - *Pseudo code of the SASS algorithm.*

Although the algorithm is very simple, it has been shown that it is capable to find near optimal solutions without the need of experimenting with different control parameter combinations.

4. Experimental Results

SASS has been applied 50 times in order to find the optimum set of profiles. The rolling program consists of 14 different slabs, therefore the average fitness for this 14 slabs had to be calculated. For SASS, previous experiments suggested that the number of particles should be of the same area of magnitude as the number of independent input parameters of the problem at hand. In this work, the number of particles has arbitrarily chosen to be 10 and was not fine-tuned, in order to prove that SASS can be used as a black-box method for practical applications.

From Table 1 it can be seen that the average fitness achieved during the experiments was 0.9649 out of 1.0 for SOMA and 0.9694 for SASS. For both algorithms, the small standard deviations indicate that in most of the searches the same optimum has been found, i.e. both algorithms have converged towards the global optimum. SOMA needed on average 4418 fitness evaluations until it reached that optimum, whereas SASS converged slightly faster, i.e. after 4072 fitness evaluations.

	SOMA		SASS	
	Average Fitness	Fitness Evaluations	Average Fitness	Fitness Evaluations
Average	0.9649	4418	0.9694	4072
Standard Deviation	0.00030	164	0.00036	464

Table 1 – *Search results.*

Table 2 compares the strip quality achieved using the original profile specification with the strip quality achieved using the best sets found by SOMA and SASS.

	Original Profiles		SOMA		SASS	
	Average	Standard Deviation	Average	Standard Deviation	Average	Standard Deviation
Crown error [mm]	0.064	0.03	0.02	0.03	0.06	0.02
Flatness edge [I-Units]	13.2	14.9	2.5	7.0	2.8	3.9
Flatness quarter [I-Units]	32.6	41.0	29.2	42.0	26.9	42.1
Flatness middle [I-Units]	22.3	52.2	26.9	53.9	21.6	53.4

Table 2 – *Strip quality with original profiles.*

Table 3 shows the improvement achieved by using the optimised sets of profiles found by SOMA and SASS.

	SOMA		SASS	
	Average [%]	Standard Deviation [%]	Average [%]	Standard Deviation [%]
Crown error	62.3	11.1	9.9	25.5
Flatness edge	81.0	52.9	78.5	73.9
Flatness quarter	10.5	-2.4	17.5	-1.3
Flatness middle	-20.6	-3.3	2.9	0.9

Table 3 –*Improvement of strip quality.*

The results for SOMA show that the average crown error was reduced dramatically by 62.3% and the corresponding standard deviation by 11.1%. The strip flatness at the edges was improved by 81.0 %, the flatness in the quarter line by 10.5%. Only the average flatness in the middle of the slabs has decreased by 20.6%. The improvements in crown error achieved by using SASS were not as great as the results produced by SOMA, but on the other hand, the improvements in flatness at the quarter line and in the middle were significantly better compared to SOMA.

5.   Conclusion

This paper introduced SASS, a novel population based Hill-Climbing algorithm with a self-adaptive step size, and reports on its application to the problem of finding optimum profiles for a rolling mill. SASS has only one control parameter, which is the population size. The population size was set in this work using a simple heuristic.

Although the algorithm is very simple, the results presented in this paper have demonstrated that SASS is capable of finding solutions near the global optimum with a very high reproducibility. It was shown that the best set of profiles found by SASS clearly outperformed that the original set and that the algorithm performed equally well compared to SOMA, but without the need of tuning a large number of control parameters. Other optimisation algorithms usually require a large number of experiments in order to find a suitable control parameter set, which can be seen as an optimisation problem itself and hence requires a considerable amount of time and afford. This is a real obstacle for practitioners who simply want to use heuristic search as a problem-solving black-box tool.

As it was demonstrated in this work, SASS offers an alternative for practical applications, because it helps avoiding expensive experimenting without compromising the quality of the results obtained.

References

1. Goldberg, D.E.: Genetic Algorithms in Search, Optimization and Machine Lerning, Addison-Wesley, 1989
2. Kirkpatrick, S., Gelatt Jr, C. D., Vecchi, M. P.: Optimization by Simulated Annealing, Science, 13 May 1983, Vol. 220, No. 4598, pp 671-680
3. Larke, E. C.: The Rolling of Strip Sheet and Plate, Chapman and Hall Ltd, London, 1963
4. Winkler, W.: Grundlagen des Breitbandwalzens, Stahl u. Eisen 63 (1943) Nr. 40, pp 731-735
5. Emicke, Lucas: Einflüße auf die Walzgenauigkeit beim Warmwalzen von Blechen und Bändern, Neue Hütte, 1. Jg. Heft 5, 1956, pp 257-274
6. Wilms, Vogtmann, Klöckner, Beisemann, Rohde: Steuerung von Profil und Planheit in Warmbreitbandstraßen, Stahl u. Eisen 105 (1985) Nr. 22, pp 1181-1190
7. Nolle, L., Armstrong, D.A., Hopgood, A.A., Ware, J.A.: Optimum Work Roll Profile Selection in the Hot Rolling of Wide Steel Strip Using Computational Intelligence, Lecture Notes in Computer Science, Vol. 1625, Springer, 1999, pp 435-452
8. Nolle, L., Armstrong, D.A., Hopgood, A.A., Ware, J.A.: Simulated Annealing and Genetic Algorithms applied to Finishing Mill Optimisation for Hot Rolling of Wide Steel Strip, International Journal of Knowledge-Based Intelligent Engineering Systems, Volume 6, Number 2, April 2002, pp 104-111
9. Nolle, L.: On the Effect of Step Width Selection Schemes on the Performance of Stochastic Local Search Strategies, Proceedings of the 18th European Simulation Multiconference ESM 2004, Magdeburg, Germany, 13-14 June 2004, pp 149-153
10. Nolle, L.: On a Hill-Climbing Algorithm with Adaptive Step Size: Towards a Control Parameter-Less Black-box Optimisation Algorithm, To appear in: Proceedings of the 9th Fuzzy Days International Conference on Computational Intelligence, Dortmund, Germany, 18-20 September, 2006
11. Nolle, L., Zelinka, I.: SOMA Applied to Optimum Work Roll Profile Selection in the Hot Rolling of Wide Steel, Proceedings of the 17th European Simulation Multiconference ESM 2003, Nottingham, UK, 9-11 June 2003, pp 53-58

SESSION 3:

AGENTS AND SEMANTIC WEB

Agents in Safety Related Systems Including Ubiquitous Networks

Lars Strandén

Swedish National Testing and Research Institute,
Borås, Sweden

lars.stranden@sp.se
www.sp.se

Abstract

The ADM (Autonomous Decision Maker) concept concerns the possibility of including intelligent interfaces, agent like, for supporting the use of ubiquitous networks, such as the Internet, in safety related applications. The need for such interfaces is inevitable if remote surveillance and control shall be supported. The single most important aspect of ADM is its capability of handling limited resources when making intelligent decisions. Intelligence in ADM is manifested in reasoning and learning. This paper outlines the role of ADM and especially in relation to the standard IEC 61508 and presents the overall properties that result. These are exemplified by a presentation of ADM demonstrator.

1. Introduction

As can be seen from day to day, everyone becomes more and more dependent on the Internet i.e. a ubiquitous network that is involved in our professional and personal lives. This trend will continue and be more important in the future when network QoS (Quality of Service) requirements will be higher and more trust is put on the Internet. However, the Internet is indeterministic, designed without overall control and exposed to different forms of attacks e.g. DoS (Denial of Service) and thus special care must be taken if safety related systems shall be able to use the Internet [1]. As part of the PIITSA[1] project the ADM (Autonomous Decision Maker) concept was developed for addressing safety aspects of a real-time system using a ubiquitous network as the communication network. The main ADM contributions are:

- Specification of an architecture for the ADM concept.
- Creation of a logical demonstrator with basic functionality

---

[1] The PIITSA project is a research and demonstration project funded by VINNOVA (Swedish Agency for Innovation Systems). PIITSA is conducted by AerotechTelub, Blekinge Institute of Technology, Swedish National Testing and Research Institute and the Swedish Road Administration in Stockholm.

ADM shall be seen as a functional unit capable of performing intelligent and autonomic decisions also when resources are limited. The purpose of using ADM is to handle some or all safety aspects on behalf of the application i.e. the principal idea is to separate safety handling from ordinary functionality. However, ADM can also be used in systems where the possible damage is small or none at all. In these cases the use of ADM can anyhow be motivated by that

- in the future the application may be modified to become more critical.
- allocation of safety between ADM and other parts of the application may change in the future.
- the separation of ADM functionality and ordinary functionality improves system quality since developers can focus on a more limited scope at a time.
- intelligent and autonomic behaviour is needed in the system (possibly also as a part of the ordinary functionality)

Since safety and ordinary functionality are separated it means that development of each can occur relatively independent of the other. This is in line with the definition of *safety functions* in IEC 61508 [2] and the ideas of *Aspect Oriented Software Development* [3].

The picture below shows an example of an application using ADMs.

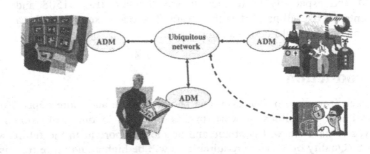

Figure 1 Application example

Here a machine (upper right) is normally controlled by a stationary operator (upper left) having overall control but with a mobile operator (lower left) having limited control (e.g. for maintenance). The mobile operator could connect to the ubiquitous network at different physical locations. Directly from the figure the following hazards are visible; an attack on the ubiquitous network (lower right), decision conflict between operators, inconsistent system views and performing actions in spite of not having complete information.

An ADM based system has two main goals given in priority order:

1. to not cause any safety violation.
2. to keep up the assigned job.

ADM analyzes when there is, or will be, a dangerous situation and ADM can then shut down the system in a safe way (according to the associated fault model) before the situation gets out of control. This is an important quality of ADM; to realise that the situation is becoming too complex to be handled and then let the system enter a safe state.

In this paper it is discussed how an ADM based system is able to handle safety and especially in relation to the IEC 61508 standard which is a domain independent, generic, comprehensive and established standard. In this project the same definition of safety is used as in IEC 61508 i.e. to avoid

- harm or death to people
- damage on equipment
- environmental damage/pollution
- economical damage (short term or long term effects)

Further, there could also be different degrees of severity in each case.

The crucial aspect of the ADM concept is resource boundedness i.e. the possibility of producing optimal decisions also in the case when there are not enough resources. This makes decision making more complex and involves aspects such as:

- How much execution time shall be spent on analysing use of resources?
- How much execution time shall be spent on evaluating different decision strategies?
- How shall resources be handled if there is a sudden change in deadline for decision (shortened/prolonged)?

This paper addresses the applicability of the ADM concept in safety-related systems and discusses resulting properties. Section 2 gives an overview of ADM and Section 3 discusses the important aspect of how to transfer safety to the ADM. Section 4 describes ADM aspects related to intelligence. A matching with IEC 61508 is made in Section 5 and, finally, the logical demonstrator is described in Section 6.

2. Overview

Generally, a system can be separated into two parts; *application* and *infrastructure* where the latter, which is application independent, makes it possible to execute the former. An ADM based distributed system is loosely connected in the sense that there is no infrastructure support for overall control by a master node. Within each node there is ordinary functionality (not handled by ADM) and safety handling (handled by ADM to an extent defined by the application). From the start, an ADM has no application specific role except enabling an intelligent interface to the application. The application has to specify requirements for the ADM and the ADM has to be instantiated. The partitioning of safety is defined by the application, however, there is always the possibility of ADM performing a safe system shut-down (according to the defined fault model). The figure below shows the internal structure of a node with ADM where a solid line shows a scheduling relation and a dashed line shows an application relation i.e. where an exchange of application information takes place.

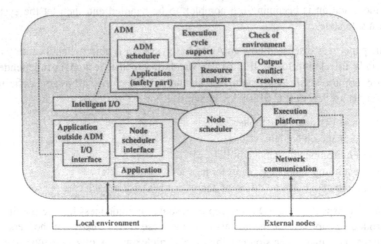

Figure 2 Node structure

A node consists of the following parts:

- ADM – The following parts are included:
    - *ADM scheduler* – It handles available resources allotted to ADM by *Node scheduler*. The idea is that *ADM scheduler* shall be capable of making optimal decisions.
    - *Execution cycle support* – It is used for executing application related tasks in ADM.
    - *Check of environment* – It is used for analysing if the environment of the node behaves in an unexpected way e.g. too fast.
    - *Application (safety part)* – It contains all safety handling allocated to ADM. Safety handling can be split between ADM and *Application outside ADM* but ADM does not consider ordinary application functionality.
    - *Resource analyzer* – It is used for analysis of available resources and resource needs within ADM. The results are used by the *ADM scheduler.*
    - *Output conflict resolver* – It handles conflicts between different settings of outputs in ADM.
- *Application outside ADM* – The following parts are included:
    - *Application* – It contains the major part of the application (all concerning ordinary functionality and possibly some of the safety handling).
    - *I/O interface* – ADM communicates with *Application outside ADM* concerning application behaviour via its *I/O interface.* ADM can use I/O for the local environment via *Application outside ADM* and use I/O for communication with *Application outside ADM*. In the former case handling is made more or less transparent from the perspective of *Application outside ADM* and

in the latter case I/O is directly used by *Application outside ADM*.

o *Node scheduler interface* – *Application outside ADM* communication with *Node scheduler* takes place via the *Node scheduler interface*.

- *Execution platform* – All communication aspects are handled by the *Execution platform*. Notice that there might be conflicts between ADM and *Application outside ADM* since both can send messages and both can control *Execution platform*.
- *Intelligent I/O* – ADM uses *Intelligent I/O* for improved quality of decisions. *Intelligent I/O* shall be seen as a plug-in unit and possibly being a COTS product e.g. an intrusion detection system.
- *Node scheduler* – The *Node scheduler* handles execution control of the following resources:
  o Execution time
  o Time to deadlines
  o Bandwidth for ubiquitous network

Scheduling information exchange with ADM takes place via the *ADM scheduler*. If output conflicts occur between ADM and *Application outside ADM* they are handled by *Node scheduler*.

ADM decisions are governed by execution of layers; *Reactive layers* are used for making fast decisions, *Deliberative layers* make it possible to reason before making decisions and *Proactive layers* support improvement of decision quality. *Proactive layers* cannot directly affect outputs but *Reactive layers* and *Deliberative layers* can. This structure could be compared with the *subsumption architecture* [4] especially concerning the reactive layers.

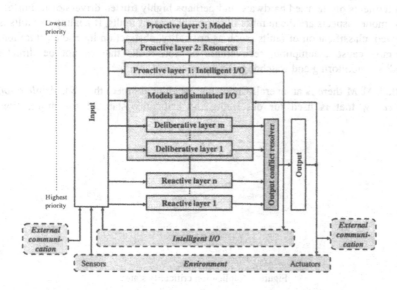

Figure 3 I/O view of ADM decision structure

126

The execution of layers is scheduled in the following way:

1. The reactive layers are executed first and according to priority and available resources.
2. The execution of deliberative and proactive layers could be interleaved and is defined by the application.

For reactive and deliberative layers an application specified number of layers is defined. The reactive and deliberative layers are related to the functionality of the system and can directly affect outputs. Since more than one layer may set outputs there is a risk of conflicts between outputs and these are handled by the *Output conflict resolver. Models and simulated I/O* are used for the deliberative layers and can be executed without affecting reality i.e. the consequences of different strategies can be analysed before being accepted. There are several models and one of them, the *Environment Model* is also used for analysing if the local environment is changing too fast to be accurately handled by ADM. For proactive layers there could be a maximum of three associated layers as shown in the figure. ADM uses *Intelligent I/O* for improved quality of decisions and the proactive layers *Resources* and *Model* are used for improving resource handling and models respectively.

The hierarchy of layers supports an incremental development of the application and also rapid prototyping. The most obvious handling can be first defined in reactive layers and later on refined or moved to deliberative layers.

The ADM fault model is application dependent and specifies how faults are manifested (actually an assumption) or, correspondingly, how components (software and hardware) fail. One important part is containment regions which define if and how an error, caused a by a specific fault, can propagate to other regions. The only fault model assumption related to ADM that is compulsory is that it shall always be possible to shut down the system. Eventually this comes down to requirements on the used hardware and perhaps highly trusted drivers of it. Further fault model aspects are the number of currently present faults, if healing of faults is allowed, classification of faults (such as criticality, abstraction level etc), duration, common cause assumption, recoverable or not, faults that cannot be directly handled (monitoring and watchdogs could be needed) etc.

Within ADM there is an overall finite state machine defined, the *FSM Application criticality,* that is used for describing the criticality state of the application.

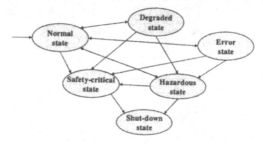

Figure 4 Application criticality states

Normal state is the state where the application is functioning without restrictions and there are no safety problems. This is also the initial state. *Error state* is the state where a fault, according to a defined fault model, has been manifested. *Degraded state* is the state where the application is functioning but with reduced performance and/or quality but there are no safety problems. A reason for entering this state could be reduced available bandwidth for communication with other nodes. *Hazardous state* is the state where actions *might* lead to safety critical situations. However, recovery from this state could be possible. *Safety-critical state* is the state where the application performs actions that are safety-critical. The motivation for this state is the possibility of reducing the damage before entering the (safe) shut-down state. Since damage is made, which must be handled somehow, recovery from this state is not possible. *Shut-down state* is the state from which there is no return, putting the application in a safe but non-functioning state.

3. Handling Safety

As mentioned above an ADM has to be configured and instantiated and the most fundamental aspect is how to transfer safety handling information to ADM. The layered approach implies that different techniques can be needed for reactive, deliberative and proactive handling. Expressing safety is also applicable internally within ADM e.g. for models used for deliberative layers and for learning. A further area for expressing safety is to support the development of infrastructure. Some examples are the handling of resource boundedness, scheduling principles (within layers and between layers) and support for degradation and recovery.

Safety is transferred to ADM using a language with the following quality criteria:

- *Expressiveness* i.e. what is the capability of the language, what is possible to express? Some of the most important aspects to support are
  - o Functional and temporal behaviour e.g. parallelism, deadlines
  - o Abstractions, hierarchies and ADM specific structures
  - o Dependability e.g. criticality, trustiness, authority, authentication, redundancy, monitoring
  - o State handling
  - o Network QoS (Quality Of Service) parameters
  - o Configuration
  - o Design guide
- *Limitations* i.e. does the language contain healthy limitations that guides the developer? Are the limitations too severe? Can limitations be checked automatically?
- *Strictness* i.e. are syntax and semantics well defined (among other things this is important for verification)?
- *Understandability* i.e. is the language and the application instantiation understandable for a non-expert? The more persons that can understand the better will requirements be designed and verified especially concerning completeness and unambiguity.
- *Flexibility and scalability* i.e. can the language be extended and can it be used for learning at runtime?

- *Execution effectiveness* i.e. can the application instantiation be executed effectively? Can learning be executed effectively?

A further enhancement, especially for the deliberative layers, is to support probabilities and utility functions that can be used to guide optimal decisions.

For this project the logical demonstrator uses *production rules* together with specific structures for reactive layers for expressing safety. Production rules have the advantage of being intuitive and effective and by letting rules affect execution of other rules a rich variability of behaviour can be expressed. Extensions can be made easily and use of pattern matching also improves the possibilities. Further, production rules can be used as a lower level implementation of higher level representations. For example, state machines, decision trees [5], belief networks [5] etc can be implemented using production rules.

Of crucial importance for the acceptance of the ADM concept is the possibility of verification. As far as possible verification shall be made offline since there is no time penalty then. Verification concerns application safety, configuration, execution principles (e.g. scheduling, resource handling, conflict resolution), deliberative models etc. Special aspects to handle are

- verification of behaviour and properties. The latter are generally more difficult to verify e.g. when is a system scalable?
- verification of whole distributed system since execution occurs in each node individually (there is no overall master node)
- verification of learned knowledge at runtime. It is difficult to guarantee correctness starting from an initially correct state
- verification under resource boundedness. Runtime verification may not be allowed or cannot be made with available resources. This can also be dependent on the criticality and the current state of the application.
- verification of models used for deliberative layers (this might also include improvements of models during runtime)

Support is needed for handling these activities and concerns application and infrastructure behaviour as well as development processes for them. Important criteria for verification are to:

- detect inconsistencies within a node and between nodes
- detect incompleteness. Since this is generally difficult the most important aspect is that the whole ADM is understandable also by non-experts.
- handle parts with less strictness e.g. expressed in plain English

Formal verification, i.e. using a formal language, is naturally a candidate for verification since it should be possible to put high quality requirements on an ADM. Proofs and model checking are verification means for formal verification and *invariants,* that shall always hold, can then be defined for application and/or infrastructure.

4. Intelligence

Intelligence is difficult to define and is here only considered as related to rational, but probably complex, overall behaviour. Intelligence is applied in the following areas:

- *Decision making* – ADM shall perform intelligent decisions at runtime
- *Learning* – ADM shall be capable of improving itself at runtime
- *Infrastructure* – ADM shall provide intelligent application independent support for *Decision making* and *Learning*

A general complexity aspect that affects ADM is the uncertainties involved with the ubiquitous network and these affect all three aspects above. ADM must always be prepared for unexpected events concerning communication with other nodes.

The basic functionality of ADM is to make decisions as intelligently as possible. The ADM separation of layers according to response time results in the following behaviour, for

- *short response time*: a reasonably good decision in time is better than a better one coming too late
- *medium response time*: there is time to evaluate different alternatives, however, the situation might unexpectedly change and a *short response time* decision might be required instead
- *long response time*: there is time to figure out strategies and improve properties. Again, the situation might unexpectedly change and a *short response time* decision might be required instead.

The resulting behaviour mimics human i.e. intelligent behaviour. For *Reactive layers* intelligence is limited since there is no time for analysis. For *Deliberative layers* simulations can take place using a number of models, actual inputs and simulated I/O. Intelligence is manifested as evaluation of different alternatives and choosing the one that is best under the current (dynamic) circumstances. Of crucial importance is then that models are representative, i.e. express what they are supposed to do with a suitable granularity, and use of them could be made in an intelligent way.

An important aspect of ADM is also to be able to improve over time and this is considered in the *Proactive layers*. For *Intelligent I/O* learning cannot be specified generally, instead it depends completely on the purpose and implementation of *Intelligent I/O*. For improvement of decision quality the proactive layer *Model* is defined and used for improving the models used for deliberative layers. How models shall be improved effectively at runtime while maintaining their functionality and properties is a specific topic in itself. There must also be a strategy in which order and when models shall be updated. Improvement of resource handling is defined in the proactive layer *Resources* and is also a specific topic in itself. An extra complexity is that this concerns the whole node i.e. also parts outside ADM.

The main intelligent aspect of the infrastructure support is to handle resources in an intelligent way. As mentioned above the main types of resources are

- Available execution time.

- Time to deadline.
- Bandwidth for ubiquitous network.

In principle, resource handling involves three tasks: to decide the amount of resources allocated to each resource consuming part, to perform analysis of resources (current and in the future) and to analyse resource handling itself with respect to consumed resources. Resource handling also needs to adapt to the needs of a used *Intelligent I/O* component which possibly is a COTS product. Since an ADM based system is exposed to unexpected events, e.g. faults, attacks, resource handling needs to be highly dynamic and adaptable to new situations. In a crisis situation a decision might have to be taken even if resources actually do not exist e.g. in the case when there is no time left to deadline. The result is then a hazardous or safety-critical situation. Intelligent infrastructure support is also needed for membership agreement of nodes i.e. which of the other nodes are trusted and which are possible to communicate with. Since an ADM based system is loosely connected the analysis of such aspects is the responsibility of each node. Scheduling of layers, interaction between *ADM Scheduler - Node Scheduler* and determination of *Execution cycle* size also need intelligent infrastructure support. The *Execution cycle* is a clock cycle used throughout ADM and the size could be shortened or prolonged according to circumstances. Finally, the principles for resolving output conflicts in an intelligent way are important since they will define one case of limitation of ADM i.e. when a situation is too complex to be handled.

5. Matching IEC 61508 and ADM

There are many development standards specifying requirements for safety. IEC 61508 is a suitable reference standard since IEC 61508 is a well-known, often used, established and stable standard. The definition of safety was given in Section 1 above and is according to IEC 61508. As can be seen in IEC 61508 there are a number of definitions and principles directly applicable for ADM:

- Safety is freedom from unacceptable risk of injury / damage
- Functional safety depends on a system or equipment operating correctly in response to its inputs.
- Neither safety nor functional safety can be determined without considering the systems as a whole and the environment with which they interact.
- A safety-related system contains specific functions, *safety functions*, to ensure risks are kept at an acceptable level. A safety function is specified by
    o   Behavior (what the function shall do)
    o   Safety Integrity Level (SIL 1-4), the likelihood of being able to perform the safety function.
- All subsystems and components, when combined to implement the safety function, are required to meet the SIL.
- SIL for software concerns techniques and measures while SIL for hardware concerns statistical reliability.
- The safety handling part of a system may be separate from the equipment under control (i.e. the part of the system performing ordinary functionality).

- If a safety-related system implements more than one safety function and if the safety integrity requirements for these differ, unless there is sufficient independence of implementation between them, the requirements applicable to the highest relevant safety integrity level shall apply to the entire system.

Dependent on SIL there are techniques and measures for software, listed in Appendix A and B of IEC 61508 Part 3 with associated recommendations, concerning:

- fault and error detection and diagnosis
- recovery block, forward and backward recovery
- graceful degradation
- use of specification tools
- strongly typed language
- certified (or proven in use) translator
- use of trusted components
- use of defensive programming
- modular approach; information hiding/encapsulation
- design and coding standards
- formal proof
- complexity metrics
- failure analysis and common cause failure analysis
- equivalence classes and input partitioning
- modelling: data flow, finite state machines, formal/semi-formal methods, performance modelling, timed Petri nets, structure diagrams, logic/function block diagrams, sequence diagram

These aspects can, in a straightforward way, be mapped to the ADM concept. For some of the aspects ADM can alternatively be seen as a development tool used for a specific high level language, i.e. like an intelligent editor / compiler / linker, which can be validated using certificate or according to "proven in use". ADM takes a specific approach concerning safety functions of different criticalities; always considering all functions as critical as the most critical function. In this way independence evaluation of safety functions is not necessary to perform (which could be a complex issue). As a summary IEC 61508 is applicable for ADM based systems but there are specific aspects to consider:

- hardware SIL is not within the current scope of ADM
- the notion of software as something that can be directly executed is not directly applicable to ADM
- ADM does not necessarily cover all handling of safety since safety can alternatively be handled outside ADM
- most software aspects of IEC 61508 concerns techniques and measures, i.e. process related issues, and not the functionality which is the current scope of ADM

6. Demonstrator

Apart from defining the ADM architecture a logical demonstrator has been developed. It consists of approximately 100 classes of Java code and is executed on the ECLIPSE platform [6]. The idea of the demonstrator is to create a non-trivial application, simulate varying conditions and provide a user friendly GUI for elaboration. The purpose of the demonstrator is to motivate and exemplify the use of ADM for safety-related applications. The system consists of application and infrastructure and since the system is reactive, deliberative and proactive layers are not included. The demonstrator also contains extra control possibilities (e.g. varying randomness), debugging support and fault injection capability. The application is described by the following:

An operator remotely controls a chemical plant via the Internet. There are three control actions: start of production, stop of production and emergency stop.

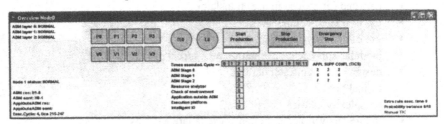

Figure 5 Operator GUI

The operator controls and gets status over the Internet. The controlled system, in Node 1, is a chemical plant where one liquid placed in tank T0 is pumped using pump P0 through valve V0 to tank T4. Another liquid in tank T1 is pumped using pump P1 through valve V1 also to tank T4 where the liquids are mixed to form the product that is pumped, after some chemical reaction time, by pump P3 via valve V3 to tank T3. During the process heat is generated in tank T4 and the temperature is checked by sensor TE0. If level indicator L0 is active it means that the level in tank T4 is too high. In case of emergency, pump P2 can pump the product via valve V2 to tank T2 but then the product is wasted.

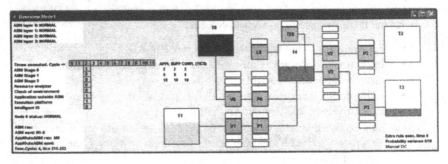

Figure 6 Chemical plant GUI

The process is automated but surveyed and overall controlled by the operator at Node 0. There are two ADMs; one at operator side and one at chemical plant side. ADM handles all safety aspects and *Application outside ADM* handles all production aspects. A principal fault model is defined according to:

- A fault setting is static (i.e. a stuck-at fault).
- A fault detected on an input signal means that the value of the input signal is not to be trusted.
- A fault detected on an output signal means that the value of the output signal is not to be trusted.
- If an input, *without fault*, is used as feedback from an output, *with fault*, the input shows the current value of the output (thus including the effect of the fault). The input *does not indicate* if the output is faulty or not.
- For trusting an output setting it is necessary to get a fault free feedback via the corresponding input (the output setting as such is not enough).
- The number of concurrent faults is not limited.

Application and infrastructure are separated in the demonstrator and thus another application can be instantiated directly. The demonstrator can be executed with injected faults and results are then shown on the two GUIs. For example, output conflicts are indicated for each valve and pump and scheduling is shown cyclically.

7. Conclusions

When using the Internet in safety-related applications for surveillance and control the ADM concept, in one form or another, is inevitable. The major issue that ADM addresses is that there are new risks when including a ubiquitous network in an application. This stems both from the public nature as such (e.g. being vulnerable to attacks) and the network QoS properties (e.g. unpredictable delays, no upper delay limit etc.). It is especially important to note that even if, hypothetically, all other problems could be solved there is always the possibility of a DoS (Denial of Service) attack resulting in inconsistencies and isolation of units. Thus there will always be a need for the functionality and capability addressed by the ADM concept. The role of ADM is to handle safety aspects on behalf of the application and to an extent defined by the application. The most important reasons for this transfer of responsibility are:

- ADM can become a standard component supporting standardised behaviour and design, making each node behave according to the same principles.
- The separation of safety functions and ordinary functions improves understanding and enables development in parallel which result in higher quality.
- A close relationship with IEC 61508 *safety functions* is directly supported.

It seems that the ADM concept is a novel idea and this concerns mainly the proposal to put agent like entities in a safety critical system. At first it may look contradictory but with carefully designed prerequisites it is certainly an applicable and useful idea. Further, the use of ADM also in non-safety critical applications becomes natural e.g. when intelligent and autonomous control is required and the control, in a natural way, can be separated from the other functionality of the system. Even though the PIITSA project (with its logical demonstrator) was focussed on machine/plant control, via a remote operator, ADM has a much larger application domain. Some examples are surveillance of patients at home, alarm system, decision support (guidance) etc. In the most general domain ADM can be applied whenever autonomous and intelligent decisions are needed in order to avoid some kind of harm, not necessarily critical, in a distributed system.

References

1. Lars Strandén, Johan Hedberg and Håkan Sivencrona, Machine Control via Internet - A holistic approach, SP, Swedish National Testing and Research Institute, Electronics, Report SP 2002:30
2. IEC 61508 – 1:4 First edition December 1998 – 2000
    Functional Safety of Electrical/Electronic/Programmable Electronic Safety-Related Systems, www.iec.ch/functionalsafety
3. Bruno Harbulot and John R. Gurd. Using AspectJ to Separate Concerns in Parallel Scientific Java Code. Proceedings of the 3rd International Conference on Aspect-Oriented Software Development (AOSD). Lancaster, UK, March 2004.
4. R. Brooks, A Robust Layered Control System for a Mobile Robot, IEEE Journal of Robotics and Automation, April 1986
5. Russel S, Norvig P, Artificial Intelligence: A Modern Approach, 1995, Prentice-Hall
6. ECLIPSE organisation www.eclipse.org

Using Semantic Web technologies to bridge the Language Gap between Academia and Industry in the Construction Sector

M. Argüello, A. El-Hasia, M. Lees
Research Institute for the Built and Human Environment (BUHU)
M.Arguello-Casteleiro@salford.ac.uk
www.salford.ac.uk

Abstract

Semantic Web technologies are emerging technologies which can considerably improve the information sharing process by overcoming the problems of current Web portals. Portals based on Semantic Web technologies represent the next generation of Web portals, however, before industry is willing to adopt Semantic Web technologies it is essential to demonstrate that Semantic Web portals are significantly better than Web portals. This paper focuses on a case study which compares the performance of a traditional Web portal using a keyword-based search engine and a Semantic Web portal using an ontology-based search engine. The empirical results of the comparison performed between these two search engines over an input data set of 100 data provides strong evidence of the tangible benefits of using Semantic Web technologies.

1. Introduction

The World Wide Web (WWW or the Web for short) has made a huge amount of information electronically available and it is a successful story in terms of both available information and growth rate of human users. Nevertheless, current Web technology has serious limitations in making information accessible for users in an efficient manner. The general problem in finding information on the Web is summarized in [1]: searches are imprecise, often yielding matches to many thousands of hits. Moreover, users face the task of reading the documents retrieved in order to extract the information desired. These limitations naturally appear in existing Web portals based on this technology, making information searching, accessing, extracting, interpreting and processing a difficult and time-consuming task.

Semantic Web portal (SW portal for short) is the next generation of web portals that are powered by Semantic Web technologies for improved information sharing and exchange for a community of users. An initial survey on SW portal can be found in [2]. Generally speaking, information in a SW portal is organized by a domain ontology and stored in a Knowledge Base (KB). Therefore, ontologies are central components of a SW portal, however, before industry is willing to adopt

135

Semantic Web Technologies it is essential to provide strong evidence of the tangible benefits of SW portals and ontology-based search engines.

This paper focuses on a case study which compares a Web portal using a traditional keyword-based search engine and a SW portal using an ontology-based search engine. To compare these two search engines, an input of 100 data were selected and the outcome data obtained. This was then analysed and represented graphically.

The paper is organised as follows. Section 2 explains the motivation and initial requirements imposed on the Web development. An initial approach, a Web portal with a search engine based on keywords is presented is section 3. A new approach involving a SW portal with a semantic search engine is described in section 4. The empirical results and bar graphs used to compare the outcome data of both search engines are shown in section 5. Conclusions are in section 6.

2. Motivation and initial requirements

The construction sector in the United Kingdom has an output of approximately £102 billion (DTI Construction stats, 2005). The UK construction sector has become increasingly fragmented over the years and more and more work is being subcontracted to specialist, often small, companies. Successive governments have commissioned reports on the performance of the sector and all these reports have highlighted the need for radical change in the performance of the sector. The challenge that still faces the sector is to improve the performance of the very large number of Small to Medium Enterprises (SMEs). It is recognised that most SMEs can not afford a research department, therefore an improvement in the links and connections between research rich organisations, like universities, and industry will benefit the SMEs. However to mention one of the many difficulties to overcome, there is no an available document (like a "yellow pages") which states the construction expertise within UK universities.

In the UK, the University of Salford commenced the *Construction Knowledge Exchange (CKE)* project in August 2004. The project has the vision to promote knowledge exchange between industry and universities in the UK construction sector by enabling networks and links that reach out to all levels of business and higher education. To gather the necessary knowledge to capture the construction expertise within universities and make this knowledge available to industry as well as to academia is the most immediate purpose of the Web development for the *CKE* project. The main goal is to make the academic expertise "readable and understandable" to industry.

It is recognised that the two identified communities in the UK construction sector: industry and academia use different languages. An integrated view from the user's perspective is an initial requirement imposed to the Web development for the *CKE* project to integrate both communities and create one virtual community. Therefore, this requirement implies bridging the language gap between the academic community and the industrial community in the construction sector.

The *CKE* project mostly focuses on the information available online where the UK academic community states its expertise/research areas in the construction sector. The requirement imposed on the Web development is to adequately encode these stated areas of expertise. To accomplish this requirement, there are two issues to face: (a) 'who has the knowledge', and (b) 'who knows what'.

To sum up the Web development for the *CKE* project aims to make the areas of expertise of the UK academic community in the construction sector available and understandable for the industrial community. The next section presents an initial attempt to fulfil the two requirements mentioned above: (1) adequately encode the areas of expertise of the UK academic community in the construction sector, and (2) bridge the language gap between the academic community and the industrial community in the construction sector.

3. A Web portal with a keyword-based search engine

The use of conceptual models of stored information has a long tradition in database research. The most well-known approach is the Entity Relationship approach. Such conceptual models normally have a tight connection to the way the actual information is stored, because they are mainly used to structure information about complex domains. This connection has significant advantages from information sharing, because the conceptual model helps to access and validate information.

Based on the information available online about the UK academic community two entities were easily identified: *Universities* and *Construction topics* (see figure 1). From the very beginning it was clear that each UK university, which is deeply engaged in activities relevant to the construction sector, has developed interest in at least one main construction topic. On the other hand, each construction topic has attracted interest from at least one university.

Figure 1 The three main activities considered to capture online UK academic information

The three main activities considered to acquire online information about the UK academic community and encode its areas of expertise are depicted in figure 1. These activities are formalized as much as possible to facilitate the inclusion of techniques to automate the information acquisition in the near future, and a brief description of them is the following:

1. *Filter* URLs available from Internet. Each university is a hierarchy where different levels can be identified: (a) the university itself is at the top-level, (b) departments, institutes, schools, etc are at a middle-level, and (c) academics are at a lower-level and outside the current scope of this

research study. These different levels are reflected in the information available online, where the filter activity performed can be considered as a discovery activity performed manually. Each university is attached to only one top-level URL (university *home* page) which contains general information about the university. Each university organisation (department/etc) is attached to two middle-level URLs: (i) one university organisation *home* page which contains general information about the university organisation, and (ii) one *expertise* page which contains specific information about the expertise/research areas of the university organisation – which initially was not explicitly incorporated.

2. *Extract* the information relevant to encode the areas of expertise of the academic community in the construction sector. The difficulty lies in the wide variety of formats used in the URLs selected in the previous activity, and the need to identify relevant information with an extremely high degree of accuracy overcoming all the differences between the different construction terminologies in use. The different construction topics found were classified in two levels: (a) main topics at a high-level, and (b) subtopics of main topics at the low-level.

3. *Store* the extracted information in a relational database. Figure 2 shows the Entity Relationship Diagram (ERD) developed in an earlier stage as part of the initial database design. Figure 3 shows the Web portal and the visualization of the relationships defined in figure 2.

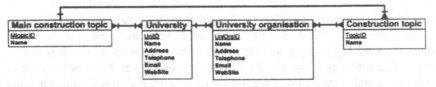

Figure 2 The ERD developed in an earlier stage

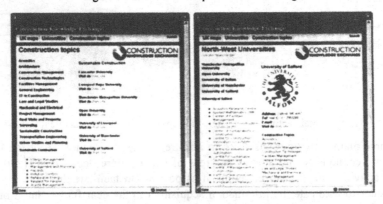

Figure 3 The Web portal of the *Construction Knowledge Exchange*: exploring construction topics (left) and exploring universities/university organisations (right)

Keyword searching is the most common form of text search on the Web. Most search engines do their text query and retrieval using keywords. The unsuitability of current commercial keyword-based search engines such as Google forced the development of a keyword-based search engine for the *CKE* project which focuses on the factual on-line information about the academic expertise. To illustrate the problem, Google [3] combines *Google Search software* (PageRank) with sophisticated text-matching techniques to find pages that are both important and relevant to the search. PageRank [3] is calculated roughly as follows:

$$PR(A) = (1\text{-}d) + d\ (\ PR(T1)/C(T1) + \ldots + PR(Tn)/C(Tn)\ )$$

where: PR(A) is the PageRank of a page A, PR(T1) is the pageRank of a page T1, C(T1) is the number of outgoing links from the page T1, and d is a dumping factor in the range $0 < d < 1$, usually sets to 0.85. Therefore, the PageRank of a Web page is calculated as a sum of the PageRanks of all pages linking to it (its incoming links), divided by the number of links on each of those pages (its outgoing links). The main reason to dismiss Google is because PageRank relies on the vast link structure as an indicator of an individual page's value and not in the content of the page. The *CKE* project needs a search engine which finds pages among the discovered ones based on the expertise/research areas stated in their content and not based on theirs links to other pages.

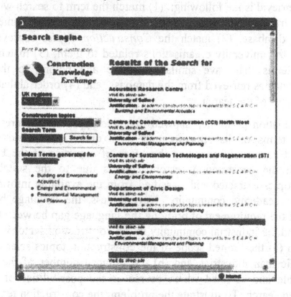

Figure 4 The keyword-based search engine: searching for *environment*

The search engine designed for the Web portal is a keyword-based search engine and only one term per search is allowed. Figure 4 shows the keyword-based search engine where two dropdown lists appear: a dropdown list to select the UK region and a dropdown list to select a construction topic. The list of main construction topics also allows the option *ALL* that performs the search over all construction topics. The keyword-based search engine has two interesting features:

1. *Context* – the index of construction short statements generated for the term to search (a) shows the term in combination with other terms (term context) to help to determinate in which context the term is relevant to the search, and (b) allows refining the search by clicking in any of the index of construction short statements generated. This feature and also the match performed between the term to search and terms with similar structure (e.g. *environment* and *environmental*) have been evaluated very positively.

2. *Justification* - the university organisations result of the search are listed alphabetically and for each of them a justification is supplied with the intention of increasing the user's confidence in the answer provided. The justification shows a list in alphabetic order of low-level construction topics, which are the subtopics of main construction topics, relevant to the current search. The user determines whether to show or hide justifications. To reinforce the user's confidence, and in line with how other keyword-based search engines work, when there is a match between the term to search and a word in the university organisation's name, the university organisation's name is highlighted.

A brief summary of the main steps involved in the keyword-based search using information retrieval is the following: (1) match the term to search with terms that have similar structure and belong to the *Construction Topics'* names which are stored in the database, (2) match the *Construction Topics* retrieved from the database with the university organisations related to them, (3) match the term to search with terms that have similar structure and belong to the university organisations' names retrieved from the database, and (4) order alphabetically and display the results of the search.

An initial evaluation performed showed that this approach captures information semantics in terms of its structure and it is quite appropriate to fulfil the requirement of adequately encoding the areas of expertise of the UK academic community in the construction sector. This is due to the suitability of the construction topics extracted and classified from the available information online about the UK academic community. Nevertheless, the language barrier is not overcome and the requirement of bridging the language gap between the academic community and the industrial community in the construction sector is not fulfilled. This is due to (a) the limited scope of the construction topics selected which are more academic than industrial, and (b) the reduced number of the construction topics available and selected which decreases the possibilities of a successful keyword-based search. To illustrate the problem, the construction term "bridge" is a particular term that is recognised to be related to several main construction topics such as: *Construction Technologies, General Engineering, Project Management, Construction Management,* and *Transportation Engineering.* However, it is not explicitly mentioned in a suitable construction context in any of the Web pages related to the expertise of the university organisations discovered for the North-West region, and consequently produces no search results, although a user from industry will expect many results for the general construction term "bridge" in a search engine which claims to be specific for the construction sector.

The next section presents a Web portal which uses Semantic Web technologies and attempts to fulfil the remaining requirement: to bridge the language gap between the academic community and the industrial community in the construction sector.

4. A SW portal with an ontology-based search engine

In the context of Knowledge Based Systems (KBS), an ontology provides the basic structure for constructing a Knowledge Base (KB). Some advantages identified in constructing a KB by reusing existing ontologies are: (1) the development step is facilitated if the structure of conceptualisations provided by an ontology to encode pieces of knowledge is used, (2) the formal ontology underlying the knowledge base clarifies the representation semantics, and (3) the knowledge base can be shared more reliably.

In the context of the World Wide Web, ontologies are the backbone technology for the Semantic Web and - more generally - for the management of formalised knowledge in the context of distributed systems. In 2004, the Web Ontology Language OWL [4] was adopted by the W3C as the standard for representing ontologies on the Web. A case study carefully designed by [5] has empirically proved that Semantic Web enhanced search accomplishes significantly better search results than other information retrieval techniques. In this sense, portals based on Semantic Web technologies, Semantic Web portals (SW portals for short), represent the next generation of Web portals where information is organised by a domain ontology and stored in a Knowledge Base (KB).

To exchange knowledge in the construction sector, i.e. semantic exchange, requires a shared mechanism to classify domain knowledge-items or information into interrelated concepts, i.e. ontology. Ontologies may be used for achieving a common consensus within a user community about conceptualising, structuring and sharing domain knowledge. It is expected that ontologies can help give an integrated interface with the construction sector, which has become increasingly fragmented over the years and has allowed the coexistence of more that one common language. It is recognised that one ontology alone is not going to facilitate the exchange of knowledge between the two identified communities in the construction sector: academia and industry. It is anticipated that an ontology that bridges the two communities will be required, as there are differences between the languages that they use.

A core purpose for the use of ontologies is the exchange of data not only at a common syntactic, but also at a shared semantic level. On the World Wide Web, more and more ontologies are being constructed and used. They are beginning to replace the old-fashioned ways of exchanging business data via standardised comma-separated formats with standards that adhere to semantic specifications given through ontologies. Thus, in the near future more and more ontologies will be made available on the World Wide Web. Therefore, experts no longer talk about a single ontology, but rather about a network of ontologies. Although, ontology engineers frequently have a core ontology that is extended, or adapted.

For the reasons mentioned above, this approach is adhered to - a modular ontology design. Existing methodologies and practical ontology development experiences have in common that they start from the identification of the purpose of the ontology and the need for domain knowledge acquisition [6], although they differ in their focus and steps to be taken. In this study, to develop a Knowledge Base for the SW portal (the β-CKE portal), the three basic stages of the knowledge engineering methodology of CommonKADS [7] coupled with a modularised ontology design have been followed:

1. *Knowledge identification*: in this stage, several activities have been included: explore all domain information sources in order to elaborate the most complete characterisation of the application domain, and list potential components for reusing, where the following knowledge sources have been identified: (a) the construction topic classification previously developed from online information about the UK academic community, (b) the SWRC ontology [8] which generically models key entities relevant for typical research communities and their relationships, and (c) classification standards and exchange protocols for the construction industry: aecXML [9], bcXML [10], BS6100 [11], CITE [12], ebXML [13], Uniclass [14].

2. *Knowledge specification*: in this second stage the construction of a specification of the domain model has been made. *Protégé 3.2 beta* [15] has been chosen as the ontology-design and knowledge acquisition tool to build ontologies in OWL using the Protégé-OWL Plugin. From the list of classification standards and exchange protocols for the construction industry, Uniclass [14] has been selected as a classification standard for the construction industry, because: (a) was developed jointly by the Construction Confederation, the Royal Institute of British Architects, the Royal Institution of Chartered Surveyors, the Chartered Institution of Building Services Engineers, and the Department of the Environment Construction Sponsorship Directorate, (b) it is specific to the construction sector, (c) it attempts to be a consensual model of meaning for construction industry, (d) it sets out to capture the complexity and fragmentation of construction industry, and (e) it is intended to supersede CI/SfB, the most commonly used classification system for construction information which was last revised in 1976. Several activities have been carried out, the most relevant: (i) extraction and adaptation of knowledge from the SWRC ontology [8], (ii) development of the *Academic Construction ontology* from the construction topic classification developed, (iii) development of the *Industrial Construction ontology* from Uniclass [14], (iv) ontology mapping between the *Academic Construction ontology* and the *Industrial Construction ontology*, and (v) development of the *Map ontology*. Figure 5 shows the relationships between ontologies and outlines the ontology mapping performed. Figure 6 shows a screenshot of Protégé 3.2 beta during the OWL ontology development; the SWRC class *Organization* is shown.

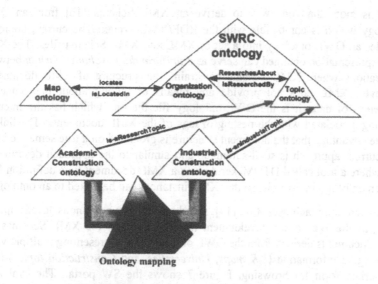

Figure 5 Relationships between ontologies

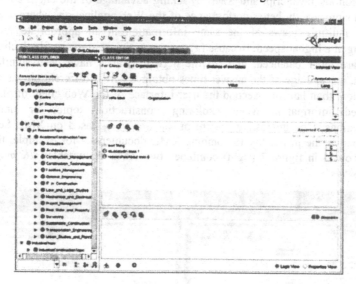

Figure 6 The SWRC class *Organization* in OWL edited with Protégé 3.2 beta

3. *Knowledge refinement*: in this third stage, the resulting domain model is validated by paper-based simulation, and more instances in OWL are added to the domain model were filled by adding.

The second and third stages are executed in an iterative process. The *Academic Construction ontology* and the *Industrial Construction ontology* could be seen as taxonomies which have about 200 and 5400 nodes respectively. These two sources have been mapped, where the 500 semantic matching performed from one source into another involves only classes (taxonomy higher levels) and not instances.

There is more than one way to derive an XML Schema [16] from an OWL ontology which is compatible with the RDF/XML syntax. The current approach encodes an OWL ontology into a set of XML and XML Schema files. The XML [17] representation obtained can serve as a *uniform data exchange format* between applications where XML Schema constrains the structure of XML documents. However, XML does not provide any means of talking about the semantics (*meaning*) of data; it is the OWL ontology file the one which has the intended meaning associated with the nesting of tags of the XML documents. The linkage has the advantage that the document structure is grounded on a true semantic basis. The current approach is semi-automatic and similar to the approach described in [18] where a tool called DTDMaker derives a XML document type definition from a given ontology in F-Logic, so that XML instances can be linked to an ontology.

The current approach uses *Ajax* [19], shorthand for Asynchronous JavaScript and XML, as the Web client development technique, where the XML Schemas and XML documents derived from the OWL ontology allow presenting multiple views of the same information (*UK maps*, *Universities*, and *Construction topics*) in an appropriate form for browsing. Figure 7 shows the SW portal. The evaluation process performed over the SW portal has proved that the combination of Asynchronous JavaScript and XML by taking advantage of the client's CPU has led to a significantly better performance of the Web application, where users can explore multiple views of the same information in an appropriate form for browsing at a higher speed. Because (a) the computing resources of both client and server are more balanced, and (b) the network traffic have been significantly reduced, an average of the answer times obtained across different clients reveals that in less than half of a second the user interface of the Web client displays the requested information when exploring construction topics or university organisations. One interesting feature of the tree view based on XML Schemas developed is the possibility to combine XML documents - for example, the tree view showed in figure 7 (right) combines two XML documents: *UK maps* and *Universities*.

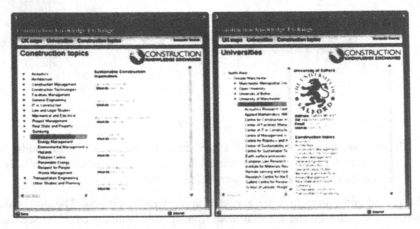

Figure 7 The SW portal of the *Construction Knowledge Exchange*: exploring construction topics (left) and exploring universities/university organisations (right)

Current methods of searching in SW portals include: (1) traditional keyword-based search using information retrieval, (2) ontology-based formal query and reasoning, and (3) simple combination of the above two methods. Method (2) is a unique feature of SW portals because traditional Web portals have no semantic information to use. Method (3) is quite basic in SW portals. For example, in OntoWeb portal [20], when an ontology-based query has no results to return, it is then automatically converted to a pure keyword search. In [21] some examples of systems which use semantic information to improve search on the (Semantic) Web are provided, and it is revealed that in general there is no tight integration of method (1) and (2). This approach is also addressed to the integration of method (1) and (2).

The proposal presented in this paper to bridge the language gap between the academic community and the industrial community in the construction sector, is to use both textual and semantic information. The main idea is that a keyword (a term, i.e. textual information) triggers off a search to find terms with similar structure in different contexts, and each context provides the semantic (*meaning*) of the search. The tight integration of textual information and semantic information is due to the construction main topics selected for the search as they determine the different contexts apply to the search. Figure 8 schematically represents the integration performed between keyword searching and ontology mapping where ovals, rectangles, arrows respectively represent activities, data sets, INPUT (thin arrows) and OUTPUT (thick arrows). Figure 9 shows the semantic search engine.

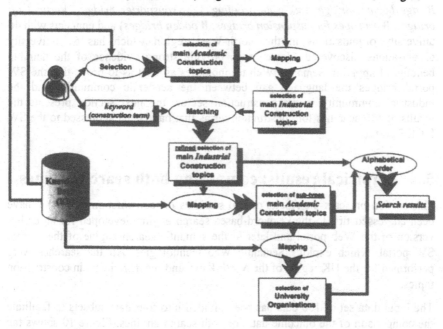

Figure 8 The integration performed between keyword searching and ontology mapping

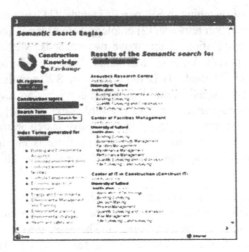

Figure 9 The semantic search engine: searching for *environment*

An initial evaluation performed showed that the SW portal fulfils the requirement that the initial Web portal failed to fulfil: bridge the language gap between the academic community and the industrial community in the construction sector. To initially illustrate this, the general construction term "bridge" as expected generates a quite long index of 51 construction short statements (such as *Arch bridges*, *Bridge beams*, *Bridge deck waterproofing*, ..., *Transporter bridges*, *Vertical lift bridges*, *Wire ropes for suspension bridges*, *Wooden bridges*) and connects with 46 university organisations in the North-West region which has 61 university organisations discovered. However, to provide strong evidence of the tangible benefits of applying Semantic Web technologies as well as to prove that the SW portal bridges the language gap between the academic community and the industrial community in the construction sector, the next section presents the results of 100 searches for construction terms that have been addressed to the SW β-CKE portal.

5.   Empirical results: comparing both search engines

This section presents the results of 100 searches for construction terms that have been addressed first to the keyword-based search engine developed for an earlier version of the Web portal and later to the semantic search engine of the current SW portal, which exploits Semantic Web technologies. All the searches were performed for the UK region of the *North-West*, and for *ALL* the main construction topics.

The input data set of 100 data has been divided into four data subsets to facilitate the comparison of the outcome data for both search engines. Figure 10 shows the empirical results and the bar graphs depicted where two parameters have been considered: (1) the number of construction short statements generated for the term to search – light grey rectangles -, and (2) the number of university organisations found to be connected with the term to search – dark grey rectangles -.

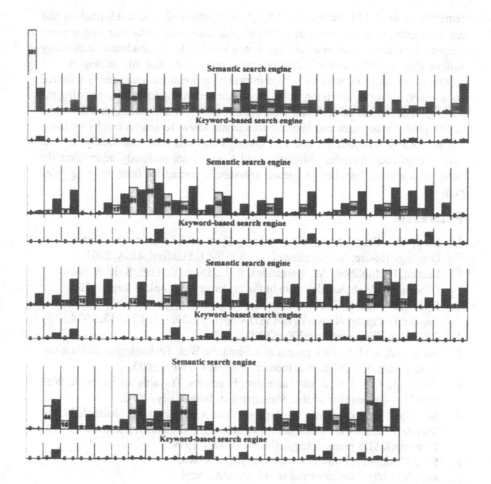

Figure 10 Empirical results: outcome data of the search

6. Conclusions

The case study presented here provides strong evidence of the advantages of using Semantic Web technologies in Web portals: (1) the SW portal allows the exploration of construction topics and university organisations and how they are connected quicker than a standard Web portal, and (2) the semantic search engine of the SW portal connects construction terms with relevant areas of academic knowledge and with the university organisations that possess that knowledge far better and more accurately than a keyword-based search engine. The proposal presented in this paper attempts to make the academic knowledge "readable and understandable" for industry by bridging the language gap between the academic community and the industrial community in the construction sector. The main idea is that a keyword (a term, i.e. textual information) triggers off a search to find terms with similar structure in different contexts, and each context provides the semantic (*meaning*) of the search. The tight integration of textual information and semantic information is mainly achieved by executing a dynamic mapping process keeping the autonomy of two ontologies: one specific to the academic community and another specific to the industrial community. The use of ontologies is a promising approach in order to capture information semantics and specify a shared vocabulary, however, a striking lack of sophisticated methodologies supporting the development and use of ontologies has been found. It is undeniable that Semantic search methods augment and improve traditional keyword search results by using not just words, but concepts and relationships between concepts. Lately, several major companies, including Microsoft and Google, are seriously addressing the issue of semantic searches to garner semantic information from existing Web pages.

References

1. Ding, Y. & Fensel, D. Ontology Library Systems: The key to successful Ontology Re-use. In Proceedings of SWWS-01, Stanford, USA, 2001.
2. Lausen, H., Stollberg, M., Hernandez, R. L., Ding, Y., Han, S.-K. & Fensel, D. Semantic Web Portals - state of the art survey. Technical Report, 2004.
3. Brin, S. & Page, L. The Anatomy of a Large-Scale Hypertextual (Web) Search Engine. Computer Networks and ISDN Systems, 30(1-7):107-117, 1998.
4. OWL, http://www.w3.org/2004/OWL/
5. Sure, Y. & Iosif, V. First results of a Semantic Web Technologies Evaluation, Proceedings of the Common Industry Program, Irvine, 2002.
6. Davies, J., Fensel, D. & van Harmelen, F. editors. Towards the Semantic Web: Ontology-Driven Knowledge Management. John Wiley. 2002.
7. Schreiber, A., Akkermans, H., Anjewierden, A.A., Hoog, R., Shadbolt, N.R., Van de Velde, W. & Wielinga, B. Engineering and managing knowledge. The CommonKADS methodology. The MIT Press, 1999.
8. SWRC ontology, http://ontoware.org/projects/swrc/
9. aecXML, http://xml.coverpages.org/aecXML.html
10. bcXML, http://xml.coverpages.org/econstructSummary.html
11. BS6100, http://www.idef.com/idef0.html
12. CITE, http://www.cite.org.uk
13. ebXML, http://www.ebxml.org/
14. Uniclass, http://www.productioninformation.org/Uniclass.html
15. Protégé, http://protege.stanford.edu/
16. XML Schema, http://www.w3.org/XML/Schema
17. XML, http://www.w3.org/XML/
18. Erdmann, M. & Studer, R. Ontologies as conceptual models for XML documents. In Proceedings of KAW'99, Banff, Canada, October 1999.
19. Ajax, http://adaptivepath.com/publications/essays/archives/000385.php
20. OntoWeb portal, http://www.ontoweb.org
21. Zhang, L., Yu, Y., Zhou, J., Lin, C., & Yang, Y. An Enhanced Model for Searching in Semantic Portals, 2005, http://www.www2005.org/cdrom/docs/

Acknowledgements - We thank to **Angel Avalos Boado**, from *A.C. Sistemas*, who contributed to essential parts of this work presented.

Ontology based CBR with jCOLIBRI [*]

Juan A. Recio-García, Belén Díaz-Agudo,

Pedro González-Calero, Antonio Sánchez-Ruiz-Granados

Dep. Sistemas Informáticos y Programación

Universidad Complutense de Madrid

Madrid, Spain

email: {jareciog,antonio.sanchez}@fdi.ucm.es, {belend, pedro}@sip.ucm.es

Abstract

jCOLIBRI[1] is a Java framework that helps designing Case Based Reasoning systems. This paper presents the incorporation of Description Logics reasoning capabilities to the new release of the framework. With this extension jCOLIBRI facilitates the development of Knowledge Intensive CBR applications. Ontologies are useful regarding different aspects: as the vocabulary to describe cases and/or queries, as a knowledge structure where the cases are located, and as the knowledge source to achieve semantic reasoning methods for similarity assessment and case adaptation that are reusable across different domains.

1   Introduction

jCOLIBRI is an object-oriented framework in Java for building Case Based Reasoning (CBR) systems. This framework promotes software reuse integrating the application of well proven Software Engineering techniques with a knowledge level description that separates the problem solving method (PSMs), that defines the reasoning process, from the domain model, that describes the domain knowledge.

This paper presents the incorporation of Description Logics (DLs) reasoning capabilities to the framework. With this extension jCOLIBRI can acquire the domain knowledge from ontologies defined in DLs, allowing the development of Knowledge Intensive CBR (KI-CBR) applications [5],[10]. This approach solves the traditional problem of knowledge acquisition in CBR systems and improves the framework functionally with new PSMs for retrieving and adapting cases.

The next section presents an overview of the framework, whereas Section 3 presents ontology based reasoning methods in a conceptual level. Section 4 shows how these methods have been implemented and included in jCOLIBRI, explaining real examples of KI-CBR applications. Ontologies used by these

---

[*] Supported by the Spanish Committee of Science & Technology (TIN05-09382-C02-01)
[1] http://sourceforge.net/projects/jcolibri-cbr/

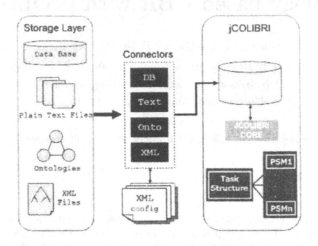

Figure 1: Connectors as abstraction of the storage medium

applications are formalized in the OWL language and are available through our web page [2] together with the framework and its documentation.

2 The jCOLIBRI Architecture

In this section we present an overview on the main features of jCOLIBRI architecture. A more complete description about these topics can be found in the web page [3].

jCOLIBRI is distributed as a core module, which provides the basic functionality for building CBR applications, and several optional modules, which supply specific features useful only in some kind of systems (for example, the extension for Textual CBR [14]).

jCOLIBRI is built using three layers: interface, reasoning logic and persistence. The framework logic is composed by Java classes and interfaces, and some XML configuration files. Developing a new CBR system is made by writing some Java classes that extend classes of the framework, and configuring some XML files. To make easier this process the interface layer provides several graphical tools that help users in the configuration of a new CBR system.

Case Base management is split in two separate although related concerns: persistence and in-memory organization. This two-layer organization of the Case Base is a powerful approach that allows a number of different strategies for accessing the cases.

Persistence is built around connectors, objects that know how to access and retrieve cases from the medium and return them to the CBR system in a uniform way, giving flexibility against the physical storage (Figure 1). Using a

---

[2] http://gaia.fdi.ucm.es/ontologies/index.html
[3] http://gaia.fdi.ucm.es/projects/jcolibri

similar idea, the Case Base component implements a common interface for the CBR application to access the cases. This way the organization and indexation chosen for the Case Base will not affect the implementation of the reasoning methods.

The steps for designing a new CBR system in jCOLIBRI are:

1. Define the case structure. A case is composed by three components: description (describes the problem), solution (represents a possible solution approach) and result (reveals if the proposed solution is able to solve the problem). Description and solution are collections of simple or compound attributes, letting us to build a hierarchical case structure.

2. Choose similarity functions. These functions computes the similarity between the query and a case, and are used to choose the most similar case to the query. There are two types of similarity functions: local (compute the similarity between simple attributes) and global (compute some kind of average over the local similarities).

3. Case Base management. The designer should choose a connector for persistence and the in-memory organization of the case base.

4. Task/Method decomposition. The developer selects the tasks the system must fulfill and for every task assigns the PSM that will do the job. There are two kind of methods: decomposition (solve a task by decomposing it in simpler subtask) and resolution (solve the task directly). As PSMs are domain-independent they must be configured with the domain information.

3 Ontology based CBR

For the last few years our research group has been working in Knowledge Intensive CBR using ontologies [8, 4, 5, 6]. We claim that ontologies have an important role in the context of KI-CBR systems. We state that ontologies are useful for designing knowledge intensive CBR applications because they allow the knowledge engineer to use knowledge already acquired, conceptualized and implemented in a formal language, like Description Logics, reducing considerably the knowledge acquisition bottleneck. Moreover, the reuse of ontologies from a library also benefits from their reliability and consistency.

Our approach proposes the use of ontologies to build models of general domain knowledge. Although in a CBR system the main source of knowledge is the set of previous experiences, our approach to CBR is towards integrated applications that combine case specific knowledge with models of general domain knowledge. The more knowledge is embedded into the system, the more effective is expected to be. Semantic CBR processes can take advantage of this domain knowledge and obtain more accurate results.

Several investigations have suggested the use of DLs to organize, represent and retrieve cases in CBR systems like MRL [11], CATO [2], RESYN/CBR [13], and a diagnosis system for the French telephone network [15]. The common ground is to take advantage of the DLs reasoning mechanisms for solving some of the CBR tasks.

We state that the formalization of ontologies is useful for the CBR community regarding different purposes, namely:

1. Persistence of cases and/or indexes using individuals or concepts that are embedded in the ontology itself.

2. As the vocabulary to define the case structure, either if the cases are embedded as individuals in the ontology itself, or if the cases are stored in a different persistence media as a data base.

3. As the terminology to define the query vocabulary. The user can express better his requirements if he can use a richer vocabulary to define the query. During the similarity computation the ontology allows to bridge the gap between the query terminology and the case base terminology.

4. Retrieval and similarity [7, 15, 13], adaptation [8] and learning [1].

The main usage of ontologies in the CBR community has been centered on similarity assessment. However, we think the usage of ontologies is specially interesting for case adaptation. Ontologies facilitate the definition of reusable, rich and semantic adaptation methods. In our modular architecture the reasoning methods are reusable because they rely on domain specific knowledge models from ontologies –that are interchangeable. This approach contrasts with most CBR systems that have traditionally relied on an enormous amount of built-in adaptation knowledge in the form of adaptation rules.

Among the contributions of this paper we include the implementation of all these features in the modular and reusable architecture of jCOLIBRI. This modular approach solves one of the main usability inconveniences of the previously cited approaches. Namely, the use of DLs as an ad-hoc persistence media that is not well suited if we have to deal with previously existing case bases. We propose the explicit separation between the case persistency media and the reasoning mechanisms to be used over a case base.

We abstract the case persistency details so the same CBR method can be used over different types of case bases. This approach allows much more flexible uses of ontologies and DLs reasoning. For example, section 5 describes an example where the case base is stored in a SQL database, the retrieval and similarity computation methods are configured as NN based on numeric and standard similarity functions, while adaptation is defined as a substitution method that relies on DLs to find suitable substitutes on the domain model.

Section 4 explains in a detailed way how jCOLIBRI manages separately the persistency and reasoning layers and the mechanisms we use to connect both layers. In this section we abstract from the case persistency layer and describe the reasoning methods in a conceptual level.

3.1 Ontologies as the CBR system vocabulary

Regarding the *case vocabulary*, there is a direct approach consisting on the use of a domain ontology in an object-oriented way: concepts are types, or classes, individuals are allowed values, or objects, and relations are the attributes describing the objects. There are also simple types like string or numbers that are considered in the traditional way. The case structure is defined using types from the ontology even if the cases are not stored as individuals in the ontology. For example, the *Destination* concept can be used as a type where every one of its instances are the type values: *Lanzarote, Fuerteventura, Gran Canaria,...*

Another approach consists on using specific types (for example, value enumerations) to define the case structure. This approach is specially useful if we want to deal with existing databases where we can not expect to have exactly the same set of values, for example, the same set of destinations in the cases than in the ontology.

Regarding the *query vocabulary* we have two options to define the queries:

- Using exactly the same vocabulary used in the cases, i.e, the same types used in the case structure definition.

- Using the ontology as the query vocabulary, what allows richer queries. The user can express better his requirements if he can use a richer vocabulary to define the query. During the similarity computation the ontology allows to bridge the gap between the query terminology and the case base terminology.

Example: In the travel domain, lets suppose we have an existing case base where it is defined an enumerated type for the *Destination* attribute where the allowed values are countries: Spain, France, Italy and others. Suppose that $case_i$ is a case whose destination is Spain. We do not want to restrict the query vocabulary to the same type but allow broader queries, for example:

- Query1: "I want to go to **Lanzarote**"

- Query2: "My favorite destination is **Europe**"

- Query3: "I would like to travel to **Spain**"

In the three queries and using the ontology of Figure 3 we could find $case_i$ as a suitable candidate. Similarity assessment described in next section measures if it is the best candidate.

3.2 Case Retrieval using Ontologies

Every case retrieval method includes a similarity assessment method to measure the adequacy between the query and cases that are candidate to be retrieved. When we deal with ontologies it is clear that the concept hierarchy influences similarity assessment. Intuitively, it is obvious that the class hierarchy contains knowledge about the similarity of the objects. There are different approaches:

- *Classification based retrieval* using DLs classification capabilities. There are two different approaches:

$$fdeep\_basic(i1,i2) = \frac{\max(prof(LCS(i1,i2)))}{\max\ (prof(Ci)),\ Ci \in CN}$$

$$fdeep(i1,i2) = \frac{\max\ (prof(LCS(i1,i2)))}{\max\ (prof(i1),\ prof(i2))}$$

$$cosine(i_1,i_2) = sim(t(i_1),t(i_2)) = \frac{\left|\left(\bigcup_{d \in t(i_1)} super(d_i,CN)\right) \cap \left(\bigcup_{d \in t(i_2)} super(d_i,CN)\right)\right|}{\sqrt{\left|\bigcup_{d \in t(i_1)} super(d_i,CN)\right|} \cdot \sqrt{\left|\bigcup_{d \in t(i_2)} super(d_i,CN)\right|}}$$

$$detail\,(i_1,i_2) = detail\,(t(i_1),t(i_2)) = 1 - \frac{1}{2 \cdot \left|\left(\bigcup_{d \in t(i_1)} super(d_i,CN)\right) \cap \left(\bigcup_{d \in t(i_2)} super(d_i,CN)\right)\right|}$$

Where

super(c, C) is the subset of concepts in C which are superconcepts of c
CN is the set of all the concepts in the current knowledge base
LCS(i1,i2) is the set of the least common subsummer concepts of the two given individuals
Prof(Ci): deepth of the concept Ci
Prof(i): deepth of the individual i

Figure 2: Concept based similarity functions in jCOLIBRI

1. Retrieval based on *concept classification*, where a concept description c_q is built using the restrictions specified in the query. This concept is then classified, and finally all its instances are retrieved.

2. Retrieval based on *instance recognition*, where an individual is built and a number of assertions are made about it based on the features specified in the query. Instance recognition is applied to retrieve the most specific concepts of which this individual is an instance, and then all the instances of these concepts are retrieved.

- *Computational based retrieval* where numerical similarity functions are used to assess and order the cases regarding the query. The use of structured representations of cases requires approaches for similarity assessment that allow to compare two differently structured objects, in particular, objects belonging to different object classes. Similarity measures for structure case representations are often defined by the following general scheme [3]: The goal is to determine the similarity between two objects, i.e., one object representing the case (or a part of it) and one object representing the query (or a part of it). We call this similarity object similarity (or global similarity). The object similarity is determined recursively in a bottom up fashion, i.e., for each simple attribute, a local similarity measure determines the similarity between the two attribute values, and for each relational slot an object similarity measure recursively compares the two related sub-objects. Then the similarity values from the local similarity measures and the object similarity measures, respectively, are aggregated (e.g., by a weighted sum) to the object similarity between the objects being compared.

In this paper we are dealing with numerical similarity functions based on ontologies. In general, the similarity computation between two structured cases

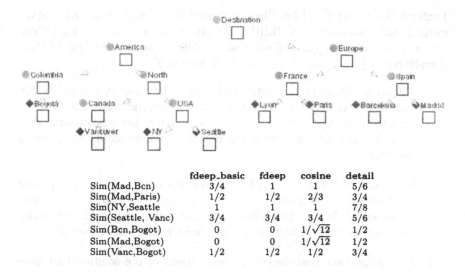

	fdeep_basic	fdeep	cosine	detail
Sim(Mad,Bcn)	3/4	1	1	5/6
Sim(Mad,Paris)	1/2	1/2	2/3	3/4
Sim(NY,Seattle)	1	1	1	7/8
Sim(Seattle, Vanc)	3/4	3/4	3/4	5/6
Sim(Bcn,Bogot)	0	0	$1/\sqrt{12}$	1/2
Sim(Mad,Bogot)	0	0	$1/\sqrt{12}$	1/2
Sim(Vanc,Bogot)	1/2	1/2	1/2	3/4

Figure 3: Example of application of the similarity functions

can be divided into two components that are aggregated [8]: the computation of *a concept based similarity* that depends on the location of the cases in the ontology (or intra-class similarity [3]) and the computation of a *slot-based similarity* (or inter-class similarity [3]) that depends on the fillers of the common attributes between the compared objects. This scheme is recursively applied until we reach individuals without slots, whose similarity is computed only by the concept-based similarity term (local similarity function).

There are different approaches for local similarity measures based on ontologies that are provided in jCOLIBRI. It initially offers four functions to compute the *concept based similarity* that depends on the location of the cases in the ontology. Of course, other similarity functions can easily be included. These similarity functions are shown in Figure 2 whereas Figure 3 explains how they work with a small ontology taken as example.

3.3 Case Adaptation based on Ontologies

Many authors agree about the fundamental role of case adaptation in the problem solving capabilities of CBR systems. However, it is in many ways the Achilles' heel of CBR. Case adaptation is a knowledge-intensive task and most CBR systems have traditionally relied on an enormous amount of built-in adaptation knowledge in the form of adaptation rules. In order to determine which rules must be included in the system, a deep analysis of the domain is required. Unfortunately, CBR is often applied to domains poorly understood or difficult to codify in the form of rules. So the leaders in the field have sometimes argued for postponing or avoiding the automatic adaptation.

In this section we propose an ontology based model and an adaptation scheme based on substitutions based on the method we described in [9]. Section

4 extends this example and describes implementation details of this adaptation method that is included in jCOLIBRI. We illustrate the method using a CBR system to recommend training exercise sessions to users according to their characteristics (this example is extended in Section 5).

1. The list L of items in the solution that need to be adapted is obtained. We find these items following a *relation path + a concept*. For example, if we want to substitute *training exercises* I would give the relation path that joins the case individual with the individuals representing the *training exercises*.

2. Every item in L is substituted by a proper new item. The search of proper substitutes is accomplished as a kind of *specialized search* which takes advantage of the DL knowledge base organization and applies similarity functions to find a substitute that is similar to the substituted one.

3. Substitute items that depend on other items of the solution that have already been adapted. For example, if we substitute the "biceps training exercise" we should change the warm-up exercises that are related to biceps.

Specialized search, as described in [12], is a way of finding candidates for substitutions in a case solution, where instructions are given about how to find the needed item. In our model memory instructions are given using the language that is explained in Section 5.

4 KI Case Representation and Retrieval in jCOLIBRI

In Section 2 we have introduced the architecture of jCOLIBRI based on 3 layers: persistence, reasoning logic and presentation. We also explained that one of the most important features of jCOLIBRI is that it allows to persist the cases independently of the applications logic. When a developer creates a new CBR system, he must define the structure of the cases using a graphical tool (shown in Figure 4) that generates a XML file with the structure information. In jCOLIBRI cases follow a composite pattern where an attribute (represented as a Java class) can be composed by other attributes, obtaining an easily extensible tree structure. Each attribute has a data type so jCOLIBRI can determine its persistence features, allowed similarity functions, etc.

When the developer has defined the case structure he configures a connector that uses that information for mapping the cases to the chosen persistence media. This mapping is also saved to a XML file. This approach allows us to create framework components than can be parameterized with these XML files containing the case structure and the connector configuration. This way, the CBR cycle is going to be independent of the persistence media.

With this architecture as the starting point our goals for integrating ontologies capabilities into the framework were: the use of ontologies as persistence media on one side, and to take advantage of DLs reasoning process to perform the retrieval, similarity and adaptation process on the other side. In a first approach we implemented the DLs extension following the idea that any case structure could be mapped into the persistence layer. But we noticed that this simple idea has side effects when using ontologies. For example, it has no sense to store in an ontology attributes like numbers (floats, integers, ...) because you should have an instance per each number, have order capabilities in the ontology... For solving this problem our final design divides case structures into two groups:

- Standard cases are composed by several attributes with different data types and can be stored into all the persistence medias excepting ontologies. If an attribute represents an instance of an ontology it has the *Concept* data type. This data type can be stored in any persistence media and connected with its instance into the ontology when loading the case.

- Pure ontological cases are completely composed by Concept-typed attributes. These cases don't need the connector information because are directly embedded into the ontology.

The Concept data type allows developers to indicate that the slot-filler of an attribute is going to be an instance of an ontology. This data type can also be stored in any kind of persistence media as a string of characters. It uses JENA[4] to link the attribute with the instance loaded by a DLs reasoner.

This approach allows us to offer persistence, similarity and adaptation capabilities for the standard cases composed for attributes with different data types. Similarity and adaptation methods could connect a Concept typed attribute to the reasoner and then compute the algorithms exposed in previous sections.

The pure ontological case structure allows to store cases embedded into the ontology structure and perform several algorithms (like the classification based retrieval method described in Section 3.2) that cannot be used in other persistence medias. There is another reason for having this special case structure: we are representing the case structure twice. jCOLIBRI represents cases using Java classes to represent the attributes (slots), and then, the connector configuration relates these slots with the slot-fillers of the persistence media. However, using ontologies as persistence media means that the slots of the case structure are defined by the concepts and properties of the ontology and the slots-filler are the instances of these concepts. This way, it has no sense to do a jCOLIBRI representation of the case structure and then map it (using the connector) with the same case structure that is in the ontology. To solve this problem our pure ontological case structure represents directly the concepts and properties of the ontology using the Java classes that jCOLIBRI uses for reasoning. With this approach the connector for DLs does not need any configuration file and can load the cases from the ontology using only the case structure information. As

---

[4]JENA is a Java framework for building Semantic Web applications. It provides a programmatic environment for RDF, RDFS and OWL. http://jena.sourceforge.net

Figure 4: Case Attributes mapping with Ontologies

cases are directly mapped to the ontology, jCOLIBRI can execute methods that don't use numerical approaches to compute similarities, retrievals, etc.

As result of the development process jCOLIBRI 1.1 includes the required components to develop a KI-CBR application using Description Logics. The main component of this extension is a component that allows developers to connect with a DLs reasoner. This component, called OntoBridge, uses the JENA library to implement most of the required methods for accessing an ontology loaded in a reasoner and perform inferences. The OntoBridge is used by the DLs Connector for loading the cases, and by the retrieval, similarity and adaptation methods that connect with the reasoner to link the Concept attributes with their corresponding instances and then perform their task.

When a developer creates a case structure he needs to choose between a standard or ontological structure. If a standard structure is selected any attribute can be typed as Concept and then choose its corresponding ontology mapping as shown in Figure 4 (left). Then, the developer can select a similarity function for computing the similarity of the instances. As explained before, the similarity functions use the information stored in the attribute to access the ontology using the *OntoBridge* component. If the developer needs a pure ontological structure, he must completely map between the jCOLIBRI case structure an the concepts of the ontology that defines the case. To perform this action he must select the concepts and the ontology relations of the ontology as shown in Figure 4 (right).

jCOLIBRI includes the ontology-based retrieval methods explained in section 3.2: *classification-based retrieval* and *computational based retrieval*. This last method applies the similarity functions explained in Figure 2 to compute the most similar cases of the given query.

```
IDONTO:= /(Concept/Relation)* /Concept
IDPROPERTY:= (Relation/Concept)*
IDCASE:= "CASE."(attribute[.])*
RULE:= IDONTO,@,CONDITION,@,ADAPTATION
CONDITION:= (IDPROPERTY (=|!=) IDCASE) | (IDCASE (=|!=) String)
            | [not] (IDPROPERTY instanceOf Concept)
ADAPTATION:= SUBSTITUTION | MODIFY [FOLLOWDEPENDENCIES Relation]
SUBSTITUTION:= "SUBSTITUTE" [#CONDITION#]
MODIFY:= DIRECTMODIFICATION | ANYOTHERINSTANCEMODIFICATION
DIRECTMODIFICATION:= "DIRECT":IDPROPERTY:instance
ANYOTHERINSTANCEMODIFICATION:= "ANYOTHERINSTANCEOF":IDPROPERTY:concept
                        [#CONDITION#]
```

IDONTO identifies the path to the instance to adapt.
IDPROPERTY identifies a property of a concept.
IDCASE identifies an attribute of the case
SUBSTITUTION substitutes the instance by another one chosen randomly. Accepts
can include a condition that the substitute instance must obey.
DIRECTMODIFICATION substitutes an attribute of the instance with the instance
indicated by the developer.
ANYOTHERINSTANCEMODIFICATION substitutes an attribute of the instance by
another instance of a concept. Accepts a condition for the substitute instance.
FOLLOWDEPENDENCIES applies the rule recursively to the instances related with the
specified relation.

Figure 5: Adaptation rules syntax

5   Ontology-based Adaptation in jCOLIBRI

This method was described in Section 3.3 and can perform several transformations in an instance that represents the solution of a case. To implement
this functionality in an extensible way we have defined a small but powerful
ontology adaptation language. This language allows developers to create rules
for adapting solutions and store them in textual files that will be loaded and
interpreted by our generic adaptation method.

These rules are composed by 3 parts. The first one identifies the instance (I)
to adapt following a <concept,relation> chain. Then the rule has a condition
that will be evaluated for deciding if the adaptation of I should be performed.
The last part defines the adaptation process. By now the method supports the
following adaptations:

- Substitution of I by another instance specified by the developer. It is also
  possible to indicate conditions that the substitute instance must obey.

- Direct substitution of an instance that is related with I using a property of
  the ontology. Note that this related instance should define a characteristic
  of I. This option allows to indicate directly the substitute instance.

- Substitution of an related instance indicating conditions for the substitute
  instance.

These rules can also follow dependencies (i.e. properties) that relates instances
to perform the adaptation process recursively.

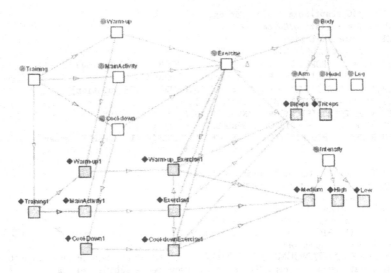

Figure 6: Sport Training Ontology

The generic adaptation method of jCOLIBRI explained in this paper uses several rules defined by the developer that indicates how to adapt the solution of the cases. Rules are composed by three parts: identification of the instance to adapt, condition to evaluate for performing the adaptation, and modification of the instance. They are stored in a text file and loaded and executed at runtime. Figure 5 shows their syntax. To illustrate how it works we are going to use a jCOLIBRI application named "Personal Sports Trainer" that recommends exercise sessions to the users. The query contains information about the user: age, sex, state of health, lesions, ... and the case base contains several cases with its solution stored in an ontology. The concept referenced by the solution is "Training" which is composed by: "Warm-up", "Main Activity" and "Cool-down". Each of these parts contains several exercises ("Exercise") that have many properties: "hasIntensity", "exercisedMuscles"... The exercises of the main activity are connected with the corresponding exercises in the warm-up and cool-down depending on the exercised muscles. Figure 6 shows a simplified view of the ontology. Now imagine the scenario where a user with a lesion in the arm sends a query and the system returns a training that contains exercises that use that body part. The following rule will adapt the retrieved solution changing the inappropriate exercises:

```
/Training/hasMainActivity/MainActivity/hasExercise/Exercise@
exercisedMuscles/Body == CASE.Description.lesion@
ANYOTHERINSTANCEOF:exercisedMuscles/Body:Body
                    #exercisedMuscles/Body not instanceof Arm#
                    FOLLOWDEPENDENCIES relatedExercise
```

Here "exercisedMuscles" is a property with domain "Exercise" and range "Body". *Body* is a concept of the ontology that has subconcepts like *head*, *arm*, *leg,...* In the condition we are comparing with the attribute of the case that stores the lesion. "relatedExercise" is the ontology property that relates the exercises in the main activity with the exercises of the warm-up and cool-down.

Next rule adjusts the intensity of the exercises depending on the state of health of the user. The state of health is included in the query (CASE.-Description.HealthState). The adaptation changes directly the property "has-Intensity" of the exercises with the instance "Low" of the concept "Intensity". As in the previous rule we propagate the transformations to the related concepts in the warm-up and cool-down.

```
/Training/hasMainActivity/MainActivity/hasExercise/Exercise@
CASE.Description.HealthState == low@
DIRECT:hasIntensity/Intensity: Low FOLLOWDEPENDENCIES relatedExercise
```

6   Conclusions

jCOLIBRI is a Java framework that helps during the development of Case Based Reasoning systems. The main advantage of using jCOLIBRI is mainly an easier development of CBR systems. To reach this goal we propose a design process that is based on reusing existing CBR knowledge (terminology, designs, tasks, methods, implementations), and on the integration of new components and the extension of existing components and their collaborations.

This paper describes the advantages that ontologies provide when they are used in CBR systems. The advantages are referred to different aspects: ontologies as the cases/queries definition languages independently of the persistence media we use for cases; ontologies as the knowledge structure where the cases are embedded, so that the persistence media for the case base uses the ontology formalization language; and ontologies as the knowledge source to get semantic reasoning processes, like retrieval, similarity and adaptation.

jCOLIBRI provides a well-defined and usable implementation of KI-CBR through ontologies. Though these ideas have repeatedly appeared in the literature this is to our knowledge the first general purpose standard-based implementation. This should promote the development of ontology-based CBR applications, but that is not only in our hands.

Besides the use of ontologies, jCOLIBRI 1.1 also includes new features for improving the development of CBR systems. The Web Interface extension includes several methods for launching a Tomcat server and communicate data between the PSMs of jCOLIBRI and the web applications running on the server. The Evaluation module test the efficiency of the CBR applications using the typical N-fold, Hold-Out or LeaveOneOut evaluation algorithms. This extension is designed for being extended by users that want to create their own evaluation algorithms, provides facilities for storing partial results and displays graphically the results.

References

[1] A. Aamodt. Knowledge intensive case-based reasoning and sustained learning. In *Procs. 9th European Conference on Artificial Intelligence (ECAI-90)*, pages 1–6, 1990.

[2] K. D. Ashley and V. Aleven. A Logical Representation for Relevance Criteria. In *EWCBR '93: Selected papers from the First European Workshop on Topics in CBR*, volume 837 of *LNCS*, pages 338–352, London, UK, 1994. Springer-Verlag.

[3] R. Bergmann and A. Stahl. Similarity Measures for Object-Oriented Case Representations. In B. Smyth and P. Cunningham, editors, *Procs. of the 4th European Workshop on Advances in Case-Based Reasoning (EWCBR '98)*, volume 1488 of *LNCS*, pages 25–36. Springer-Verlag, 1998.

[4] B. Díaz-Agudo and P. A. González-Calero. An Architecture for Knowledge Intensive CBR Systems. In E. Blanzieri and L. Portinale, editors, *Proceedings of the 5th European Workshop on Advances in Case-Based Reasoning (EWCBR '00)*, volume 1898 of *LNCS*, pages 37–48. Springer-Verlag, 2000.

[5] B. Díaz-Agudo and P. A. González-Calero. Knowledge Intensive CBR through Ontologies. In B. Lees, editor, *Procs of the 6ht UK CBR Workshop*. 2001.

[6] B. Díaz-Agudo and P. A. González-Calero. *Ontologies in the Context of Information Systems*, chapter An ontological approach to develop Knowledge Intensive CBR systems, page 45. Springer-Verlag, 2006.

[7] P. A. González-Calero, M. Gómez-Albarrán, and B. Díaz-Agudo. Applying DLs for Retrieval in Case-Based Reasoning. In *Procs. of the 1999 Description Logics Workshop (Dl '99)*. Linkopings universitet, Sweden, 1999.

[8] P. A. González-Calero, M. Gómez-Albarrán, and B. Díaz-Agudo. A Substitution-based Adaptation Model. In *Challenges for Case-Based Reasoning - Proc. of the ICCBR'99 Workshops*. Univ. of Kaiserslautern, 1999.

[9] P. A. González-Calero, M. Gómez-Albarrán, and B. Díaz-Agudo. A Substitution-based Adaptation Model. In *Procs. of the ICCBR'99 Workshops*. University of Kaiserslautern, Germany, 1999.

[10] G. Kamp. Using Description Logics for KI-CBR. In B. Faltings and I. Smith, editors, *Third European Workshop on Case-Based Reasoning (EWCBR'96)*, volume 1168 of *LNCS*, pages 204–218. Springer-Verlag, Switzerland, 1996.

[11] J. Koehler. An Application of Terminological Logics to CBR. In J. Doyle, E. Sandewall, and P. Torasso, editors, *KR'94: Principles of Knowledge Representation and Reasoning*, pages 351–362. Morgan Kaufmann, 1994.

[12] J. Kolodner. *Case-Based Reasoning*. Morgan Kaufmann, San Mateo, 1993.

[13] A. Napoli, J. Lieber, and R. Courien. Classification-Based Problem Solving in CBR. In I. Smith and B. Faltings, editors, *Proceedings of the Third European Workshop on Advances in Case-Based Reasoning (EWCBR '96)*, volume 1168 of *LNCS*, pages 295–308. Springer-Verlag, 1996.

[14] J. A. Recio, B. Díaz-Agudo, M. A. Gómez-Martín, and N. Wiratunga. Extending jCOLIBRI for textual CBR. In *Procs. of 6th International Conference on CBR, ICCBR 2005*, volume 3620 of *LNCS*, pages 421–435. Springer–Verlang, 2005.

[15] S. Salotti and V. Ventos. Study and Formalization of a CBR System using a Description Logic. In *Advances in Case-Based Reasoning (EWCBR'98)*, volume 1488 of *LNCS*, pages 286–301. Springer-Verlag, 1998.

Domain Dependent Distributed Models for Railway Scheduling[*]

M.A. Salido[1], M. Abril[1], F. Barber[1], L. Ingolotti[1], P. Tormos[2], A. Lova[2]

[1]DSIC, Universidad Politécnica de Valencia, Spain

[2]DEIOAC, Universidad Politécnica de Valencia, Spain

{msalido, mabril, fbarber, lingolotti}@dsic.upv.es

{ptormos, allova}@eio.upv.es

Abstract

Many combinatorial problems can be modelled as Constraint Satisfaction Problems (CSPs). Solving a general CSP is known to be NP-complete; so that closure and heuristic search are usually used. However, many problems are inherently distributed and the problem complexity can be reduced by dividing the problem into a set of subproblems. Nevertheless, general distributed techniques are not always appropriate to distribute real life problems. In this work, we model the railway scheduling problem by means of domain dependent distributed constraint models and we show that these models maintained better behaviors than general distributed models based on graph partitioning. The evaluation is focussed on the railway scheduling problem, where domain dependent models carry out a problem distribution by means of trains and contiguous set of stations.

keywords: Constraint Satisfaction Problems, Railway Scheduling.

1 Introduction.

Many real problems in Artificial Intelligence (AI) as well as in other areas of computer science and engineering can be efficiently modelled as Constraint Satisfaction Problems (CSPs) and solved using constraint programming techniques. Some examples of such problems include: spatial and temporal planning, qualitative and symbolic reasoning, diagnosis, decision support, scheduling, hardware design and verification, real-time systems and robot planning.

Most of the work is focused on general methods for solving CSPs. They include backtracking-based search algorithms. While the worst-case complexity of backtrack search is exponential, several heuristics to reduce its average-case complexity have been proposed in the literature [2]. However, many of the problems solved by using centralized algorithms are inherently distributed. Some works are currently based on distributed CSPs (see special issue of Artificial Intelligence, Volume 161).

[*]This work has been partially supported by the research projects TIN2004-06354-C02-01 (Min. de Educacin y Ciencia, Spain-FEDER), FOM-70022/T05 (Min. de Fomento, Spain) and by the Future and Emerging Technologies Unit of EC (IST priority - 6th FP), under contract no. FP6-021235-2 (project ARRIVAL).

Furthermore, many researchers are working on graph partitioning [3], [5]. The main objective of graph partitioning is to divide the graph into a set of regions such that each region has roughly the same number of nodes and the sum of all edges connecting different regions is minimized. Graph partitioning can be applied on telephone network design, sparse gaussian elimination, data mining, clustering and physical mapping of DNA. Fortunately, many heuristic may solve this problem efficiently. For instance, graphs with over 14000 nodes and 410000 edges can be partitioned in under 2 seconds [4].

Partition of a CSP can be performed in a general (domain independent) way (see Figure 1 (2)), by using graph partitioning techniques. For instance, we can divide a CSP into several subCSPs so that constraints among variables of each subCSP are minimized. Otherwise, a domain dependent partition can be used (see Figure 1 (3)). This requires a deeper analysis of the problem to be solved. In this paper, we show that in several problems, a domain dependent partition obtains a more adequate distribution so that a higher efficiency is obtained. Moreover, cooperation among the distributed CSP solvers can be also improved.

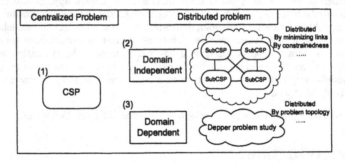

Figure 1: Centralized&Distributed Problem.

A general graph partitioning software called METIS [4] can be applied to compare its behavior in the CSP environment against a domain dependent distributed model.

Our aim is to model the railway scheduling problem as a Constraint Satisfaction Problems (CSPs) and solved using different models of distributed CSPs. Due to deregulation of European railways operators, long inter-country journeys must be scheduled. These journeys involve many stations at different countries with different railway policies. For instance, for travelling from London to Madrid, the train must run for three different countries, which different characteristics and different policies. Furthermore, each railway operator maintains strategic/private information that should not be revealed to competitors. These reasons have motivated us to distribute the railway scheduling problem.

The overall goal of a long-term collaboration between our group at the Polytechnic University of Valencia (UPV) and the National Network of Spanish Railways (RENFE) is to offer assistance to help in the planning of train scheduling, to obtain conclusions about the maximum capacity of the network, to identify bottlenecks, etc.

In this work, we compare several ways to distribute the railway scheduling problem. It is partitioned into a set of subproblems by means of graph partitioning, by means of types of trains and by means of contiguous constraints.

In the following section, we summarize some definitions about distributed CSP as well as our distributed model. In section 3, we summarize the railway scheduling problem. In section 4, we present different partition proposals. An evaluation among different models is carried out in section 5. Finally we summarize the conclusions in section 6.

2 Distributed CSPs.

This section presents numeric CSPs in a slightly non-standard form, which will be convenient for our purposes, and will unify works from constraint satisfaction communities. Furthermore, we present our distributed model.

2.1 Definitions.

A *CSP* consists of: a set of variables $X = \{x_1, x_2, ..., x_n\}$; each variable $x_i \in X$ has a set D_i of possible values (its domain); a finite collection of constraints $C = \{c_1, c_2, ..., c_p\}$ restricting the values that the variables can simultaneously take.

A solution to a CSP is an assignment of values to all the variables so that all constraints are satisfied; a problem with a solution is termed *satisfiable* or *consistent*.

State: one possible assignment of all variables.

Partition : A partition of a set C is a set of disjoint subsets of C whose union is C. The subsets are called the blocks of the partition.

Distributed CSP: A distributed CSP (DCSP) is a CSP in which the variables and constraints are distributed among automated agents [12].

Each agent has some variables and attempts to determine their values. However, there are interagent constraints and the value assignment must satisfy these interagent constraints. In our model, there are k agents $1, 2, ..., k$. Each agent knows a set of constraints and the domains of variables involved in these constraints.

A **block agent** a_j is a virtual entity that essentially has the following properties: autonomy, social ability, reactivity and pro-activity [11].

Block agents are autonomous agents. They operate their subproblems without the direct intervention of any other agent or human. *Block agents* interact with each other by sending messages to communicate consistent partial states. They perceive their environment and changes in it, such as new partial consistent states, and react, if possible, with more complete consistent partial states.

A **multi-agent system** is a system that contains the following elements:

1. An environment in which the agents live (variables, domains, constraints and consistent partial states).

2. A set of reactive rules, governing the interaction between the agents and their environment (agent exchange rules, communication rules, etc).

3. A set of agents, $A = \{a_1, a_2, ..., a_k\}$.

2.2 The Distributed Model.

In the specialized literature, there are many works about distributed CSPs. In [12], Yokoo et al. present a formalization and algorithms for solving distributed CSPs. These algorithms can be classified as either centralized methods, synchronous backtracking or asynchronous backtracking [12].

Our model can be considered as a synchronous model. It is meant to be a framework for interacting agents to achieve a consistent state. The main idea of our multi-agent model is based on [6] but partitioning the problem in k subproblems as independent as possible, classifying the subproblem in the appropriate order and solving them concurrently.

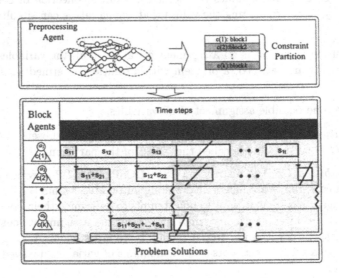

Figure 2: Multi-agent model.

In all our proposals, the problem is partitioned in k blocks or clusters in order to be studied by agents called *block agents*. Furthermore, a partition agent is committed to classify the subproblems in the appropriate order depending on the selected proposal. For instance, if Metis is selected to partition the problem, the partition agent must classify the subproblems such as the most interrelated problem is studied first.

Once the constraints are divided into k blocks by a *preprocessing agent*, a group of *block agents* concurrently manages each block of constraints. Each *block agent* is in charge of solving its own subproblem by means of a search algorithm. Each *block agent* is free to select any algorithm to find a consistent partial state. It can select a local search algorithm, a backtracking-based algorithm, or any other, depending on the problem topology. In any case, each *block agent* is committed to finding a solution to its particular subproblem. This subproblem is composed by its CSP subject to the variable assignment generated by the previous *block agents*. Thus, *block agent* 1 works on its group of constraints. If *block agent* 1 finds a solution to its subproblem, then it sends the consistent partial state to *block agent* 2, and both they work concurrently to solve their specific subproblems; *block agent* 1 tries to find other solution and *block agent* 2 tries to solve its subproblem knowing that its *common variables* have been assigned by *block agent* 1. Thus, *block agent* j, with the variable assignments generated by the previous *block agents*, works concurrently with the previous *block agents*, and tries to find a more complete consistent state using a search algorithm. Finally, the last *block agent* k, working concurrently with *block agents* $1, 2, ...(k - 1)$, tries to find a consistent state in order to find a problem solution.

Figure 2 shows the multi-agent model, in which the *preprocessing agent* carries out the network partition and the *block agents* (a_i) are committed to concurrently finding partial problem solutions (s_{ij}). Each *block agent* sends the partial problem solutions to the following *block agent* until a problem solution is found (by the last *block agent*). For example, state: $s_{11} + s_{21} + ... + s_{k1}$ is a problem solution. The concurrence can be seen in Figure 2 in *Time step* 6 in which all *block agents* are concurrently working. Each *block agent* maintains the corresponding domains for its *new variables*. The *block agent* must assign values to its *new variables* so that the block of constraints is satisfied. When a *block agent* finds a value for each *new variable*, it then sends the consistent partial state to the next *block agent*. When the last *block agent* assigns values to its *new variables* satisfying its block of constraints, then a solution is found.

3   Railway Scheduling Problem.

Train timetabling is a difficult and time-consuming task, particularly in the case of real networks, where the number of constraints and the complexity of constraints grow drastically. A feasible train timetable should specify the departure and arrival time of each train to each location of its journey, in such a way that the line capacity and other operational constraints are taken into account. Traditionally, train timetables are generated manually by drawing trains on the time-distance graph. The train schedule is generated from a given starting time and is manually adjusted so that all constraints are met. High priority trains are usually placed first followed by lower priority trains. It can take many days to develop train timetables for a line, and the process usually stops once a feasible timetable has been found. The resulting plan of this procedure may be far from optimal.

The literature of the 1960s, 1970s, and 1980s relating to rail optimization was relatively limited. Compared to the airline and bus industries, optimization was generally overlooked in favor of simulation or heuristic-based methods. However, Cordeau et al. [1] point out greater competition, privatization, deregulation, and increasing computer speed as reasons for the more prevalent use of optimization techniques in the railway industry. Our review of the methods and models that have been published indicates that the majority of authors use models that are based on the Periodic Event Scheduling Problem (PESP) introduced by Serafini and Ukovich [8]. The PESP considers the problem of scheduling as a set of periodically recurring events under periodic time-window constraints. The model generates disjunctive constraints that may cause the exponential growth of the computational complexity of the problem depending on its size. Schrijver and Steenbeek [7] have developed CADANS, a constraint programming- based algorithm to find a feasible timetable for a set of PESP constraints. The scenario considered by this tool is different from the scenario that we used; therefore, the results are not easily comparable. The train scheduling problem can also be modeled as a special case of the job-shop scheduling problem (Silva de Oliveira [9], Walker et al. [10]), where train trips are considered jobs that are scheduled on tracks that are regarded as resources.

Our goal is to model the railway scheduling problem as a Constraint Satisfaction Problems (CSPs) and solved using constraint programming techniques. However, due to the huge number of variables and constraints that this problem generates, a distributed model is developed to distribute the resultant CSP into a semi-independent subproblems such as the solution can be found efficiently.

3.1 Constraints in the Railway Scheduling Problem

There are three groups of scheduling rules in our railway scheduling problem: traffic rules, user requirements rules and topological rules. A valid running map must satisfy the above rules. These scheduling rules can be modelled using the following constraints:

1. **Traffic rules** guarantee crossing and overtaking operations. The main constraints to take into account are:

   - *Crossing constraint*: Any two trains (T_i and T_j) going in opposite directions must not simultaneously use the same one-way track. That is, train i arrivals to station A before than train j departures from station A ($T_iA_A < T_jD_A$) or train j arrivals to station B before than train i departures from station B ($T_jA_B < T_iD_B$).

     $$T_iA_A < T_jD_A \text{ or } T_jA_B < T_iD_B$$

     The crossing of two trains can be performed only on two-way tracks and at stations, where one of the two trains has been detoured from the main track (Figure 3).

- *Overtaking constraint*: Any two trains (T_i and T_j) going at different speeds in the same direction can only overtake each other at stations.

$$T_i D_A < T_j D_A \rightarrow T_i A_B < T_j A_B$$

The train being passed is detoured form the main track so that the faster train can pass the slower one (see Figure 3).

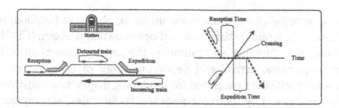

Figure 3: Constraints related to crossing and overtaking in stations

- *Expedition time constraint*. There exists a given time to put a detoured train back on the main track and exit from a station (see Figure 3 right).

- *Reception time constraint*. There exists a given time to detour a train from the main track so that crossing or overtaking can be performed (see Figure 3 right).

2. **User Requirements**: The constraints due to user requirements are:

- *Type and Number of trains* going in each direction to be scheduled.

- *Path of trains*: Locations used and *Stop time* for commercial purposes in each direction.

- *Scheduling frequency*. Train departure must satisfy frequency requirements in both directions. This constraint is very restrictive because, when crossings are performed, trains must wait for a certain time interval at stations. This interval must be propagated to all trains going in the same direction in order to maintain the established scheduling frequency. The user can require a fixed frequency, a frequency within a minimum and maximum interval, or multiple frequencies.

- *Departure interval* for the departure of the first trains going in both the up and down directions.

- *Maximum slack*. This is the maximum percentage δ that a train may delay with respect to the minimum journey time.

3. **Railway infrastructure Topology and type of trains** to be scheduled give rise to other constraints to be taken into account. Some of them are:

- Number of *tracks in stations* (to perform technical and/or commercial operations) and the number of tracks between two locations (one-way or two-way). No crossing or overtaking is allowed on a one-way track,
- *Time constraints*, between each two contiguous stations,
- Added *Station time constraints* for technical and/or commercial purposes.

The complete set of constraints, including an objective function, transform the CSP into a constraint satisfaction and optimization problem (CSOP), where the main objective function is to minimize the journey time of all trains. Variables are frequencies, arrival and departure times of trains at stations and binary auxiliary variables generated for modelling disjunctive constraints. Constraints are composed by user requirements, traffic rules, and topological constraints.

(1) **Min** $\sum_{i=1}^{i=n}(T_iA_r - T_iD_1) + \sum_{j=1}^{j=m}(T_jA_1 - T_jD_r)$;

Subject To

/frequency constraint $\quad \forall i = 1..n, \forall k = 1..r$

(2) $T_{i+1}D_k - T_iD_k = Frequency$;

/Time Constraints $\forall i = 1..n, \forall k = 1..r$

(3.1) $T_iA_{k+1} - T_iD_k = Timei_{k-(k+1)}$;

(3.2) $T_jA_k - T_iD_{k+1} = Timei_{k-(k+1)}$;

/Stations Time Constrains $\quad \forall i = 1..n, \forall k = 1..r$

(4) $T_iD_k - T_iA_k - TSi_k = CSi_k$;

/Constrains to limit journey time $\quad \forall i = 1..n, \forall j = 1..m$

(5.1) $T_iA_r - T_iD_1 \leq (1 + \frac{4}{100}) * Timei_{1-r}$;

(5.2) $T_jA_1 - T_jD_r \leq (1 + \frac{4}{100}) * Timej_{r-1}$;

/Crossing Constrains $\quad \forall i = 1..n, \forall j = 1..m, \forall k = 1..r$

(6.1) $T_jA_k - T_iD_k <= 86400 * Y_{i-j;k-(k+1)}$;

(6.2) $T_iA_{k+1} - T_jD_{k+1} <= 86400 * (1 - Y_{i-j;k-(k+1)})$;

/Expedition time constrains $\quad \forall i = 1..n, \forall j = 1..m, \forall k = 1..r$

(7.1) $T_jA_k - T_iD_k - 86400 * (X_{i-j} - Y_{i-j;k-(k+1)} + Y_{i-j;(k+1)-(k+2)} - 1) + ET_i <= 0$;

(7.2) $T_iA_k - T_jD_k - 86400 * (X_{i-j} - Y_{i-j;k-(k+1)} + Y_{i-j;(k+1)-(k+2)} - 2) + ET_j <= 0$;

/Reception time constrains $\quad \forall i = 1..n, \forall j = 1..m, \forall k = 1..r$

(8.1) $T_iA_k - T_jA_k - 86400 * (X_{i-j} - Y_{i-j;k-(k+1)} + Y_{i-j;(k+1)-(k+2)} - 1) + RT_i <= 0$;

(8.2) $T_jA_k - T_iA_k - 86400 * (X_{i-j} - Y_{i-j;k-(k+1)} + Y_{i-j;(k+1)-(k+2)} - 2) + RT_j <= 0$;

/Binary Constraints

X_{i-j}; $\quad \forall i = 1..n, \forall j = 1..m$

$Y_{i-j;k-(k+1)}$; $\quad \forall i = 1..n, \forall j = 1..m, \forall k = 1..r$

Figure 4: Formal Mathematical Model of the Railway Scheduling Problem..

The complete CSOP is presented in Figure 4. Let's suppose a railway network with r stations, n trains running in the down direction, and m trains running in the up direction. We assume that two connected stations have only one line connecting them. T_iA_k represents that train i arrives at station k; T_iD_k means that train i departs from station k; $Timei_{k-(k+1)}$ is the journey time of train i to travel from station k to $k+1$; TSi_k and CSi_k represent the technical and commercial stop times of train i in station k, respectively; and ET_i and RT_i are the expedition and reception time of train i, respectively.

4   Partition Proposals

4.1   Domain Independent: Partition Proposal 1.

A natural way to distribute the problem is carried out by means of a graph partitioning software called METIS [4]. METIS provides two programs *pmetis* and *kmetis* for partitioning an unstructured graph into *k* equal size parts. In this way, the railway scheduling problem can be modelled as a constraint network. This network can be partitioned in semi-independent subproblems by means of METIS. However, this software does not take into account additional information about the railway infrastructure or the type of trains to guide the partition, so the generated clusters may not be the most appropriate and the results are not appropriate. Figure 5 shows the distribution carried out by METIS. Red agent is committed to assign variables to train 0 and train 1 at the beginning and finishing of its journeys. Green agent studies two trains in disjoint part of the same train. METIS carries out a partition of the constraint network generated by the corresponding CSP. However, we can observe visually that the best partition generated by a well-known software is not the most appropriate for this problem. To improve the partition procedure, we extract additional information from the railway topology to obtain better partitions such as partition proposal 2 and 3.

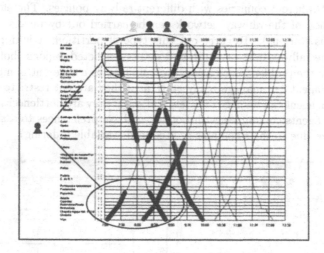

Figure 5: Distributed Railway Scheduling Problem: Proposal 1.

4.2   Domain Dependent: Partition Proposal 2.

This model extracts additional information from the railway topology to obtain a better partition by distributing the original problem by means of train type. The problem can be considered as a scheduling problem where trains are tasks so that the partition is carried out by trains (task-driven). Each agent is committed to assign values to variables regarding a train or trains to minimize the journey travel. Depending on the selected number of partitions, each agent will manage one o more trains. Figure 6 left, shows a running map with 20 partition, each agent manages one train. This partition model has two important advantages: Firstly, this model allow us to improve privacy. Currently, due to the policy of deregulation in the European railways, trains from different operators work in the same railway infrastructure. In this way, the partition model gives us the possibility of partition the problem such as each agent is committed to a operator. Thus, different operators maintains privacy about strategic data. Secondly, this model allow us to manage efficiently priorities between different types of trains (regional trains, high speed trains, freight trains). In this way, agents committed to priority trains (high speed trains) will firstly carry out value assignment to variables, in order to achieve better journey travels

4.3   Domain Dependent: Partition Proposal 3.

This model is based on distributing the original railway problem by means of contiguous stations. The problem can also be considered as a scheduling problem where stations are resources and the partition is carried out by stations (resource-driven). Due to deregulation of European railways operators, long journeys may be scheduled. However, long journeys involve large number of stations at different countries with different railway policies. Therefore, a logical partition of the railway network can be carried out by means on regions (contiguous stations). To carry out this type of partition, it is important to analyze the railway infrastructure and detect restricted regions (bottlenecks). To balance the problem, each agent is committed to a different number of stations. An agent can manage many stations if they are not restricted stations, whereas an agent can manage only few stations if they are bottlenecks. Furthermore, the agents committed with bottleneck have preferences to assign values to variables due to their domains are reduced (variable ordering).

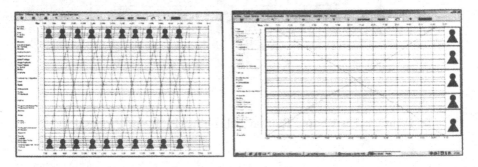

Figure 6: Distributed Railway Scheduling Problem. Proposal 2 (left) and proposal 3 (right).

Thus, the running map to be scheduled between two cities is decomposed in several and shorter running maps. Figure 6 (up) shows a running map to be scheduled. The set of stations will be partitioned in block of contiguous stations and a set of agents will coordinate to achieve a global solution (Figure 6 (down)). Thus, we can obtain important results such as railway capacity, consistent timetable, etc.

5 Evaluation.

In this section, we carry out an evaluation between our distributed model and a centralized model. Furthermore, we evaluate the behavior of a distributed model generated by a general software called METIS and two proposed partition models. To this end, we have used a well-known CSP solver called Forward Checking (FC)[1].

This empirical evaluation was carried out with both different types of problems: random problems and benchmark problems.

Random problems.

In our evaluation, each set of random CSPs was defined by the 3-tuple $< n, a, p >$, where n was the number of variables, a the arity of binary constraints and p the number of partitions. The problems were randomly generated by modifying these parameters.

In Table 1 we compare the running time of the distributed model by METIS with the centralized problem. In Table 1 left, we fixed the arity of binary constraints and the size of the partition, and the number of variables was increased from 100 to 500. We can observe that the running time for small problems was worse by the distributed model than the centralized problem. However, when the number of variables increased, the behavior of the distributed problem was better. In Table 1 right, we fixed the number of variables and the arity of binary constraints and the size of the partition was increased from 3 to 20. We can observe that the size of the partition is important to distributed the problem. For small problems, the number of partition must be low. However, for large CSPs (railway Scheduling Problems) the size of the partition must be higher. In this case, the appropriate number of partition was 7.

As we can observe, the distributed model using METIS works well for random instances. However in real scheduling problems, a domain dependent distributed models are necessary to optimize running times.

Benchmark problems.

This empirical evaluation was carried out over a real railway infrastructure that joins two important Spanish cities (La Coruna and Vigo). The journey between these two cities is currently divided by 40 stations. In our empirical evaluation,

---

[1] Forward Checking were obtained from CON'FLEX. It can be found in: http://www-bia.inra.fr/T/conflex/ Logiciels/adressesConflex.html.

174

Table 1: Random instances $< n, a, p >$, n: variables, a: arity and p: partition size.

Problem	Distributed Model (sc.)	Centralized Model (sc.)	Problem	Distributed Model (sc.)	Centralized Model (sc.)
$< 100, 25, 10 >$	12	14	$< 200, 25, 3 >$	26	75
$< 200, 25, 10 >$	16	75	$< 200, 25, 5 >$	19	75
$< 300, 25, 10 >$	19	140	$< 200, 25, 7 >$	14	75
$< 400, 25, 10 >$	30	327	$< 200, 25, 9 >$	16	75
$< 500, 25, 10 >$	42	532	$< 200, 25, 20 >$	22	75

each set of random instances was defined by the 3-tuple $< n, s, f >$, where n was the number of periodic trains in each direction, s the number of stations and f the frequency. The problems were randomly generated by modifying these parameters.

General graph partitioning softwares work well in general graphs. However, in the railway scheduling problem, we did not obtain good results using these softwares. We evaluate the partition proposal 1 by using METIS in several instances $< n, 20, 120 >$. Figure 8 left, shows that the obtained results were even worse in the distributed model than in the centralized model. For a low number of trains, the behavior was better than the complete model. However, with more than 8 trains, the distributed model was unable to solve the problem in 1000000 seconds, so that the program was aborted. We studied the partitions generated by METIS and we observed that the journey of a train is partitioned in several clusters, and each cluster was composed by tracks of trains in opposite directions. This cluster is easy to solve but very difficult to propagate to other agents. Furthermore, the following partition proposals make the contrary, that is, they never join tracks of trains in opposite directions.

Figure 7 shows the behavior of the partition proposal 2, where the number of partition/agents was equal to the number of trains. In both figures, we can observe that the running time increased when the number of trains increased (Figure 7 left) and when the number of stations increased (Figure 7 right). However, in both cases, the distributed model maintained better behavior than the centralized model.

The partition proposal 2 (distributed by trains) was better behavior but similar to partition proposal 3 (distributed by stations) (see Figure 8 right), mainly when the number of trains increased. However, partition proposal 3 maintained an uniform behavior.

6 Conclusions.

Distributed CSP is a promising research area in CSP, where graph partitioning techniques can be applied. However, we show that domain dependent distributed constraint models maintained better behaviors than general dis-

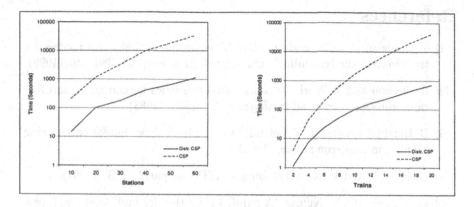

Figure 7: Running Time when the number of trains and stations increased (proposal 2).

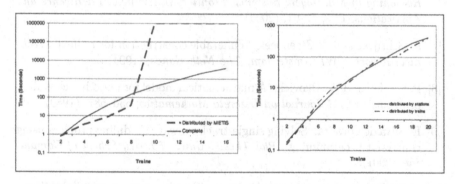

Figure 8: Running Time using Metis and Complete (left). Comparation of proposal 2 and 3 (right).

tributed models. Our study has been focused on the railway scheduling problem, where specific railway characteristics make the problem domain-dependent. Each instance depends on the number of trains in each direction, the number of stations, the distance among stations, etc. The evaluation shows that general distributed models had a better behavior than the centralized model, but domain dependent distributed models are more efficient than general ones. Our domain dependent model makes a distribution based on trains (which can be assimilated to task to do) and on stations (which can be assimilated to resources). Research on models for domain-based distribution is a promising research area to distributed CSP which can also be applied to a distributed architecture where each subCSP competes among them for a global solution.

References

[1] J. Cordeau, P. Toth, and D. Vigo, 'A survey of optimization models for train routing and scheduling', *Transportation Science*, **32**, 380–446, (1998).

[2] R. Dechter and J. Pearl, 'Network-based heuristics for constraint satisfaction problems', *Artificial Intelligence*, **34**, 1–38, (1988).

[3] B. Hendrickson and R.W. Leland, 'A multi-level algorithm for partitioning graphs', in *Supercomputing*, (1995).

[4] G. Karypis and V. Kumar, 'Using METIS and parMETIS', (1995).

[5] G. Karypis and V. Kumar, 'A parallel algorithm for multilevel graph partitioning and sparse matrix ordering', *Journal of Parallel and Distributed Computing*, 71–95, (1998).

[6] M.A. Salido, A. Giret, and F. Barber, 'Distributing Constraints by Sampling in Non-Binary CSPs', *Distributed Constraint Problem Solving and Reasoning in Multi-agent Systems. Frontiers in Artificial Intelligence and Applications*, **112**, 77–91, (2004).

[7] A. Schrijver and A. Steenbeek, 'Timetable construction for railned', *Technical Report, CWI, Amsterdam, The Netherlands*, (1994).

[8] P. Serafini and W. Ukovich, 'A mathematical model for periodic scheduling problems', *SIAM Journal on Discrete Mathematics*, 550–581, (1989).

[9] E. Silva de Oliveira, 'Solving single-track railway scheduling problem using constraint programming', *Phd Thesis. Univ. of Leeds, School of Computing*, (2001).

[10] C. Walker, J. Snowdon, and D. Ryan, 'Simultaneous disruption recovery of a train timetable and crew roster in real time', *Comput. Oper. Res*, 2077–2094, (2005).

[11] M. Wooldridge and R. Jennings, 'Agent theories, arquitectures, and lenguajes: a survey', *Intelligent Agents*, 1–22, (1995).

[12] M. Yokoo and K. Hirayama, 'Algorithms for distributed constraint satisfaction: A review', *Autonomous Agents and Multi-Agent Systems*, **3**, 185–207, (2000).

SESSION 5:

NATURAL LANGUAGE

Bringing Chatbots into Education: Towards Natural Language Negotiation of Open Learner Models

Alice Kerly[1], Phil Hall[2] and Susan Bull[1]

[1] Electronic, Electrical and Computer Engineering, University of Birmingham, Edgbaston, Birmingham, B15 2TT, UK
[2] Elzware Ltd, 70 Mendip Road, Windmill Hill, Bristol, BS3 4NY
[1] {alk584, s.bull}@bham.ac.uk   [2] phil.hall@elzware.com

Abstract. There is an extensive body of work on Intelligent Tutoring Systems: computer environments for education, teaching and training that adapt to the needs of the individual learner. Work on personalisation and adaptivity has included research into allowing the student user to enhance the system's adaptivity by improving the accuracy of the underlying learner model. Open Learner Modelling, where the system's model of the user's knowledge is revealed to the user, has been proposed to support student reflection on their learning. Increased accuracy of the learner model can be obtained by the student and system jointly negotiating the learner model. We present the initial investigations into a system to allow people to negotiate the model of their understanding of a topic in natural language. This paper discusses the development and capabilities of both conversational agents (or chatbots) and Intelligent Tutoring Systems, in particular Open Learner Modelling. We describe a Wizard-of-Oz experiment to investigate the feasibility of using a chatbot to support negotiation, and conclude that a fusion of the two fields can lead to developing negotiation techniques for chatbots and the enhancement of the Open Learner Model. This technology, if successful, could have widespread application in schools, universities and other training scenarios.

1 Background

This paper unites work in chatbots, natural language processing in an educational context, intelligent tutoring systems and learner modelling. We briefly introduce these fields below, and propose how this combined approach might be used to support learners.

1.1   Chatbots

Conversational agents, or chatbots, provide a natural language interface to their users. Their design has become increasingly sophisticated and their use adopted in education, (e.g. [1]), commerce (e.g. [2], [3]), entertainment (e.g. [4]) and the public sector (e.g. [5], [6]).

ELIZA [7], was regarded as one of the first chatbots. ELIZA analysed input sentences and created its response based on reassembly rules associated with a decomposition of the input. This produced an impression of caring about its users, but it held no memory of the conversation and so could not enter into any form of targeted collaboration or negotiation. The syntactic language processing used by ELIZA has been developed significantly, leading to the development of a number of language processing chatbots (an exhaustive list can be found at [8]).

A.L.I.C.E. [9] is a chatbot built using Artificial Intelligence Markup Language (AIML), developed over the past 10 years. The chatbot is based on categories containing a stimulus, or pattern, and a template for the response. Category patterns are matched to find the most appropriate response to a user input. Further AIML tags provide for consideration of context, conditional branching and supervised learning to produce new responses. A.L.I.C.E. is a viable and experienced system but has not to our knowledge, as yet, been applied in a commercial environment.

The Jabberwacky [10] chatbot has as its aim to "simulate natural human chat in an interesting, entertaining and humorous manner". Jabberwacky learns from all its previous conversations with humans. It functions by storing everything that is said to it, and uses contextual pattern matching techniques to select the most appropriate response. It has no hard-coded rules, instead relying entirely on previous conversations. It is explicitly not intended to do anything 'useful', instead being simply to chat [10].

Modern commercial chatbots, such as those developed with Lingubot™ [11] technology, offer sophisticated development environments allowing the building of intelligent conversational agents with complex, goal driven behaviour. In 'Lingubots' both the words and the grammatical structure of the user's input are analysed using customised templates. This facilitates the development of a user model, which is used in conjunction with the conversational context and specific words in the dialogue to determine the chatbot's response. Responses might include further conversation with the user, reading or writing to external systems (for instance to open a web page or update a database), or a combination of these. This rich range of responses allows for intelligent conversation with the user, and provides the ability to steer the user back to the task in hand if they stray from the designated discussion content for too long.

As computing technology and the underlying language processing software progresses, we can expect to see potentially exponential growth in the delivered complexity of chatbots. Already, they have come a long way from their roots in systems that were more about fun, flirtation or simple 'chat'. We are now approaching a time where the technologies such as Lingubot can, through extensive syntactic structures developed for natural language processing and some complex methodological data structuring, begin to display behaviour that users will interpret as understanding.

1.2 Intelligent Tutoring Systems

The field of Intelligent Tutoring Systems emerged from earlier work on generative computer-assisted instruction, for example Uhr's [12] work on generating arithmetic problems. Other systems were able to adaptively select problems based on the student's performance (e.g. Suppes, 1967, cited by Sleeman and Brown [13], pg 1). These systems maintained basic models of the student's behaviour, but did not tend to store representations of the student's actual knowledge [13]. Uhr advocates systems that were able to generate new problems according to a small set of axioms, in order to provide problems that were suited to the level the learner was performing at [12]. Sleeman and Brown also argued that to tutor well the system must constrain the student's instructional paths by a system of student modelling [13].

Intelligent Tutoring Systems (ITS) researchers were able to exploit developments within both the cognitive sciences and in hardware to produce systems which took into account the learner's state, e.g. Clancey's GUIDON [14] and Burton's DEBUGGY [15] systems. There are a variety of learner modelling techniques, such as overlay models which model the learner as a subset of the expert; perturbation models that also allow misconceptions to be modelled; Bayesian networks to allow more complex inferences (see [16] for an overview). Work in learner modelling has continued to be central to research in intelligent tutoring systems (e.g. [17], [18], [19]), with researchers exploring issues such as learner control over the learner model contents, modelling learner misconceptions, peer-group modelling, presentation of models, and learner models for mobile computing.

Thus learner modelling has developed as the practice of creating a model of the learner's understanding based on their interaction with an ITS. This allows for personalisation of the user experience, and to provide individualised feedback to the user on their progress.

1.3 Learner Modelling and Open Learner Modelling

Intelligent Tutoring Systems employ a learner model to infer the learner's knowledge and to provide an adaptive interaction. While many ITSs do not reveal the contents of the learner model to the learner, it has been argued that opening the learner model to the ITS users can in fact provide opportunities for learner reflection and deep learning that enhances the learning experience (e.g. [20], [21], [22], [23] and [24]).

Open learner models are therefore accessible to the user. They are inferred from the learner's interaction with the system (as in any ITS), and may also include contributions obtained directly (explicitly) from the student. As a pedagogical goal, learner reflection is endorsed by many theories, including Dewey [25], Schön [26], and Kolb [27]. Bull & Pain [28] and Dimitrova [21] proposed that both learner reflection and model accuracy could be increased through a process of negotiation of the learner model contents and implemented the Mr. Collins and STyLE-OLM systems respectively. In this method the learner model is collaboratively constructed and maintained by both the system and the learner. In both the above systems, the learner was required to discuss their beliefs with the system, arguing against the system's assessment if they disagreed with it, and providing supporting evidence or argument for their own beliefs when they differed from the system. This interaction supported the increased learner reflection intended to benefit learning, and produced a more accurate learner model on which to base system adaptivity.

In order to support the negotiation functionality, the learner model must store distinct records of the learner's and the system's beliefs about the learner's knowledge. Two separate belief measures were maintained in the Mr. Collins [28] system, each of which was taken into account by the system in providing adaptive interactions. Baker's notion of interaction symmetry [29] was applied to the system, ensuring that all dialogue moves necessary for negotiation were available to both the student and the system. Laboratory studies of the Mr. Collins system [28] found that students were interested in being able to see the contents of their learner model. They were keen to use negotiation to improve the accuracy of the learner model and most students also wanted the system to challenge them if it disagreed with their attempts to change their confidence in their performance.

Previous open learner model systems have employed menu-selection or conceptual graphs to achieve negotiation of the learner model contents. While laboratory trials ([28], [21]) of these systems suggested the potential for engaging learner reflection and enhancing the accuracy of the learner model, the negotiation methods used may be restrictive or unnatural. We propose that natural language negotiation through a Chatbot may offer users the flexibility to express their views in a naturalistic and intuitive way. For the early exploratory design of the Chatbot structure we have opted to follow the negotiation strategies provided in Mr. Collins as these offer a structured and limited architecture on which to base our protocols.

1.4 Intelligent Tutoring Systems that use Natural Language

Intelligent tutoring systems that use natural language have largely tended to be either tutors, pedagogical agents or avatars. Avatars provide an engaging, personalised and simple interface, often (though not always) with an animated human character (e.g. an avatar to improve child users' engagement in a web-based game to teach home and city safety [30]).

Pedagogical agents are autonomous agents that occupy computer learning environments and facilitate learning by interacting with students or other agents (e.g. [31], [32], [33], and [34]). They may act as peers, co-learners, competitors, helpers or instructors. For effective pedagogy, agents should be able to ask and respond to questions, give hints and explanations, monitor students and provide feedback [35]. Tutoring may be provided by pedagogical agents, avatars, or other simpler mechanisms (e.g. staged textual hints) and is tailored to the individual learner to help them progress through the immediate task.

This paper presents a study involving a simulated chatbot to investigate combining the benefits of natural language interaction with negotiation of the learner model. This is a new direction for the use of natural language in ITS, drawing on work on pedagogical agents, avatars and natural language tutoring.

2 Using a Chatbot for Negotiated Learner Modelling

Kay [22] states that open learner models may enhance the student experience by encouraging effective learning (rather than merely browsing), by creating opportunities for the learner to disagree or negotiate with the system, by asking the student to reflect on their knowledge and compare this with their student model, and by asking the student to use their model to identify areas to revise. Kay also suggests that offering different presentations of the same information may help students to think about their knowledge in different ways. It is envisaged that all of these goals could be facilitated by a chatbot suitably integrated into an open learner model system.

Natural language dialogue has not previously been used in an ITS to support the creation or maintenance of an open learner model. Given the benefits that negotiation can bring to learner model construction and to encouraging learner reflection, and the capabilities of modern chatbots, the present study aimed to explore the feasibility of integrating a natural language conversational agent into an open learner model system to enable student-system negotiation over the contents of the learner model.

2.1 The Choice of Chatbot

The technology for negotiation of an open learner model requires the following characteristics:

- Keeping the user 'on topic' – preventing them from deviating too long from the issue at hand
- Database connectivity – to allow reading and writing of data to and from the learner model
- Capability to be event driven by database changes – to allow the chatbot to initiate negotiation if there are conflicts in the learner model
- Web integration – to allow easy deployment to maximum possible users
- An appropriate corpus of semantic reasoning knowledge.

The open source foundations of AIML [9] have provided an interesting and useful application for AI development. We believe that while the A.L.I.C.E. solution could be used to create this system, writing of AIML on this scale would be challenging for the non-developer, and that the richness of processing is limited in comparison to Lingubots [11]. Both Lingubots and AIML have a wide corpus, but Lingubot's is more focussed on goal driven conversation. The Lingubot Creator editorial interface allows for more in-depth developmental objectives and facilitates the building of this complex system.

The Lingubot technology has generated a significant corpus of external scripts and applications, providing functionality relevant to conversations, such as abuse counters, theme metrics and directed conversational abilities, as well as integration with many web technologies. It has the capability to generate and manipulate variables and information regarding the conversation, and also for retrieving and posting information to other web enabled applications such as search engines and databases. The commercial nature of the technology also ensures that it is well tested.

Lingubot technology is the most appropriate AI technology for this development due to the ability for the human to remain in the loop due to its ease of update and open reporting structures. It also meets the requirements of a user-centred experience, easy web integration and database connectivity. By allowing the AI researcher to focus more on the delivery or outcomes of conversation, rather than the underlying pattern matching effectiveness we hope to build a bridge towards a more complex understanding of the dynamics of humans with machines.

3 Wizard-of-Oz study

3.1 The Wizard-of-Oz Paradigm

In this study, as a precursor to development of a chatbot, we used the Wizard-of-Oz method (discussed below) to conduct an experiment where the role of the chatbot was taken by the experimenter; the 'Wizard'. The fact that the chatbot was actually a person was not revealed to the participants until after the study to ensure that data collected from their interaction would be pertinent to human-computer conversational design.

Wizard-of-Oz experiments are studies where participants are told that they are interacting with a computer system, when in fact the interaction is mediated by a human operator, the 'Wizard' [36]. The dialogues required to negotiate over a learner model are expected to be complex and varied in terms of language, tasks, and domain content [37]. The Wizard-of-Oz method has been shown to be appropriate for collecting data about user interaction in such complex domains [38] cited by [39]. The approach is also valuable in that computer-mediated human-human interaction data can be an unreliable source of information for some important aspects of human-computer dialogue design as humans and computers can be expected to perform differently in conversation [38]. As a technique it is good at eliciting application-specific linguistic characteristics, and is also significant as keyboard interaction appears to be a mode that alters the normal organization of discourse [36], thus rendering non-computer mediated data less valuable.

The Wizard-of-Oz paradigm necessarily involves deception of the participants about the nature of the experiment. This study was conducted within British Psychological Society Ethical Principles for Research with Human Participants guidelines [40], including debriefing participants by explaining the purposes of the deception and answering their questions or concerns about the process.

3.2 The Learner Modelling System

In order to investigate the potential for negotiation over the learner model, we needed an open learner model system capable of independently storing the system's and student's beliefs. The system employed was a modified version of Flexi-OLM [41], an open learner model in the domain of C programming. The system infers its beliefs from students' answers to multiple-choice and short-answer questions, and computes and displays the learner model as a result, in a choice of 7 formats to suit the learner's preferences for how to access the information: 2 knowledge map views; 2 hierarchical structures; 2 list views; and a textual description. Figure 1 shows the concept map view as an example, with the colour of the nodes portraying the knowledge level of each concept. The learners were also able to record their own beliefs about their knowledge, and this data was stored in parallel with the system's inferences, and could be viewed in the same 7 formats as the system's beliefs, for direct comparison. These two belief sets (system inferences and student-provided information about their beliefs) provided the necessary data for comparisons of beliefs leading to negotiation of the learner model.

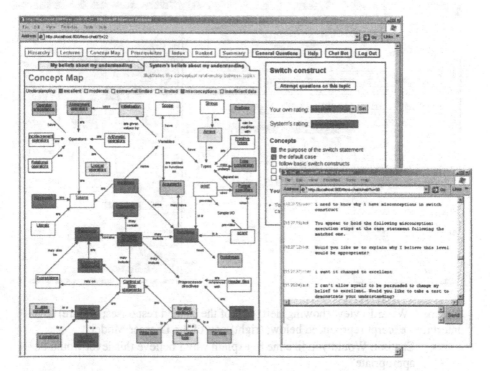

Figure 1. User's screen in Concept Map view of System beliefs of student knowledge & chat interface [41]

3.3 Experimental setup

The participants were 30 students from the University of Birmingham Electronic, Electrical and Computer Engineering Department. 11 were final year undergraduates and 19 were MSc students. All had previously taken courses in educational technology and C programming. All were competent English language speakers, though in some cases English was not their first language.

Mr. Collins [28] provided a range of strategies for negotiation: ask user if they wish to accept the system's viewpoint; offer compromise; ask user to justify their belief (e.g. by taking a test to demonstrate knowledge); system justify its belief; or offer student the opportunity to view the learner model. These strategies were adopted as the initial conversational basis of the 'chatbot'. The 'Wizard' was provided with a decision tree to allow the consistent selection of appropriate responses, and 350 pre-authored 'chatbot' negotiation initiations and responses to user inputs [37]. These 'canned responses' can be seen in the left part of Figure 2, while the right shows the wizard's view of the learner model. This view of the model enabled the wizard: (i) to compare the user and system beliefs for each topic in two columns using colour to represent the student's and system's beliefs about the learner's knowledge level; (ii) to see the student's answers to questions; and (iii) to select unanswered questions to offer the student a test by which to demonstrate their knowledge.

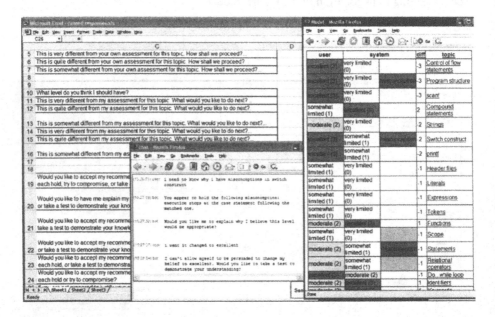

Figure 2. Wizard's view showing (left) part of the canned responses; (centre) Chat interface - excerpt reproduced below; (right) part of the Learner Model

- Chatbot: Would you like me to explain why I believe this level would be appropriate?
- User: I want it changed to excellent.
- Chatbot: I can't allow myself to be persuaded to change my belief to excellent. Would you like to take a test to demonstrate your understanding?

The users were instructed that they would be able to use a chatbot feature of Flexi-OLM to discuss their learning of C programming which could lead to modification of the learner model. They were not constrained as to how they should interact with the 'chatbot'. They were provided with an interface to allow them to answer questions related to C programming; view the system's model of their knowledge or their own belief model; attempt to edit their own beliefs (though the 'chatbot' may challenge them) and negotiate over the model by challenging the chatbot about the system's beliefs. Students completed post-interaction questionnaires with responses required on a 5-point Likert Scale. All interactions were logged by the system.

It is acknowledged that providing the Wizard with 350 pre-authored phrases substantially restricted the content that the 'chatbot' could handle. However, this limitation was necessary in order to remain manageable for the Wizard. We also recognise the limitations of the relatively small population, their restricted demographic, and their prior experience of educational technology.

3.4 Outcomes

In the 30 logged student-'chatbot' conversations there were 164 negotiation fragments (elements of conversation where a topic is introduced, discussed and resolved). Users initiated the conversation on 94 occasions; the 'chatbot' began the discussion 70 times. Interaction times ranged from 18 to 64 minutes, (mean 30.17 minutes, median 29.5 minutes). Negotiation fragments lasted a mean of 4.65 minutes (median 4 minutes).

Table 1 User opinions of the Chatbot and negotiation facility

	< strongly agree....strongly disagree >					Mean score
	(1)	(2)	(3)	(4)	(5)	
The negotiation changed my view of my understanding	6	13	8	3	0	2.3
I used the Chatbot to help me understand my learner model *	7	16	4	1	1	2.1
I always challenged the Chatbot when I disagreed with it (or I would)	13	11	5	1	0	1.8
I liked the Chatbot when it disagreed with me	4	16	6	2	2	2.4
I liked the Chatbot when it agreed with me *	6	16	7	0	0	2.0
I enjoyed interacting with the Chatbot *	12	11	6	0	0	1.8
I was able to achieve the negotiation tasks I wished with the Chatbot	6	18	5	0	1	2.1
The Chatbot made negotiation easy	7	17	4	1	1	2.1
The Chatbot was a convenient way to provide my opinions to the system *	8	14	6	1	0	2.0
It was easy to interact with the Chatbot	7	13	7	2	1	2.2

(* indicates one user did not respond, therefore total responses is 29)

Table 1 summarises the questionnaire responses. For each of the above statements the mean score shows that users were either positive or neutral in their reaction. Particularly noteworthy are the 13 strongly agree and 11 agree responses to "I always challenged the Chatbot when I disagreed with it" as this willingness to engage in discussion is essential to the concept of negotiating a learner model. Also of interest are the 12 strongly agree and 11 agree responses to "I enjoyed interacting with the Chatbot". This enjoyment in the interaction is crucial in keeping users engaged and involved. Interestingly, most students claimed to like the chatbot even when it disagreed with them. It is also important that 17 users agreed and 7 strongly agreed that "the Chatbot made negotiation easy". It is our aim to provide a user-friendly interface to negotiation, and this finding supports our proposal that chatbots are a fitting tool in this endeavour. Of key interest to the pedagogical aims of this work are the first two statements. 13 students agreed and 6 strongly agreed that "the negotiation changed my view of my understanding" and 16 agreed and 7 strongly agreed that "I used the Chatbot to help me understand my learner model". There were also positive results for statements regarding usability of the chatbot, including being able to achieve the negotiation tasks wished, being a convenient way to provide opinions to the system, and ease of interaction.

Our investigations suggested that allowing students to additionally discuss content not related to their learner model may be useful in helping them to build a rapport with the chatbot. This is important in keeping students engaged in the discussion for as long as possible and to permit the maximum possible on-topic negotiation. Students in the Wizard-of-Oz study commented that they would like to be able to "discuss other stuff, e.g. weather, just for a little break from working!" Users also often asked the chatbot "how old are you?" and "what is your name?" One user asked "what will you do this evening?" and several others asked "what's the time?"

From the transcripts of the Wizard-of-Oz study we were able to identify a number of questions that frequently arose in users' conversations with the chatbot. Therefore, we believe that in a learner modelling environment, key inputs that the chatbot should be able to respond to include:

- What should I do next?
- Can you help me?
- What should I study?
- What am I good at?
- What am I bad at?
- What's the answer?
- What are my misconceptions?

These findings suggest that implementation of a chatbot to facilitate negotiation of the learner model is a worthwhile next step in open learner modelling.

4 Lessons for implementation

As a result of our investigations, we have established a set of requirements for a system that is to provide negotiation functionality, particularly within a learner modelling environment.

4.1 System Requirements

- **Links to external databases**. This is essential in order to provide accurate and current modelling capabilities. The chatbot must be able to write to the database, for example to record the outcomes of a negotiation fragment, and must also be able to read data from the database in order to insert into its text outputs, for example to ask the user a test question.
- **Common user requests**. The chatbot should be able to respond appropriately to requests identified as frequent or of particular importance.

- **Privacy of data.** The focus here is on reassuring users that data is secure.
- **Keeping the user on topic.** This is a particular skill of the Lingubot technology, and is important for this system to be pedagogically successful. While a degree of smalltalk is considered beneficial to the interaction (see below) the essence of the system is negotiation over the learner model. If the learner is allowed to be distracted from their educational goals, this will be detrimental to the success of the learning episode. Therefore, the chatbot must be able to manage a small amount of "extra-curricular" discussion before pleasantly but firmly returning the user to the topic at hand.
- **The need for smalltalk.** We intend to use the power of the Yhaken conversational core (a specific Lingubot implementation) [42] to allow the user an effective smalltalk experience and deal with flak that arises when we push the user back to the point at hand.
- **Prevent user 'losing' chatbot.** In order to ensure the user always has access to the chatbot's conversation, it is necessary to ensure that they cannot have accidentally closed or buried the chatbot window. We propose overcoming this risk by embedding the chatbot window in a frame at the side of the learner modelling system. This will ensure it remains accessible at all times, and that users may better associate the chatbot's utterances with their behaviour and results in the learner model.
- **Understand negotiation fragments.** There is a need for the chatbot to 'know' when a negotiation fragment has been completed. This is necessary to ensure that discussions remain on target, and that the chatbot can address further outstanding issues once one has been dealt with satisfactorily.
- **Deliver an effective conversation.** We believe that this will be achieved by ensuring that the user is presented with self-referential objectives (i.e. always referring to pertinent topics from their learner model) and pushed to the edges of understanding. As a piece of educational software, this type of behaviour aims to promote the reflection that has been shown [33] to affect deep learning.
- **Feedback mechanism.** To ensure continual improvement of the system it will be necessary to incorporate methods to review the transcripts of conversations, assess their success, and make additions or alterations to the Lingubot scripts or functions as necessary.

4.2 Areas for Further Research

We have also identified a number of areas which will benefit from further research, but which are (at least initially) non-essential to the system.

- **What evidence the system can accept.** Currently the only way for users to convince the chatbot and system of their understanding of a subject is to correctly answer test questions. It would be interesting to explore what other evidence may be acceptable, for example details of courses, work, training or experience through which the user is able to demonstrate the relevant knowledge point.
- **Graphical versus text display.** In our initial implementation, the chatbot is likely to be text only, perhaps represented by a static graphic. Many

chatbots and pedagogical agents use "embodied" or graphical displays. An investigation of the effect on user perceptions of the system when the chatbot is text only or has a face/character/graphical display of "emotions", designed according to findings from other educational environments, will further benefit our understanding of user perceptions and rapport in the context of discussing one's knowledge in negotiated learner modelling.

5 Conclusion

We have presented an investigation into the potential for two new developments: the use of chatbots to provide negotiation facilities, and the incorporation of chatbots into an open learner modelling environment.

Using a Wizard-of-Oz experiment, we investigated the requirements for constructing a chatbot in a negotiated open learner model, the potential utility of a chatbot in such a scenario, and user reactions to the interaction. We established technical constraints, including database access, data privacy and a feedback mechanism, and requirements for effective dialogue, including keeping the user on-topic, incorporating smalltalk capabilities, preventing crossed dialogue threads, and successfully resolving negotiation fragments. Users in the study commented on their enjoyment of the interaction, the ease of negotiation by this method, and their willingness to engage with a chatbot, thereby improving their learner model.

We conclude that, while there are technical challenges to be met in specifying the scripts and functions of a complete system, a chatbot can provide the necessary negotiation facilities for an enhanced open learner model interaction. We have commenced work on the detailed specification and build of the system, and intend to publish further results on user interaction with our 'live' chatbot.

Acknowledgements

We thank Andrew Mabbott for extending Flexi-OLM [41] for this study, and Felix Cohen for his comments on draft versions of this paper. The first author is funded by the UK Engineering and Physical Sciences Research Council.

References

1. Jia, J., CSIEC (Computer Simulator in Educational Communication): An Intelligent Web-Based Teaching System for Foreign Language Learning, in *ED-MEDIA (World Conference on Educational Multimedia, Hypermedia & Telecommunications)*. 2004: Lugano, Switzerland.
2. De Angeli, A., G.I. Johnson, and L. Coventry, The unfriendly user: exploring social reactions to chatterbots, in *International Conference on Affective Human Factors Design*, Helander, Khalid, and Tham, Editors. 2001, Asean Academic Press: London.
3. Creative Virtual. UK Lingubot Customers. 2004-2006. Listing of major companies using Linubot technology. www.creativevirtual.com/customers.php. Accessed 14/12/05
4. Wacky Web Fun Ltd. RacingFrogz.org. c2005. Online game with chatbot capabilities. www.racingfrogz.org. Accessed 17/05/06
5. West Ham and Plainstow NDC. 2005. New Deal For Communities. "Splodge" New Deal For Communities chatbot assistant. www.ndfc.co.uk. Accessed 02/06/06

6. Bath & North East Somerset Council. 2006. Council web site Citizen Information Service Agent. www.bathnes.gov.uk/BathNES/Search/ask/default.htm. Accessed 02/06/06

7. Weizenbaum, J., ELIZA - A Computer Program For The Study of Natural Language Communications Between Man and Machine. *Communications of the ACM*, 1966. **9**(1): p. 36-45.

8. dmoz. 2006. Open Directory Project Computers: Artificial Intelligence: Natural Language: Chatterbots http://dmoz.org/Computers/Artificial_Intelligence/Natural_Language/Chatterbots/ Accessed 08/06/06

9. Wallace, R.S. Chapter 00. The Anatomy of A.L.I.C.E., in http://www.alicebot.org/documentation. Accessed 09/12/05

10. Carpenter, R. 1997-2006. Jabberwacky.com. www.jabberwacky.com. Accessed 16/05/06

11. Creative Virtual. 2004-2006. CreativeVirtual.com. Web site of UK Lingubot distributor. www.creativevirtual.com. Accessed 12/05/06

12. Uhr, L., Teaching machine programs that generate problems as a function of interaction with students, in *24th National Conference*. 1969. p. 125-134.

13. Sleeman, D.H. and J.S. Brown, eds. *Intelligent Tutoring Systems*. 1982, Academic Press: London.

14. Clancey, W.J., Tutoring Rules for Guiding a Case Method Dialogue, in *Intelligent Tutoring Systems*, D.H. Sleeman and J.S. Brown, Editors. 1981, Academic Press: London. p. 201-225.

15. Burton, R.R., Diagnosing Bugs in Simple Procedural Skills, in *Intelligent Tutoring Systems*, D.H. Sleeman and J.S. Brown, Editors. 1981, Academic Press: London. p. 157-183.

16. Holt, P., S. Dubs, M. Jones, and J. E. Greer, The State of Student Modelling, in *Student Models: The Key to Individualized Educational Systems*, J.E. Greer and G.I. McCalla, Editors. 1994, Springer-Verlag: New York.

17. Michaud, L.N. and K.F. McCoy, Capturing the Evolution of Grammatical Knowledge in a CALL System for Deaf Learners of English. *International Journal of Artificial Intelligence in Education*, 2006. **16**(1): p. 65-97.

18. Zapata-Rivera, J.D. and J.E. Greer, Interacting with Inspectable Bayesian Student Models. *International Journal of Artificial Intelligence in Education*, 2004. **14**(2): p. 127-163.

19. Reye, J., Student modelling based on belief networks. *International Journal of Artificial Intelligence in Education*, 2004. **14**: p. 63-96.

20. Bull, S., P. Brna, and H. Pain, Mr. Collins: A collaboratively constructed, inspectable student model for intelligent computer assisted language learning. *Instructional Science*, 1995. **23**: p. 65-87.

21. Dimitrova, V., STyLE-OLM: Interactive Open Learner Modelling. *International Journal of Artificial Intelligence in Education*, 2003. **13**: p. 35-78.

22. Kay, J., Learner Know Thyself: Student Models to give Learner Control and Responsibility, in *ICCE97 International Conference on Computers in Education*, Z. Halim, T. Ottomann, and Z. Razak, Editors. 1997: Kuching, Malaysia. p. 17-24.

23. Morales, R., Exploring participative learner modelling and its effects on learner behaviour. 2000, Unpublished PhD Thesis. University of Edinburgh: Edinburgh.

24. Zapata-Rivera, J.D. and J. Greer, Externalising Learner Modelling Representations, in *Workshop on External Representations of AIED: Multiple Forms and Multiple Roles. International Conference on Artificial Intelligence in Education*. 2001: San Antonio, Texas.

25. Dewey, J., *How We Think: A Restatement of the Relation of Reflective Thinking to the Educative Process*. 1933, Boston: D. C. Heath and Company.

26. Schön, D., *The Reflective Practitioner*. 1983, London: Maurice Temple Smith Ltd.

27. Kolb, D., The Process of Experiential Learning, in *The Experiential Learning: Experience as the Source of Learning and Development*, D. Kolb, Editor. 1984, Prentice-Hall: NJ.

28. Bull, S. and H. Pain, Did I say what I think I said, and do you agree with me?: Inspecting and Questioning the Student Model, in *World Conference on Artificial Intelligence in Education*, J. Greer, Editor. 1995, AACE: Charlottesville, VA. p. 501-508.

29. Baker, M.J., Negotiated Tutoring, an Approach to Interaction in Intelligent Tutoring Systems. 1990, Unpublished PhD Thesis. Open University: Milton Keynes, UK.

30. Sheth, R., Avatar Technology: Giving a Face to the e-Learning Interface. *E-Learning Developer's Journal*, 2003 (August 25 2003).

31. André, E., T. Rist, and J. Müller. WebPersona: A Life-Like Presentation Agent for Educational Applications on the World-Wide Web. in *Workshop on Intelligent Educational Systems on the World Wide Web at Artificial Intelligence in Education*. 1997. Kobe, Japan.

32. Shaw, E., W.L. Johnson, and R. Ganeshan, Pedagogical Agents on the Web, in *International Conference on Autonomous Agents*. 1999, ACM Press: Seattle, WA, USA. p. 283-290.

33. Graesser, A.C., K. Moreno, J. Martineau, A. Adcock, A. Olney, and N. Person. AutoTutor improves deep learning of computer literacy: Is it the dialogue or the talking head? in *Artificial Intelligence in Education*. 2003. Amsterdam: IOS Press.

34. Lester, J.C., B.A. Stone, and G.D. Stelling, Lifelike Pedagogical Agents for Mixed-Initiative Problem Solving in Constructivist Learning Environments. *User Modeling and User-Adapted Interaction*, 1999. 9: p. 1-44.

35. Person, N.K. and A.C. Graesser, Pedagogical Agents and Tutors, in *Encyclopedia of Education*, J.W. Guthrie, Editor. 2006, Macmillan: New York. p. 1169-1172.

36. Dählback, N., A. Jönsson, and L. Ahrenberg. Wizard of Oz Studies - Why and How. in *International Workshop on Intelligent User Interfaces '93*. 1993: ACM.

37. Kerly, A. and S. Bull, The Potential for Chatbots in Negotiated Learner Modelling, in *Intelligent Tutoring Systems: 8th International Conference*, M. Ikeda, K. Ashley, and T.-W. Chan, Editors. 2006, Springer Verlag: Berlin-Heidelberg. p. 443-452.

38. Bernsen, N.O., H. Dybkjaer, and L. Dybkjaer, *Designing Interactive Speech Systems - From First Ideas to User Testing*. 1998: Springer. New York.

39. Fiedler, A. and M. Gabsdil, Supporting Progressive Refinement of Wizard-of-Oz Experiments, in *Workshop on Empirical Methods for Tutorial Dialogue Systems at International Conference on Intelligent Tutoring Systems*, C. Penstein Rose and V. Aleven, Editors. 2002: San Sebastian, Spain. p. 62-69.

40. British Psychological Society. 2000-2004.BPS Ethical Principles for Research with Human Participants. http://www.bps.org.uk/the-society/ethics-rules-charter-code-of-conduct/code-of-conduct/ethical-principles-for-conducting-research-with-human-participants.cfm Accessed 18/10/05

41. Mabbott, A. and S. Bull, Student Preferences for Editing, Persuading and Negotiating the Open Learner Model, in *Intelligent Tutoring Systems: 8th International Conference*, M. Ikeda, K. Ashley, and T.-W. Chan, Editors. 2006, Springer Verlag: Berlin-Heidelberg. p. 481-490.

42. Elzware Ltd. Yhaken.com. Website for Yhaken, a Lingubot built with Kiwilogic technology. www.yhaken.com. Accessed 01/06/06

Adding question answering to an e-tutor for programming languages

Kate Taylor

Research Associate
Computer Laboratory
University of Cambridge, UK
kate.taylor@cl.cam.ac.uk

Simon Moore

Senior Lecturer
Computer Laboratory
University of Cambridge, UK
simon.moore@cl.cam.ac.uk

http://www.cl.cam.ac.uk/users/ksw1000   http://www.cl.cam.ac.uk/users/swm11

Abstract

Control over a closed domain of textual material removes many question answering issues, as does an ontology that is closely intertwined with its sources. This pragmatic, shallow approach to many challenging areas of research in adaptive hypermedia, question answering, intelligent tutoring and human-computer interaction has been put into practice at Cambridge in the Computer Science undergraduate course to teach the hardware description language Verilog. This language itself poses many challenges as it crosses the inter-disciplinary boundary between hardware and software engineers, giving rise to several human ontologies as well as the programming language itself. We present further results from our formal and informal surveys. We look at further work to increase the dialogue between student and tutor and export our knowledge to the Semantic Web.

1.   Introduction

The *Intelligent Verilog Compiler (IVC) Project* teaches the Verilog Hardware Description Language (HDL) through a web-based tutorial integrated with and partly generated from an ontology of the Verilog language. The IVC draws together research from the Semantic Web, Adaptive Hypermedia, Model Checking, AI knowledge representation and Learner Reflection as well as best practice from computer language compiler design and teaching Computer Science on-line using visualisation. The IVC is part of the second year undergraduate course at Cambridge [1].

It is 'intelligent' in two ways: it helps check the syntax and the semantics of the learner's program and it finds a technical or English definition, comparison or example suitable to the error being reported in the context of the piece of code. It displays this information next to the incorrect code and errors in order to 'scaffold' learning without directly providing the answer. Current work [2] allows the learner to ask questions in English that query the same ontology as is currently used to provide 'help' text.

The IVC maintains a user concept model to keep track of how much the learner knows about each concept as they progress through the tutorial. This is used to provide them with feedback on how they are progressing.

Learning any new programming language involves grasping the basics of a language through interaction with a compiler. Once this is achieved, the next task is to understand the semantics of the language to get the program to do what is intended: practical implementations that embody fundamental concepts like state machines, Boolean arithmetic and modular composition. One to one teaching with a human tutor uses a variety of techniques to draw a student on rather than provide them directly with the answer.

Providing a conversation, albeit a simple one, helps to guide and direct the student towards completion of the programming exercises, supporting their learning as a 'sense-making' activity. Tracking the questions asked and the errors made allows dynamic modelling of the learner's understanding at this point in time for this particular area.

This paper discusses the issues in creating a dialogue with the student and early work in tracking and interpreting their responses. We justify the use of a logic system at the core of our ontology by the power it gives us to model the user's reasoning. We describe the various disciplines in Computer Science that we have drawn on together with ideas from educational theory to highlight why each facet has been included in the IVC.

2. Related Work

Our system stands in the overlap between **semantic web** [3] research which tends to define well-defined ontologies with concepts standing for objects, properties and relations [5] and **adaptive hypermedia research** oriented towards personalization techniques that adapt the content or navigation systems seen by learners. These two research areas are seen to be converging towards an **adaptive semantic web** [4],[5]. This move to separate rules from data allows an adaptive hypermedia system to reason effectively. From the opposite direction, the use of semantic metadata allows reasoning systems to participate in the semantic web.

"The Semantic Web is about two things. It is about common formats for interchange of data, where on the original Web we only had interchange of documents. Also it is about language for recording how the data relates to real world objects. "[3]

The Web Ontology Language (OWL), the Resource Description Framework (RDF) and its associated query language SPARQL defined by W3C provide the principal technologies for presenting and interpreting knowledge across platforms. Our alternative approach is to use an inference engine that can export its knowledge in RDF format to become part of the Semantic Web, following guidelines from WC3 as in [8]. Internally, our use of first order logic allows us to reason about the user's knowledge and about the knowledge itself.

Like [6] we are taking the approach of an ontology closely linked with web pages. The core of our system is HTML material we ourselves have written and structured.

We have implemented our ontology using SWI-Prolog and the WordNet [7] Prolog interface to utilise first order logic and the lexical definitions. SWI-Prolog is used as an inference engine for the Mozilla Firefox internet browser.

We have followed the style of architecture used by the AQUA [9] question answering system: a process model with a parser, a logical interpreter, a WordNet lexical resource, a failure-analysis system and a question classifier. Our architecture is shown in Figure 1. We focus on the local intranet (the web tutorial) to provide the answers to our questions and for explaining compiler messages. This is described in Section 3.4.

Many e-tutoring systems such as Andes [10] provide dialogue scripts to support solving problems. This approach works well where there are no real choices to be made. However, when learning a language or writing a mathematical proof, there are several distinct successful strategies that the student can employ as well as many unsuccessful ones so we do not use a script. A sister project to ours in the Intelligent Book research is MathsTiles [11] which does not constrain the order of tasks within mathematical proofs using tiles.

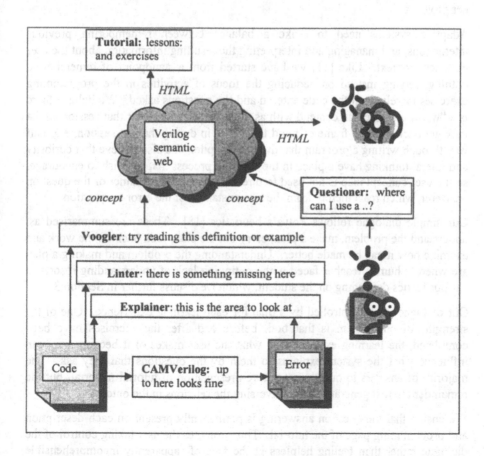

Figure 1 The IVC Architecture

Our explainer generates suggestions to complete the exercise. We phrase the explainer messages to avoid giving a direct answer, and present help from the tutorial instead. The student must read the explanation and the help to gain the understanding to correct the error themselves. This promotes *deep learning:* the critical analysis of new ideas including linking them to already known concepts. It leads to understanding and long term retention of concepts for use in unfamiliar contexts [12]. There is no automatic code completion in our system as provided by programming environments such as Eclipse [13]. However, we did use the results of these studies, for example, the use of line numbers and the colouring of the previous version of the code. We are interested in promoting *retention of information* on the learning curve rather than productivity for experts using the language in anger.

Learner reflection has been shown to be a vital component of cognitively intensive tasks, such as learning a new programming language [17]. We provide the user with a pictorial representation of the English ontology as a user concept map. The aim in showing the user this model is to make her aware of how different parts of the Verilog language relate to each other while also providing her with feedback on her progress.

Adaptive systems need to strike a balance between remembering previous interactions, and managing and interpreting the resulting information about the user in a new context. Like [11] we have started from a standpoint of remembering nothing, relying instead on deducing the focus of activities in the programming exercises merely from the code entered and the questions asked. We believe there is a "warm-up" effect to contend with as the user gets started for that session whilst they get back into the frame of mind they were in during the last session, e.g. half way through writing a program that did not compile. We also believe that curiosity and lateral thinking have a place in the learning process that we wish to encourage, so the user concept map is not used to direct the compiler explainer or the question answerer, which react merely from the circumstances of the error or question.

Our simple dialogue follows Polya's heuristics [18]. These are summarised as: understand the problem, make a plan, carry out the plan, look back on the work and examine how it can be made better. Understanding the problem and making a plan are where a human teacher faced with continuing lack of understanding resorts to various tactics depending on the student, which we discuss further in Section 3.4.

Our dialogue is not controlled by a plan for each learning experience. One of the strengths of our system is that both before and after the exercises have been completed, the learning experience is what the user makes of it because they can influence what the system explains to them by the questions that they ask. The majority of answers to questions are a re-presentation of tutorial material, but the remainder are text generated from traversing the relations in the ontology.

We ensure that the question answering is permanently present on each description and programming page of the tutorial. This promotes the user taking control of the dialogue rather than feeling helpless in the face of apparently incomprehensible error messages and explanations that still do not solve the problem for her. The compiler explainer plays its part in the dialogue by focusing on related areas of help at a suitable level as well as providing hints. The answer is never provided.

3.   IVC Architecture

3.1   Challenges in teaching Verilog

Verilog bridges a divide between hardware and software engineers. It deliberately uses syntax from the programming language C, a *lingua franca* between the two disciplines, to do this. However, the different semantics that arises from the behaviour of the hardware can trip up software engineers. Assigning a mutually acceptable meaning in the ontology is problematic from an inter-disciplinary point of view. The definitive pedagogy in terms of content and style was defined by Dr Moore from the content of the four lectures that the IVC replaced. The ontology was created using this terminology and with alternative terminology as the secondary meaning whilst retaining the emphasis of a hardware module in a Computer Science degree rather than a computing module in an electrical engineering degree.

3.2   Constructing the ontology

We have used the design techniques from the W3C committee [4] to follow best practice. It is fairly common to identify more than one sub-ontology as the design process is worked through [14], which was the case for Verilog. A programming language comes with an ontology in the form of the grammar description. The Backus-Naur Format (BNF) in our tutorial is taken from the IEEE standard 1364-2001 which defines the Verilog language. The BNF notation captures selection between alternate constructs, repetition of one or more constructs and the valid order of constructs.

However, the symbol set used in the Verilog language has several interesting challenges when creating an ontology, for example, the use of the word "and". The symbol "&" is called "and" and "ampersand". The "and" can be a unary and a binary operator, whilst "and" is also used to refer to "&&" which is another logical binary operator. To complete the possibilities for ambiguity, "and" is also a language keyword using in timing conditions

We selected the reserved words from the language and related English phrases. For each of these we wrote a glossary definition, a piece of introductory text, the corresponding fragment of the language grammar and an example. We completed the tutorial with more examples and explanation, multiple choice tests and programming exercises, being careful to stick to our own ontology.

3.3   Cross-linking the different ontologies

We have identified ontologies of symbols, language reserved words and English terms which we have linked together with synonyms to create the Verilog semantic web.

We have nominated the language keyword ontology to be the "master" ontology and related the example, glossary, grammar and introductory text to this. Synonyms can relate to all or part of concepts.

3.4 Shallow question answering

Our question classifier uses shallow parsing techniques based on interrogative pronouns and the keywords of the language. We have reduced the complexity of the question answering task because we have control of the source material and can tie it into the ontology. The definitions and comparisons which are hard to generate in attractive English are stored in the HTML text. Relating one concept to another is done by simple text generation from the ontology. We have mapped to these tactics in terms of the relationships between the concepts: hypernymic or "is a kind of" and meronymic or "is a part of". These can be illustrated by the following dialogues between a student and teacher.

A hyponymic case:

Student is puzzling over concept , which is a special case of x.

"Well, how do you do x?"

"An x does this" "Great, so y is like x which also …".

A hypernymic explanation works the other way round, working up the concept hierarchy rather than down it: "x is like y but cannot do..".

A meronymic explanation uses the "part-of" relation:

"How do I write an if..else statement" "Have you got everything you need?"

A holonymic question uses the meronym relationship from the other end:

"My if..else statement looks fine: what is the problem?" "Is it in the right place?"

3.5 User Concept Model

The user concept model in Figure 2 is made up of individual nodes which are coloured in according to how much knowledge the student has demonstrated about that particular concept. At some points in the tutorial, the user may only have read about some concepts and not necessarily have any deep understanding of them. She is then given the chance to implement the new concept a few exercises later. A concept turns green once the user has successfully used it in some Verilog that she has written herself.

The user concept model gives the user another chance to find out more about any concept she does not yet fully understand by clicking on it. The representation of the user concept model is automatically updated after every page and exercise. This self-reflection stimulates questions to ask the system as a short-cut to re-reading the material directly, saving navigation time.

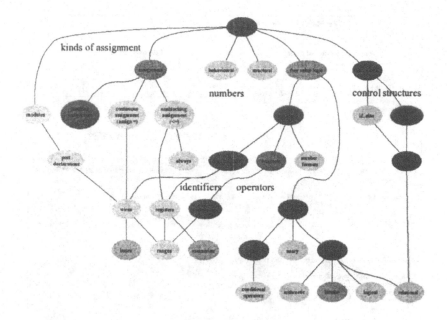

Figure 2 The user concept model

3.6   User interface

The user interface for the compiler pages has undergone three cycles of prototyping before the final interface shown in Figure 3. Our experience is that hidden functionality behind buttons is rarely noticed in the desire to get the coding done, so the final screen design makes help and question answering permanently visible. The layout also aims to model a dialogue using the idioms of current question answering systems on the Worldwide Web.

In this particular interaction, the student has realised that there is something wrong with the way she has used assign and first asks "How do you use assign?" She is told that it is used in continuous assignment and thus continues the discourse by asking "What is continuous assignment?" The answer provided solves her problem: she can see that she should be using '=' rather than '<=', and recompiles. Once the model checker has confirmed the correctness she is ready to move on to the next exercise with a deeper understanding of assignment.

200

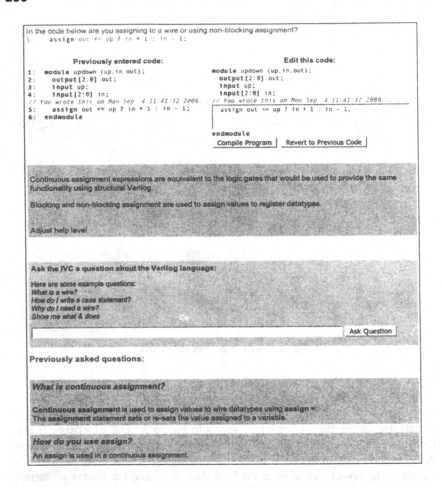

Figure 3 Help generated from the compiler error messages and questions answered

4.   Results

4.1   Research Questions

Because we are interested in *deep learning*, we have aimed to look at a number of quantitative measures over time for measuring the effectiveness of the IVC.

1: Reading the help text and/or explainer advice fixes the current error.
2: Asking a question reduces the number of compilations required to get to a correct answer in this and subsequent exercises.
3: Asking one or more questions fixes the current error.

4.2 Methodology

Any analysis of quantitative results gathered from an end user study has a number of external factors to contend with. Measuring time taken to perform a task does not take into account distractions. Measuring number of compilations is distorted by students who make a quick change and recompile as a style of learning. This may also arise from a lost novice who is trying anything, or recompiling half way through to "see how it is going" when there is not a compiler-recognisable construct there. Looking at the changes in the program from the previous recompilation indicates what the student is thinking about, and hence probably what they are confused about.

1. We measure the time taken to complete an exercise with and without question answering.

2. We plot the number of characters changed on each attempt, and the number of attempts as a cumulative plot to create an activity index. The number of characters may grow and shrink around the final program.

4.3 Question Answering Opportunities

Figure 4 shows an activity index plot for a particular user for all four exercises. We interpret a plateau as a period of thinking and cautious experimentation, whilst an increase in gradient represents a burst of typing activity which can be interpreted an idea. We note that the activity index can be skewed by activities such as re-indenting code.

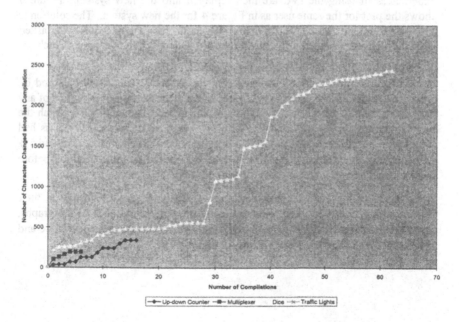

Figure 4 Activity index without question answering

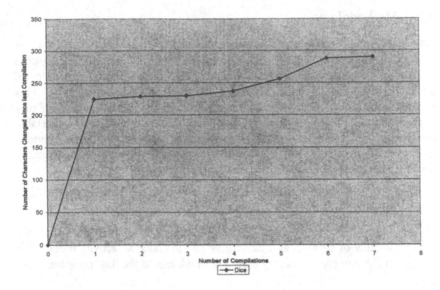

Figure 5 Activity index with question answering

To measure the effect of adding question answering, we analyse the activity index plots for the four exercises on a per user basis to select users whose graphs showed a number of plateaus. We identify these plateaus as opportunities in which to ask questions. We avoid the random set of users that were used to study the detailed edits of files to provide common errors for the explainer to work on. These users' experiences of using the IVC are then replayed into the new system. Figure 5 shows the plot for the same user as in Figure 4 for the new system. The solution is found after around 300 characters rather than 2500, with the question being asked after the first compilation. The graph is more sigmoidal than stepped, which we take to indicate a steadier progress towards the solution.

In some cases in the selected user replays, the plateau is found to be caused by errors in the logic of the exercise, where the question answering could not be of any help. Our sample also included users with unmatched begin-end pairs, which the new system checks for explicitly and advises. Around 30% of the 2005 class had issues with mismatched begin-end, 8% with case and endcase mismatches and 5% with opening and closing parentheses. One user asked all his questions before producing an answer within a reasonable number of compilations.

Around 4% of the 2005 class demonstrate a sigmoidal curve tendency in their activity index as they worked towards a solution. In around 60% of the graphs, parallel lines for different exercises show that a student has a particular tactic and sticks to it. An example of this is shown in Figure 6.

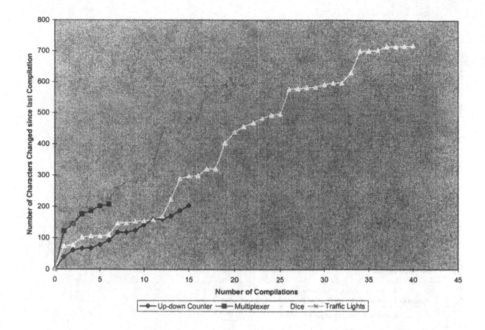

Figure 6 Activity index demonstrating similar tactics for each exercise

4.4 Average Activity Index Results

The second exercise in the IVC is a multiplexer which extends the usage of concepts taught in the first up-down counter exercise. The third dice exercise uses these concepts whilst introducing others, and the final traffic lights exercise is a more complicated version of the dice. We calculate the average activity index for each for the 2005 data as 0.27, 0.83, 0.41 and 0.59 which reflects our intuition of how challenging the exercises are in terms of new material to be learned.

4.5 Tracking User Activity

The user can now interact with the system via multiple choice questions, the user concept map, the compiler and the questioner. Figure 7 shows a log of these activities. In this particular interaction, all four styles of interaction are shown in time order. This logging will provide qualitative data to direct further work in this area once the system has been used by the 2006 students.

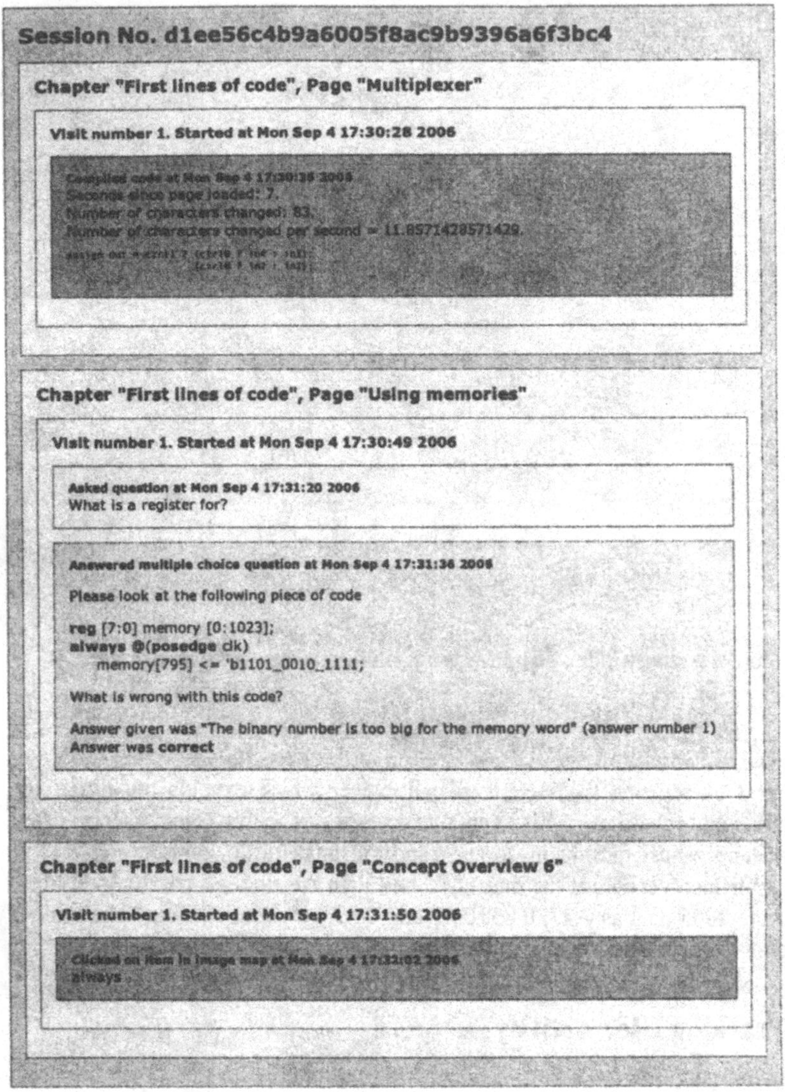

Session No. d1ee56c4b9a6005f8ac9b9396a6f3bc4

Chapter "First lines of code", Page "Multiplexer"

Visit number 1. Started at Mon Sep 4 17:30:28 2006

Compiled code at Mon Sep 4 17:30:35 2006
Seconds since page loaded: 7.
Number of characters changed: 83.
Number of characters changed per second = 11.8571428571429.

assign out = dzzb[1 ? (c[b?0 | 1b? : 1a?)
                    [c[z?b & 1a? : 1a?)

Chapter "First lines of code", Page "Using memories"

Visit number 1. Started at Mon Sep 4 17:30:49 2006

Asked question at Mon Sep 4 17:31:20 2006
What is a register for?

Answered multiple choice question at Mon Sep 4 17:31:36 2006

Please look at the following piece of code

reg [7:0] memory [0:1023];
always @(posedge clk)
    memory[795] <= 'b1101_0010_1111;

What is wrong with this code?

Answer given was "The binary number is too big for the memory word" (answer number 1)
Answer was **correct**

Chapter "First lines of code", Page "Concept Overview 6"

Visit number 1. Started at Mon Sep 4 17:31:50 2006

Clicked on item in image map at Mon Sep 4 17:32:02 2006
always

Figure 7 Tracking the student's interaction with the IVC

4.6   Results from student revision

Our proof-of-concept system which we offered to the students at revision time had
the question answering hidden behind a button and the help in sight at a level to fit
in approximately half the screen. This Eliza-like interface did provoke some
exploratory dialogue that was not directly related to the program under
construction, which could be explained by the novelty value of the interface or the
desire to use it to revise rather than to help complete the program. As we have

mentioned in Section 2, we do not wish to prevent this kind of diversion during the learning process, and believe that it is this user-directed work that may well be retained better as the material is gathered together in the order which best suits the student's style of working.

5. Conclusions

We have made some progress in laying the foundations of a dialogue. The compiler explainer provides extra material to read, whilst the questioner allows the student to take the initiative. Looking back is also supported by the user concept model. Understanding the problem and making a plan are supported by providing question answering capabilities both to re-present tutorial material and provide basic generated explanations.

We have defined an activity index as a means of identifying a student's working style and validated its results against our intuition about the exercises. We have demonstrated the benefits of adding question answering in terms of improving the activity index for students who have missed how a concept fits in or forgotten syntax. When used with user reflection, it provides a means of allowing a student to take control and adds to the enjoyment of the learning experience.

Having added question answering to our system raises users' expectations of how much is being understood and to what they are talking, which draws our work more towards a merging of search engine interaction techniques and traditional interaction between a programmer and a compiler.

One of the achievements of the IVC is the gathering of data *about* learning and the enhancement *of* learning to further develop a user model. We would like to look more at educational and cognitive science work on learning models as we believe that more can be done to increase the dialogue between the IVC and the student. In particular, a non-irritating algorithm for intervention that avoids giving away the answer requires more work.

We wish to extend the resources for question answering to the Internet and Semantic Net using appropriate search engine transformations as in [9], [16] as our logging indicates a number of questions about programming in general. At the time of writing there is no other ontology advertised for Verilog: it is one of our aims to provide one.

This work was funded by the Cambridge MIT Institute (CMI) and the evaluation performed with the assistance of the Centre for Applied Research in Educational Technology (CARET). We wish to thank the students for their enthusiasm and commitment. The final deployed version was designed and developed by the IVC team, Stephen Williams of Trinity Hall, Cambridge and Philip Bielby of Gonville and Caius College, Cambridge, who have contributed to this paper as well as brought our ideas to life.

References

1. Moore, S, Taylor K An Intelligent Interactive Online Tutor for Computer Languages, 25th Annual International Conference of the BCS Specialist Group on Artificial Intelligence (SGAI) (2005).

2. Taylor K, Moore S My Compiler Really Understands Me Adaptive Hypermedia (AH 2006) Dublin June 2006

3. www.w3.org/2001/sw/Activity Activity on the Semantic Web

4. Sparck-Jones 2004 What's new about the Semantic Web? Published in ACM SIGIR Forum, 38(2), December 2004, 18-23

5. Peter Dolog1, Nicola Henze2, Wolfgang Nejdl1,2, and Michael Sintek3 Towards the Adaptive Semantic Web Adaptive Hypermedia 2005

6. Kotis K Using simple ontologies to build personal Webs of Knowledge SGAI 2005

7. WordNet Electronic Lexical Database May 1998 ISBN 0-262-06197-X

8. Quick guide on how to publish a Thesaurus on the Semantic Web www.w3.org/tr/2005/WD-swbp-thesaurus-pubgiide-20050510/

9. Vargus-Vera A, Motta E AQUA- Ontology Based Question Answering System MICAI 2004: 468-477

10. VanLehn Fading and Deepening: the Next Steps for Andes and other Model-Tracing Tutors University of Pittsburgh

11. Billingsley W, Robinson P Towards an Intelligent On Line Textbook for Discrete Mathematics, University of Cambridge

12. http://www.engsc.ac.uk/er/theory/learning.asp

13. Storey et al Improving the usability of Eclipse for Novice Programmers OOPSLA 2003

14. Miller J, Baramidze G, Sheth A Fishwick P The Need for a Discrete Event Modelling Ontology

15. Gruber T, Olsen G An Ontology for Engineering Mathematics In J Doyle, P Torasso, & E Sandewall, Eds., *4th International Conference Principles of Knowledge Representation and Reasoning*, 1994.

16. Ding, L, Rong, P, Finin T, Anupam J Finding and Ranking Knowledge on the Semantic Web *4th International Semantic Web Conference 2005*

17. Li L, Kay J Learner Reflection in Student Self-Assessment, Technical Report Number 568, University of Sydney NSW 2006

18. George Pólya How to Solve It (ISBN 0-691-08097-6) 1945

Speech-Enabled Interfaces for Travel Information Systems with Large Grammars

Baoli Zhao, Tony Allen and Andrzej Bargiela
Nottingham Trent University
{baoli.zhao, tony.allen, andrzej.bargiela}@ntu.ac.uk
www.ntu.ac.uk

Abstract

This paper introduces three grammar-segmentation methods capable of handling the large grammar issues associated with producing a real-time speech-enabled VXML bus travel application for London. Large grammars tend to produce relatively slow recognition interfaces and this work shows how this limitation can be successfully addressed. Comparative experimental results show that the novel last-word recognition based grammar segmentation method described here achieves an optimal balance between recognition rate, speed of processing and naturalness of interaction.

1. Introduction

The main objective of this research was to investigate the issues associated with designing a robust speech-enabled query interface for the London ATTAIN* travel information system that could operate in real-time. Our previous research has focused on a creating a real-time speech-enabled interface for the equivalent Nottingham travel information system. As a result of this research, two VoiceXML based interfaces, using directed-dialogue and mixed-initiative dialogues respectively, were developed and are presented in [1] & [2]. With a recognition accuracy rate of 88.5% and a system response time of 1.2 seconds, the mixed-initiative speech-enabled interface for the Nottingham system could be accepted by users as a real time application. However, this interface used a medium sized grammar file that contained only 1355 bus stop names. If this interface were required to use a much larger grammar file, then both the system response time and the recognition performance are likely to be significantly degraded.

In recent years, PC based automatic speech recognition (ASR) systems using large vocabulary continuous ASR have claimed significant improvements [3] and there are now several commercial systems on the market (ViaVoice of IBM, SAPI of Microsoft and NaturallySpeaking of Dragon etc.). However, all of these systems only achieve their optimum performance when used in certain environments (i.e. speaker-dependant, noise-free etc). Currently, there is little published research on

---

* Advanced Traffic and Travel Information System. This research project is funded by Nottingham City Transport.

the use of large grammar files in VoiceXML based systems, especially for real time applications. This paper aims to address some of these shortfalls by investigating techniques for enabling the development of large vocabulary real-time VoiceXML based systems.

2. Large grammar issues in a London bus travel application

There are 23337 bus stop names in the London area. This is much bigger than the Nottingham system which contains only 1355 bus stop names. This increase in the number of bus stop names was expected to produce an increase in processing time and a reduction in recognition accuracy when compared to the Nottingham system's performance. To test this assertion, the 23337 London bus stop names were collected into a single large grammar file. This large grammar file was then used to replace the 1355 bus stop name grammar file in the Nottingham directed-dialogue system. An initial experiment indicated that single bus stop name recognition would take 13 seconds using this large grammar. During this processing, the users hear nothing from the system. Ideally, the demand an application places on the network should be transparent to the caller, and the system should appear to be instantaneously responsive regardless of the amount of data being processed. In reality, speech recognition is computationally intensive, and its demands increase with the complexity and size of the grammar. With a 23337 name grammar the latency of the system's response time resulting from the extensive computation required for just one single input is easily perceived and is unacceptable.

When designing speech interfaces, a common HCI problem that emerges involves the users' inability to interpret silence. In speech-only systems, silence can either mean that the speech recogniser didn't hear an utterance or that it is processing the user's input. In such situations the users tend to assume that a lengthy silence means that the system did not hear the request. The default duration of the hourglass (latency of system processing) consists of two intervals: See Figure 1.

- From end of speech detection to end of recognition.
- From end of recognition until the next prompt is reached.

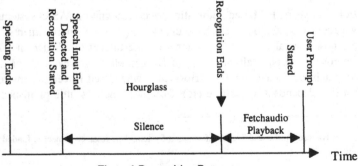

Figure 1 Recognition Response

In most small or medium grammar file applications, where the recognition time is small, the caller perceived latencies would usually occur during the second interval when the interpreter is typically fetching VoiceXML documents over the Internet. For this reason, the VoiceXML specification includes a fetchaudio attribute. This feature allows the application to specify audio that can be played from the time the fetch is attempted until the time another fetch or the next listen state is reached. In this way, the hourglass is terminated as soon as the fetchaudio begins playing. By employing fetchaudio, the user perceived duration of the hourglass only occurs during the first interval – speech detection end to speech recognition end. The system can cover this remaining latency with a percolation sound that provides the user with a hint that the system is processing the input. However, in the London bus information system case, the resulting recognition takes such a long time, that the use of a percolation audio is of no help. The users are unlikely to spend 13 seconds listening to a percolation audio whilst waiting for the system to respond to their input. Researchers state that latencies longer than 8 seconds cannot be effectively masked [4]. As it is not possible to reduce the grammar any further, other more efficient grammar constructs need to be built that can reduce this long recognition latency problem.

In terms of recognition accuracy, the experimental results also show that there was a mean sample accuracy rate of 53% in the large grammar file (23337 bus stop names) directed-dialogue system. The London interface recognition accuracy is therefore significantly worse than the Nottingham directed-dialogue interface's (1355 bus stop name grammar) average sample accuracy rate of 88.5% [2]. However, this result is reasonable because the number of bus stop names in the London system is 17 times more than for the Nottingham system. Smaller grammars are easier for a computer to recognise, while larger grammars are more difficult because of increased ambiguity between words. Deroo et al obtained common error rates in laboratory experiments on speaker-independent isolated word databases of around 1% for a 100 words grammar, 3% for 600 words and 10% for 8000 words [5]. Young obtained error rates of around 15% for a 65000 word vocabulary with a speaker-independent continuous speech recognition system [6]. This is obviously significantly better than the London bus travel information system, but the phonetic sound of the bus stop names are more similar than the words used in Young's dictation system. This leads to an increase in substitution, making the recognition accuracy worse than in a system such as Young's which uses a common word grammar. Young's experimental result was also under laboratory condition which is another reason for that system having better recognition results than the London real time system. For the public to accept the London speech-enabled bus travel information system, it is obvious that both the accuracy rate of the system and the system response time need to be improved.

3. First letter based grammar reduction system

In the large single grammar London application, the caller perceived latencies occur whilst the speech recogniser is processing the user's input against the large grammar. Dividing a large grammar file into many smaller grammar files is one possible way of reducing this latency. These smaller grammar files can then be processed individually by selecting only one of the smaller files using contextual information.

3.1 Dividing a large grammar file into many small files

The large London application grammar file can be divided into 26 small grammar files with each grammar file only containing the bus stop names that have the same first letter. The directed-dialogue speech-enabled query interface for a first letter based ATTAIN travel information system using VoiceXML is shown in Figure.2. Firstly, the users need to supply the first letter of their origin or destination to the system. After the system has recognised the first letter of the bus stop names, the system fetches the one relevant small grammar file corresponding to this recognised first letter. The system then asks the user to give the full bus stop name and processes the user's input against this fetched grammar file.

System: Please say the first letter of your origin.
User: A
(System fetches the "A" grammar file.)
System: Please say your origin.
User: Abbess Close
(System recognises the user input using the "A" grammar file.)
System: Please say the first letter of your Destination.
User: B
(System fetches the "B" grammar file.)
System: Please say your destination.
User: Bailey Mews
(System recognises the user input using "B" grammar file.)
......

Figure 2 First letter based speech interface for London

3.2 Confusion matrix for first letter recognition

In the first letter recognition system, a critical problem is that the system has to be 100% accurate in its recognition of the first letter of the user's origin or destination. If the system wrongly recognises the first letter, then the system will fetch the wrong small grammar file. Using this incorrect grammar file, the user's input will produce either an out of grammar (rejection) error or a substitution error. Because the phonetic sound of single letters is fairly ambiguous, the speech recogniser can easily misrecognise them. For example, the letter "D" sounds very like "T", whilst "F" sounds like "S" etc. If users were prepared to learn the police letter alphabet, Alpha, Bravo, Charlie, Delta etc, this would be a solution. However, in terms of usability, this method is not a good one, because the users need to put extra effort into using such a system. In addition, not everybody would know this police letter alphabet. It was therefore necessary to find a reliable way of making sure that the first letter could be 100% correctly recognised without affecting the user's motivation. Combining the small grammar files of the easily confused letters into one medium sized grammar file was considered a possible solution. This approach could be considered as negating some of the advantage of separating the original single grammar file on the basis of first letter, however, as long as there is some separation of bus stop names then there will be some improvement in recognition accuracy and processing time. Unfortunately, there is little research showing which letters are easily confused by a speech recognition system processing mobile phone (narrowband) based speech input. The following experiment was performed to construct a first letter confusability matrix. 10 native and 10 non-native United Kingdom English speakers participated in the experiment. Each speaker was simply asked to speak the letters A, B, C......Z. The system recognised these letters using a simple grammar file containing only the 26 letters. The experimental results can be seen in Figure3.

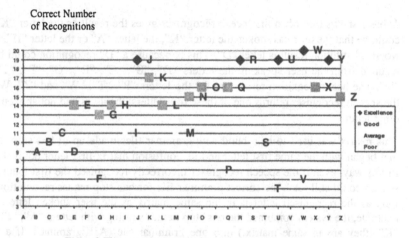

Figure3 The accuracy rates of letters recognition

Figure 3 clearly shows that the most difficult letter to recognise is "T"; which was only recognised 5 times during 20 tests. The Letter "W" was recognised correctly 100% of the time. To further evaluate the experimental result, the correlation between the letter recognition results was found. For example, when the user speaks the letter "F", the speech recogniser returns "S" 7 times and returns the correct result "F" 6 times during the 20 tests. This means that when the speech recogniser gives the result as a letter "S", the users could have spoken "F". The letters "F" and "S" are easily confused by the speech recogniser and we can put these two letters into one confusing letter matrix. The other letters have similar correlations. After consideration of all of the exceptions, the final confusing letter matrix is as shown in Table 1.

Recognised Letter	Substituted (confused) for								Recognised Letter	Substituted (confused) for		
A	J	K							N	M	F	Z
B	D	E	V	P					O	L		
C	E	T							P			
D	B	C	E	G	P	T	V		Q	U		
E	B	C	D						R	I		
F	S								S	F		
G	M								T			
H	A								U	Q	W	
I	Y								V	B		
J	G								W			
K	A	H							X	F		
L	H	O							Y	I		
M	N	O							Z			

Table 1 The Confusing Letter Matrix

Table 1 shows that when the speech recogniser gives the result as the letter "K", it could be that the user has spoken the letter "K", the letter "A" or the letter "H". The worst substitution result is letter "D". This is because a "D" recognition could have resulted from the user speaking the letters "D", "B", "C", "E", "G", "P", "T" or "V". The best recognition results are for the letters "P", "T", "W" and "Z". When the speech recogniser returns one of these four letters, the users had not spoken any other letter.

This matrix was used to help build new grammar files made up of bus stop name that began with the same first letter and its confusion matrix first letter equivalents. In this way, even if the speech recogniser incorrectly recognised the first letter, the system could still fetch the correct grammar file for bus stop names recognition, as long as the recognised letter is in the same matrix as the user spoken letter. For example, the system combined the bus stop names starting with letters "A", "J" and "K" (they are in same matrix.) into one grammar file (AJK.grammar). If a user wants to go from King's Cross and gives the first letter "K" to the system, the system could return the first letter result as letter "A" thereby fetching the AJK.grammar. Because the bus stop name "King's Cross" is still in the AJK.grammar, the system could correctly recognise it even though it had incorrectly recognised the first letter. See Figure.4.

System: *Please say the first letter of your origin.*
User: *K*
System: *Recognised as "A". System fetches the grammar AJK.grammar.*
System: *Please say your origin.*
User: *King's Cross*
System: *Recognised as "King's Cross"*
......

Figure 4 Using combined first letter grammar

3.3 Large & first letter grammar system comparison

In order to compare the performance of the first letter based grammar system against the large grammar file system, an experiment was carried out. In this experiment, the system using the large grammar file and another using many small grammar files were used to carry out the same journey information task. 50 users (25 non-native and 25 native English speakers) participated in the experiment. At the beginning of the experiment the users were informed as to the purpose of the experiment. For each system, the users were taught how to interact with the system. In the experiment, the users were required to find one bus information enquiry using both the system with a large grammar file and the system with many small grammar files using the confusion plus n-best static offline grammar file combination approach. Both of the systems utilize the Nuance V7.0.4 speech recogniser. The confidence level of this speech recogniser was configured to 0.1. This is the minimum value of confidence level; meaning the system will accept all users' input and rarely give rejection errors. The Timeout property was set to 5 seconds; the Complete Time Out property was set to 1 second.

The experimental results show that the use of small grammar files has significantly reduced the system processing time for a single entry. The processing time is reduced from 13 seconds with the large grammar file to 1.67-2.17 seconds with different small grammar files. The processing times variation for the small grammar file system is due to the different small grammar file sizes. For example, the "Z" grammar only contains 15 names. When the user inputs the bus stop names starting with the letter "Z", the system only takes 1.67 seconds to process the input. Letters "B", "C" and "D", on the other hand, use the combined grammar file containing most names (4220). When the system uses the "BCD" grammar file to recognise the bus stop names, the system takes 2.17 seconds to process it. However, even with the longest delay, the users cannot perceive the latencies associated with these delays.

Our measurement of recognition accuracy depended on whether the users' bus stop name inputs were correctly recognised; first letter recognition errors that still allowed correct bus stop name recognition were counted as correct recognition. For example, in the small grammar file, if the user wants to travel from "Oxford Street", the system will ask the user to speak the first letter of their origin. If the user says "O" and the system returns "A", so the system will fetch the AJK grammar file. When the user then says "Oxford Street", the system will definitely return one wrong substitution result because the system has fetched an incorrect grammar file (AJK grammar file doesn't contain the "Oxford Street" bus stop name). In this case, a substitution error would probably occur and be counted as a misrecognition error. Conversely, if the user said "O" and the engine returned "L", the LHO grammar file would be fetched because letters L, H and O share the same confusing letter matrix. When the user then says "Oxford Street" the desired end recognition result could still be achieved. This would be counted as a correct overall recognition result.

As stated earlier, the mean sample accuracy rate of the large grammar system is 53%. This is significantly worse than the Nottingham directed-dialogue interface's average sample accuracy rate of 88.5% [2]. Ideally, the London system using several smaller grammar files should be more accurate than the London system using the large grammar file. Unfortunately, the experimental results show that both London systems give the same accuracy rate. The major reason is that many more out-of-grammar errors occurred in the system using the small grammar files. Evaluating the results we can see that the system incorrectly recognised the first letter 17 times during the 100 users inputs. This number does not include the incorrectly recognised letters that resulted in fetching the correct small grammar files as a result of using the confusing letter matrix for the reasons stated above. The 17 times the system incorrectly recognised the first letter from the user's inputs, such that the incorrect small grammar file was fetched, directly reduced the chances of the system correctly recognising the full bus stop names. 3 of these times were caused by the user's unclear utterance and 2 times were caused by unexpected noisy interruption. Another 12 times were caused by an incomplete confusing letter matrix. For example, when the user said "A", the engine returned "H" (which is not part of the confusing letter matrix "AJK"). As a result the "AJK" grammar file would not be fetched.

It is possible that the out of grammar file errors could be reduced by producing a more representative confusing matrix. However, although recognising the first letter has significantly changed the system's performance in terms of processing time, it has introduced significant usability issues. In human-to-human communication, asking people to speak the first letter of a word and then trying to recognise a word is not a natural form of interaction. In addition to this inherent unnatural interaction format, the accuracy rate of the system, as it stands, is still not accurate enough to be used by the public. In order to achieve the goal of naturalness and robustness, the system had to be improved further.

3.4 Automatic first phoneme recognition system

To allow the user to naturally communicate with the system, it would be better for the user not to be asked any unnecessary questions (i.e. "Please say the first letter of your origin" etc). This is an unnatural communication format from a usability standpoint. In actual fact, it should be possible for the system to get this information automatically from the user's input by recording the speech input. If the system were to ask the user to speak the bus stop names once and record the user's input, the system could retrieve the first letter from the recorded audio. This method would help reduce the "unnatural" communication.

A system that could automatically recognise the first letter of a bus stop name has been built which uses a first phoneme recognition method. Initially, the speech recogniser used a grammar file that contained the letters "A" to "Z" in order to recognise the first phonemes of a prescribed segment of the recorded bus stop name speech input. Unfortunately, the results from using this grammar do not give a good recognition performance. We also tried using another grammar file that contained all 45 English phonemes. Ideally, each incoming frequency band would find the right phoneme in the grammar file. However, that also gave poor results. 20 users participated in the experiment and each was asked to speak 5 bus stop names to the system. The system incorrectly recognised the first letter up to 74 times during the 100 users' inputs using first phoneme recognition. There are so many variations in sound due to how words are spoken that it's very difficult to reliable match an incoming sound to an entry in the grammar file. Different people pronounce the same phoneme differently. In addition, in this system, the speech recogniser attempts to recognise the first phoneme from a first phoneme WAVE file that had been extracted form the complete bus stop name WAVE file using a fixed 0.35 second sampling period. This duration is long for some phonemes. During the interval in which the speech recogniser is trying to recognise the first phoneme, many phoneme frequency bands could actually be present with the result that the speech recogniser only recognises the most outstanding (stress pronounced) phoneme. To make matters worse, the environment also adds its own share of noise. The above difficulties thus cause the system to give a very poor recognition performance.

4. Last word based recognition system

The first phoneme recognition results were not encouraging. There are two probable reasons for this: i) it is inherently harder to disambiguate the small sized phoneme WAVE segments, ii) the first letter grammar file the system is using is not optimal. Whilst analyzing this problem, the idea of dividing the large London grammar on the basis of end word (i.e. Road, Street, grove etc.) inspired us to develop another system to improve the latency and accuracy of the large grammar system. A system that could automatically recognise the last word would probably work better than one based on first phoneme because the sound segments are longer and the words sounds are more distinct. Development of a last word segmentation process would mean that the system could sub-divide the large London grammar file into many smaller grammar files based on the different word endings. For example, when the system asks the user to say the original/destination bus stop names, it can record the user's input as before. The system then can try to locate and recognise the last word of the bus stop names. Using this last word recognition, the system can attempt to recognise the complete bus stop name using the appropriate small ending grammar file. Based on the first letter experiment result, this method should reduce the speech recogniser's processing time because this system also uses many small grammar files.

road	street	walk	court	bank	circus
north	lane	mall	fields	bridge	studios
mews	close	drive	gardens	grove	broadway
estate	terrace	view	parade	park	place
villas	crescent	way	avenue	buildings	row
hill	gate	south	cottages	yard	square
corner	vale	green	east	arches	passage
end	rise	croft	market	quay	chambers
west	path	almshouses	mead	village	approach
wharf	arcade	flats	mount	side	common
dene	**Special**				

Table 2 Different Bus Stop Endings Grammar Files

From the 23337 bus stop names about 633 common endings can be identified. However most of these endings are only common to one or two bus stop names. There are 61 different endings that are common to 10 or more bus stop names. The system puts any bus stop names with last words that do not belong to this 61 endings list, into one special grammar file (special.grammar). The large grammar file can thus be divided into 62 smaller grammar files based on the different bus stop endings. See Table 2.

4.1 The system design

The architecture and overall operation of this system is similar to the first phoneme recognition system. The difference is that this system automatically locates and recognises the last word of the user's input rather than the first phoneme. Firstly, the users are asked to give the bus stop names. Their responses are passed to the sound card in the system, sampled in 8 KHz 8-bit Mono and converted into digital form using PCM. The <record> element stores the user's input as WAVE (RIFF Header) format in the Documents Server. See Figure 5.

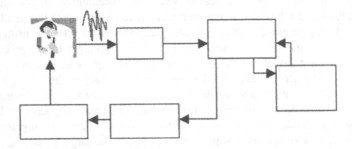

Figure 5 Automatic last word recognition based system architecture

The major issue for this system is how to locate the position where one word ends and the next one begins. Natural human speech often contains occasional pauses even in the middle of a word, thereby causes incorrect word recognition. In this system, a Last Word Processor was developed to automatically locate the last word of a user's input. LWP works similar to the First Phoneme Processor. The core issue for the Last Word Processor is how to determine the boundary between words. By analysing an average-speed speaker's sound file, we found that silence is represented as value 70-7F and F0-FF and that noise is represented as value 60-6F and E0-EF. Thus if there are more than 4 contiguous values of either 60-7F or E0-FF between data samples of other byte values, these values can be assumed to be the boundary between words. The Last Word Processor (LWP) works as follows:

1) The LWP fetches the user's FullUtterance WAVE file from the Documents Server;

2) The LWP reads the data from the last byte of FullUtterance.

3) The LWP compares these data values against the silence and noise values (60-7F and E0-FF). After the system has found 4 contiguous values which are not silence and noise value, the system have reached the end point of the last word period (Point E).

4) The LWP has found the end point of last word period and remembers this point as Point E.

5) The LWP reads the data from the end point of the last word period (Point E)

6) The LWP compares these data values against the silence and noise values (60-7F and E0-FF). After the system has found 4 contiguous values which are silence and noise value, the system have reached the starting point of the last word period (Point S).

7) The LWP has found the starting point of last word period and remembers this point as Point S.

8) The LWP copies the data from the last word starting point (Point S) to the last word end point (Point E) as a "data" Sub-chunk;

9) The LWP adds the "RIFF" Chunk data and "fmt" Sub-chunk data in front of "data" Sub-chunk

10) The LWP writes the complete chunk into LastWord WAVE file.

The Last Word Processor can correctly segment most of the last words from the users' inputs. However, some words are still difficult for the LWP to distinguish. For example, the words "Street" and "Approach". The pronunciation of "Street" [stri:t] contains three phonemes: [s], [tri:] and [t]. The data values of the first phoneme [s] are similar to noise data values and lasts for more than 4 bytes. In this case, the LWP will only write the data values of the phonemes [tri:] [t] into the LastWord WAVE File (sounds like "treet") and regards the phoneme [s] as noise. The speech recogniser will then have difficulty recognising the word using the grammar file because it doesn't contain the word "treet". The pronunciation of "Approach" [ə`prəutʃ] contains four phonemes: [ə], [p], [rəu] and [tʃ]. When a human speaker pronounces a word like "Approach", they put special emphasis on the second phoneme [p]. Before such an emphasized phoneme, humans always have a period of silence between the initial vowel [ə] and the emphasized phoneme. The length of this silence is often longer than 4 bytes causing similar problems as the word "Street". The LWP only writes the data of phonemes [p] [rəu] and [tʃ] into LastWord WAVE File (sounds like "proach") and regards the phoneme [ə] as another word. In order to address these difficulties, words such as "Street" and "Approach" are replaced in the grammar file with the words "treat" and "proach" etc.

4.2   The experimental results

A system using small grammar files that are based on the different bus stop name endings has been developed. In order to compare its performance against the large grammar file system and the system using the small grammar files based on first letter, an experiment was carried out. 50 users participated in the experiment and all the users were the same as used in the previous experiments.

The experiment results show that the last word based system takes a total of 1.37-1.89 seconds to record, submit and locate the last words in the user's response. The variation in processing time being mainly due to the variation in input time of the different length utterances. The major user perceived latency is now 4.01-5.94 seconds, this includes both origin and destination recognition (See Figure 6). These times are dependent on the size of small grammar files used and whether or not the user spoke a bus stop names with one of the special last words. For example, the "Corner" grammar only contains 14 names. When the user inputs bus stop names that end with "Corner", the system takes less time to recognise the bus stop name using the "Corner" grammar file. The "Road" grammar, on the other hand, contains the most names (6487). When a user inputs bus stop names that end with the word "Road", the system takes the most time to recognise it.

System: *Please say your origin.*

User: *King's Cross (System takes a total of **1.37-1.89** seconds to record, submit and locate the last words in the user's response. The system does **not** recognise the origin or last word at this stage.)*

System: *Please say your destination.*

User: *Bailey Mews (System takes a total of **1.37-1.89** seconds to record, submit and locate the last words in the user's response. The system does **not** recognise the destination or last word at this stage.)*

System: *please wait for a moment. (The system recognises both the origin and destination using the algorithm shown in figure 5.9. Users will perceive **4.01-5.94** seconds delay.)*

System: *Do you want to go from King's Cross to Bailey Mews?*

User: *Yes*

System: *Ok, you can catch bus......*

Figure 6 The user perceived latency in last word recognition system

In the event the user spoke a bus stop name with one of the special last words, the system does not need to fetch or recognise the last word and instead will recognise the full bus stop name at the special grammar stage. This takes the least amount of time (see Figure 6). However, even with the longest delay 5.94 seconds, the user can still accept this latency because they have been prepared for the wait.

Because the last word recognition system does not need to ask any additional questions of the user, the users can communicate naturally with the system. The first letter recognition system has to ask users to give the first letter of their origin or destination; which is not only unnatural but also wastes time. The experiments show that using the last word recognition system, the average users spent less time (34.7 seconds) accomplishing the task than using the first letter recognition system (44.8 seconds) or the one large grammar system (77.8 seconds). From a usability point, the users could therefore accomplish the task more naturally and more efficiently using the last word recognition system.

Overall there was a mean sample accuracy rate of 61% in the last word recognition system. This is an improvement of 8% on the accuracy rate of both the first letter recognition system (53%) and the large grammar system (53%). Peissner states that a 5% improvement in accuracy is much more effective at a low starting level than at a rate of 90% correct recognition [7]. Thus the last word method is seen to be a significant improvement on the other two techniques.

39 bus stop names were incorrectly recognised in the 100 tests. Among these 39 errors, 29 last word recognition errors were caused by the Last Word Processor segmentation algorithm. Among the LWP's 29 errors, 23 times were the results of the LWP failing to accurately find the last word in the FullUtterance WAVE file because of the user's very quick speaking rate. When users speak very quickly, the inter-word segments are very small. If the segments values are less than 4 bytes, the LWP will not separate the words in the user's inputs.

The experiment results also show that 22 of the 39 errors happened in noisy environments. Sudden fluctuations in noise decrease the LWP's performance by causing the algorithm to find false beginnings or ends of the last words. The algorithm in LWP only considers stationary noise. If sudden noise happens whilst the user is speaking, the algorithm will fail to segment the words correctly. The signal amplitude, or more appropriately, the ratio of the signal to noise amplitude, determines the segmentation and therefore recognition accuracy of the system. For any noise level, if the speech signal level is equal to the noise level, the last word segmentation will be relatively poor.

5. Conclusion and discussion

A directed-dialogue VXML based speech interface has been developed for London to investigate the performance of a speech-enabled interface with very large grammars. The initial version of this system used a large grammar file containing all 23337 bus stop names. Experimental results show that the system processing time takes up to 13 seconds to process one bus stop name. The experimental results also show that the recognition performance of this interface is significantly lower (53%) than the equivalent Nottingham system with its medium sized grammar. The system processing time had, therefore, to be reduced and the speech recognition accuracy rate improved for public acceptance.

A second version interface was developed that used many small grammar files that contained bus stop names grouped according to their starting letter. To facilitate this grammar file separation, this system had to ask the user to speak the first letter of their origin or destination before speaking the full bus stop name. After the system has recognised the first letter of the bus stop names, the system attempted to recognise the full bus stop names using the small grammar file that corresponded to the recognised first letter. Experimental results show that recognising the first letter does significantly improve the system's performance in terms of the processing time; which now only takes 1.67-2.17 seconds to process one user's entry. However, this methodology does leave usability issues. Asking a user to speak the first letter of a word and then trying to recognise this word is not a natural form of interaction. In order to achieve the goal of naturalness and robustness, the system had to be further improved. To ensure that the user can naturally communicate with the system, the user should not be asked to answer any 'unnecessary' (from the user's perspective) questions. Ideally, the system should automatically extract this data from user's input. Consequently, a First Phoneme Processor was developed which, in theory, should be able to automatically find the first phoneme from a user's input. Unfortunately, the first phoneme recognition results were not encouraging.

To overcome this problem, the idea of dividing the large London grammar on the basis of end words was proposed. Segmentation of the speech image into separate words should be easier than segmentation based on first phoneme because the sound segments are longer and the words sounds are more distinct. Using this methodology it was possible for the system to sub-divide the large London grammar files into many smaller grammar files based on the different word endings (street, road, avenue etc). The experimental results show that the LWP system takes a total of 1.37-1.89 seconds to record, and segment the user inputs. The major user perceived latency is now 4.01-5.94 seconds. This is when the system is attempting to recognise both the origin and destination bus stop names using the LWP processing algorithm. Because the last word recognition system does not need to ask any unnecessary questions of the user, the users can naturally communicate with the system thereby addressing the first letter version's usability issue. Experimental results also show that the recognition rate of the LWP based speech-enabled interface is improved to a sample accuracy rate of 61%. The LWP based system is thus shown to be the most efficient and effective of all the London grammar systems.

References

1. Zhao, B., Allen, T., & Bargiela, A. Evaluation of a mixed-initiative dialogue multimodal interface. In: Macintosh, A., Ellis, R. & Allen, T. (ed) Application and innovations in intelligent system XII, Springer-Verlag, London, 2004, 265–278.
2. Zhao, B., Allen, T., & Bargiela, A. Usability evaluation of a directed-dialogue speech-enabled query interface for the ATTAIN travel information system. RASC 2004, 265-278
3. Tang, M. Large vocabulary continuous speech recognition using linguistic features and constraints. PhD Thesis, MIT, USA, 2005.
4. Levow, G. Making sense of silence. Conference on Human Factors in Computing Systems, 1997, Workshop on Speech User Interface Design Challenge.
5. Deroo, O. Hidden Markov Models and neural networks for speech recognition. PhD Thesis, Faculté Polytechnique de Mons, Belgium, 1998.
6. Young, S., Adda-Dekker, M., Aubet, X., Dugast, C., Gauvain, J., Kershaw, D., Lamel, L., Leeuwen, D., Pye, D., Robinson, A., A., Steeneken, H., & Woodland, P. Multilingual large vocabulary speech recognition: the European SQALE project. Computer Speech and Language, 11:73-89.
7. Peissner,, M. What the relationship between correct recognition rates and usability measures can tell us about the quality of a speech application. WWDU 2002, 296-298.

SHORT PAPERS

Adoption of New Technologies in a Highly Uncertain Environment: The Case of Egyptian Public Banks[1]

Khedr, A. and Borgman, H.

Leiden University

khedr@liacs.nl

www.leidenuniv.nl

Abstract. What is the relation between the process of adopting new technologies, and its impact on business value, in situations of high internal and external uncertainty? Whereas technology adoption is generally fairly well understood, the models do not seem to hold in situations of high uncertainty. The aim of this paper is to investigate the impact of this uncertainty, using a case study on the introduction of a new technology in a large Egyptian public bank. After exploring the most relevant uncertainty factors and their impact on the adoption process, the paper ends with a general discussion and conclusion.

1. Introduction

Research on technology adoption processes is relatively rare [1]. Earlier studies mostly explain the process as one of political influence [2] or focus on the role of technology supporters or advocates [3]. The most comprehensive of the process studies is a study of technology adoption in small firms by Langley and Truax [4]. They go beyond the political models and provide detailed descriptions of adoption processes in five firms. They also describe the contextual elements imposed on these processes but they do not address success of adoption process.

According to the OECD [5] technology adoption processes are defined as processes that involve creating or reengineering products or services to meet new market demands by introducing new technologies to improve productivity, developing or applying new marketing techniques to expand sales opportunities, and incorporating new forms of management systems and techniques to improve operational efficiency [6]. Stoneman [7] integrated the idea that adopting a new technology is similar to or almost the same as any other kind of investment process under uncertainty and therefore can be analysed and measured [8]. The investment decision of adopting new technology is characterized by 1) uncertainty over prospect profit, 2) irreversibility that creates at least some sunk costs, and 3) the opportunity to delay [8]. The primary implication of this way of looking at the adoption of any new technology' problem is that there is "option value" to waiting:

---

[1] The financial support from LUF, The Netherlands is gratefully acknowledged.

that is, adoption should not take place the instant benefits equal costs, but should be delayed until benefits are quite above costs [8].

In this paper we explore the impact of a highly uncertain environment on the adoption of a new technology. Our analysis is based on a case study that (based on interviews, questionnaires and direct observation) in an Egyptian public bank. The outline of the paper is as follows: Section 2 presents the currently dominant technology adoption models, section 3 describes the case study using these adoption models and section 4 discusses the applicability of the existing models and explores possible future extensions.

2. Current Dominant Technology Adoption Models

Literature distinguishes between three major classes of adoption models:

- Option theory: option theorists view the opportunity to adopt a new technology as a call option with an exercise price equal to the investment outlay, and the underlying asset is the new technology [9].
- Behavioural technology acceptance models: earlier studies considered users' perceptions as critical factors that influence user acceptance and use of new technologies [10,11]. Perceived usefulness and (to a lesser extent) ease of use have been shown to play a major role in technology diffusion [10, 12]. Also, the theory of reasoned action provides a theoretical basis for the link between attitude and behaviour [13].
- Situational uncertainty models: Jensen [14] has investigated the issue of technology adoption under uncertainty. He considered a duopoly where the value of the new technology is stochastic. He presumed that the innovation could either succeed or fail depending on the reduction of marginal costs. Balcer and Lippman [15] presumed that the value of the currently available new technology is known with certainty, but that the organization faces uncertainty about the arrival of a better version. Their analysis revealed that the announcement of a new discovery could lead to a delay in the adoption of the current technology. As shown by Hendricks [16], uncertainty about the new technology capabilities of the rival organization tends to slow down the first adoption of a new technology. In the Fudenberg and Tirole [17] model, they found that this type of uncertainty prevents a complete dissipation of the potential first-mover advantage.

3. Case: Technology Adoption in Egyptian Banks

Egypt's transforming economy was following the same path of globalisation processes across the world. This worldwide globalisation of financial markets has led to creating strong relationships among financial institutions [18]. As a result, the financial institutions today face a fast-paced, dynamic, and competitive environment on a global scale. Given such a competitive environment, the financial services sector, as well as the financial institutions, is required to examine their performance because their survival depends on their productive efficiencies with their customers. Early studies [cf.19] demonstrated that, particularly in the banking sector, inefficiencies are more important than scale and scope issues.

An extensive Economic Reform and Structural Adjustment Program (ERSAP) led to a consolidation within the banking sector, as smaller public banks were unable to deal with the new competition from the private banks. In addition to scale and efficiency issues, the competition was also based on offering customers more innovative and sophisticated banking services and products. The new banks were better able to offer these new services and products, partly because of the more modern infrastructure of these banks and partly because the existing public banks were less open to introduce these new services and products such as online banking services.

In order to counter the strong competitive forces faced by the banks, many banks reacted with so-called Customer Relationship Management (CRM) initiatives to better serve existing and attract new customers. Within the bank studied for this case study, a particularly advanced new technology was introduced, called Knowledge Discovery in Databases (KDD). Because of the impact of internal and external uncertainty factors plays a vital role in accomplishing the desired consequences; a particular attention is given in this issue.

Competition, deregulation, and the applications of adopting new technologies in large organizations, such as banks, have contributed to the growth of customer's power. Customers may switch banks on a whim. To win new customers and retain existing customers, organizations may adopt new technological solutions, such as KDD and CRM, in order to analyse the customers' behaviours and needs.

Forecasting which customers are probable to leave, and then designing cost-effective strategies to convince them to stay are extremely difficult for most organizations. Egyptian public banks need to classify and analyse volumes of data that are often difficult to access and combine because of the lack of ability to support the complex KDD processes analytical tasks that are essential to ensure customer retention [20]. An effective KDD for CRM would increase the quality of customer relationships, thereby increasing retention in several ways [20].

In our study, we attempted to explore whether staff perceptions (negative or positive) of the expected benefits of a new technology affect the adoption process [21]. Staff perceptions in different departments and at different levels within the bank (users, IT staff, CRM staff and managers) were measured using questionnaires administered in 2001/2, 2004 and 2006[2].

Figure 1 shows a roadmap of the KDD adoption process within the bank and the uncertainty factors that were faced during this process. For instance, the September 11 events in 2001 greatly influenced customer's attitudes towards Western/Egyptian banks.

---

[2] Full details of the survey results have been accepted at the Symposium on Professional Practice in AI, Santiago Chile August 2006.

226

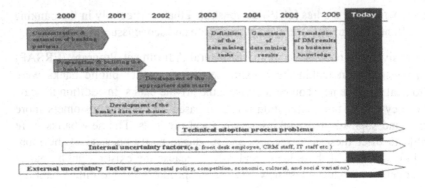

Figure 1: Adoption Process' Roadmap and Challenges

4.   Discussion and Conclusion

Up to now (2006) the adoption of KDD by the Egyptian bank is lower than initially planned. If we try to understand this using the models presented in section 2, we see that the option theory model is hardly applicable. The behavioural technology acceptance model as well as the situational uncertainty model are primarily helpful to explain the technology adoption process from a user perception and user satisfaction perspective, but they hardly account for external factors and for the role of uncertainty. Therefore, our case study underlines the need for an extended technology adoption model which explicitly takes uncertainty factors into consideration. We expect more conclusive results to be available when the bank has finished its KDD roll-out process by the end of 2006.

5.   References

1. Woiceshyn J., Technology Adoption: Organizational Learning in Oil Firms, Business & Finance, Organization Studies, Faculty of Management, University of Calgary, Canada, 2000, pp. 1-21.
2. Dean, James W., Deciding to innovate: How firms justify advanced technology, Cambridge, MA: Ballinger, 1987.
3. Burgelman, Robert A., A process model of internal corporate venturing in the diversified major firm, Administrative Science Quarterly 28, 1983, pp. 223-244.
4. Langley, Ann, and Jean Truax, A process study of new technology adoption in smaller manufacturing firms, Journal of Management Studies 31, 1994, pp. 619-652.
5. OECD, A New Economy?- The Role of Innovation and Information Technology in Recent OECD Economic Growth, DSTI/ IND/ STP/ ICCP, 2000.
6. Porter, M. and S. Stern, Innovation: Location Matters, Sloan Management Review, 2001, pp. 28-37.

7. Stoneman, Paul, Financial Factors and the Inter Firm Diffusion of New Technology: A Real Option Model, University of Warwick EIFC Working Paper No.8, 2001.

8. Dixit, Avinah, and Robert Pindyck, Investment Under Uncertainty, Princeton, New Jersey: Princeton University Press, 1994.

9. Zhu, K., & Weyant, J., Strategic exercise of real options: Investment decisions in technological systems, Journal of Systems Science and Systems Engineering, Vol.12, No.3, 2003, pp. 256-278.

10. Davis, F.D., Perceived usefulness, perceived ease of use, and user acceptance of information technology, MIS Quarterly, Vol.13, No.3, 1989, pp. 319-40.

11. Davis, F.D., Bagozzi, R.P. and Warshaw, P.R., Users acceptance of computer technology: a comparison of two theoretical models. Management Science, Vol.35, No.8, 1989, pp. 982-1003.

12. Adams, D.A., Nelson, R.R. and Todd, P.A., Perceived usefulness, ease of use, and usage of information technology: a replication, MIS Quarterly, Vol.16, No.2, 1992, pp. 227-50.

13. Fishbein, M. and Ajzen, I., Beliefs, Attitude, Intention and Behavior: An Introduction to Theory and Research, (Reading, MA: Addison-Wesley), 1975.

14. Jensen R., Innovation Adoption and Welfare under Uncertainty, Journal of Industrial Economics, Vol.40, 1992, pp. 173-180.

15. Balcer, Y. and Lippman, S. A., Technological Expectations and Adoption of Improved Technology, Journal of Economic Theory, Vol.34, 1984, pp. 292-318.

16. Handricks, K., Reputation in the adoption of a new technology, International Journal of Industrial Organization, Vol.10, 1992, pp. 663-677.

17. Fudenberg, D. and Tirole, J., Preemption and Rent Equalization in the Adoption of New Technology, Review of Economic Studies, Vol.52, 1985, pp. 383-401.

18. Ragunathan, V., Financial Deregulation and Integration: An Australian Perspective, Journal of Economics and Business, 1999, pp. 505-514.

19. Berger, A. N. and D. B. Humphrey, The dominance of inefficiencies over scale and product mix economies in banking, Journal of Monetary Economics, Vol.28, 1991 pp.117-148.

20. Filippidou, D., Keane, J.A., Svinterikou, S. and Murray, J., Data Mining for Business Improvement: Applying the HyperBank Approach, PADD'98 – 2nd Int. Conf., on the Practical Application of Knowledge Discovery and Data, 1998.

21. Khedr, A. and Kok, J., Adopting Knowledge Discovery in Databases for Customer Relationship Management in Egyptian Public Banks, IFIP TC12 and WG12.5 – Symposium on Professional Practice in Artificial Intelligence, Santiago Chile August, 21-24, 2006 (accepted paper).

RoboCup 3D Soccer Simulation Server:
A Progressing Testbed for AI Researchers

Mohammad Ali Darvish Darab
Shahriar Azad University, Tehran, Iran
ali@armanteam.org

Mosalam Ebrahimi
City University, London, England, UK
hesham@armanteam.org

Abstract

RoboCup 3D Soccer Simulation is a growing domain that makes a wide variety of AI and Multi-Agent researches possible. The RoboCup 3D Soccer Simulation Server is a Multi-Agent environment that supports 22 independent agents to play a soccer match within a real-time and complex environment. Many researchers from all over the world have been using this simulator to pursue their researches in a wide variety of areas such as multiagent learning, cooperative actions and multiagent planning. This paper illustrates the current organization of RoboCup 3D Soccer Simulation Server.

1. Introduction

Firstly, Mackworth [1] introduced the idea of using soccer-playing robots in AI researches. Unfortunately, the idea did not get the proper response until the idea was further developed and adapted by Kitano, Asada, and Kuniyoshi. Japanese proposed research program, called Robot J-League2 further changed name to the Robot World Cup Initiative or RoboCup for short [2].

Now, on the first page of the official RoboCup web-site [2] it is stated literally that "RoboCup is an international joint project to promote AI, robotics, and related field. It is an attempt to foster AI and intelligent robotics research by providing a standard problem where wide range of technologies can be integrated and examined" [3]. Furthermore it states the ultimate goal of this project as follows "By 2050, develop a team of fully autonomous humanoid robots that can win against the human world champion team in soccer". To achieve this, there are annual international RoboCup events involve technical conferences as well as RoboCup competitions.

RoboCup Soccer Simulation [4] as a substrate of RoboCup competitions is a simulated competition between soccer robots/agents to get nearer to the ultimate goal of RoboCup federation [2]. The RoboCup simulation is based on the RoboCup simulators called 2D Soccer Server and 3D Soccer Server. Unlike many AI domains, the soccer server embraces as many real-world complexities as possible.

In this paper we investigate the current state of RoboCup 3D Soccer Simulation Server. The rest of the paper is as follows. In section 2 we have an overview on the Soccer Server 3D and some important features of it. Section 3 investigates the inside of the Soccer Server 3D. Section 4 describes SPADES [7] as a middleware system for agent-based distributed simulation which is used by the 3D Soccer Server. Section 5 depicts the complete simulation of a soccer game using the 3D Soccer Server. At last, we finish the paper with concluding remarks in section 6.

2.   Characteristics of RoboCup 3D Soccer Server

The most substantial reason that the 3D Soccer Server is widely used is that it simulates soccer, which is very popular and world-wide. Similar to chess, popularity is an important factor for research applications, because researchers can share an understanding and intuition about the domain [8]. While individual players in soccer are relatively simple (this is important in simulations), the variation of team play is very wide. Therefore, we can find many open issues in it, such as opponent modelling, multiagent learning, cooperative actions, multiagent planning, resource management, agent monitoring and task allocation.

The 3D Soccer Server enables a soccer match to be played between two teams of player-programs. Soccer Server provides a virtual soccer field and simulates the movements of players and a ball.

3.   Inside of RoboCup 3D Soccer Server

The ultimate goal of the 3D Soccer Server is creating a system which can provide simulations of 3D environments. To achieve such a goal several aspects must be considered which are listed below:

1. The integration of a robust physics system

2. How agents can act and live in the environment.

3. An appropriate means must be provided to visualize the state of the 3D environment.

3.1   World and Object Representation

In the 3D Soccer Server world, there are two types of objects. Beside agents (players) which are the live entities in the world there also are some passive objects such as soccer ball. Passive objects have the lack of sensors and effectors to perceive and interact with the environment.

Each object within the environment has a set of properties which are called Object aspects. There are three categories of aspects which are given as follows [6]:

1. Physics Aspect: The physics aspect is used to provide an interface to the physics system.

2. Visual Aspects: This aspect captures what the object looks like.

3. Geometry Aspect: The geometry aspect is used to define the solidity of the object, its shape and size as it is used by a subsystem which detects and resolves collisions.

3.2 Scene Graph

The 3D Soccer Server uses a scene graph [10] to represent spatial relationships (Figure1). In the beginning the scene graph does not contain any world objects. It is only composed of the scene node as its root.

The simulator is initialized by registering a host of perceptor and effector classes. After this step the actual simulation can be initialized. At first the control aspects are added to the simulation. A control aspect investigates the legality of agents' actions [6] which almost can be considered as a referee. At this stage the world can be populated with objects and their corresponding aspects. During this step every agent aspect performs its initialization procedure, requesting perceptors and effectors.

After the world is initialized, the simulation process can be started. The simulation is performed in a so called run-loop. Every iteration of the loop corresponds to a frame being displayed by the simulator. The production of a single frame involves the interaction of all aspects to update the scene graph. The use of effectors changes the state of the environment. This brings us to the next step, where the physics engine resolves the resulting object motion using the geometry and physics aspect. At this point, collision perceptors are also notified when applicable. Updating the visual aspect of the scene graph objects begins by locating the camera. After all, rendering procedure is utilized to bring the simulation on the screen and the next iteration can begin [6].

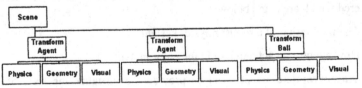

Figure 1 A Sample scene graph for two agents and a ball

4. SPADES

The 3D Soccer Server is implemented above a platform called SPADES (System for Parallel Agent Discrete Event Simulation). It implements the basic structure to allow the interaction between agents and a simulated world in such a way that the users do not have to worry about some issues such as sockets and addresses.

4.1 Component Organization

SPADES components are organized in client-server architecture (Figure 2). The Simulation Engine and the Communication Server are two parts of SPADES. The Simulation Engine is a generic piece of software that allows creating specific world models upon it. It runs on the server side and provides the interaction between agents and their world (in this case soccer simulator) via the Communication Server. On the same machine it must run the specifications of the World Model that has the characteristics of the environment where the agent will act. Distributed entities along the clients are the Agents and the Communication Server. The Communication Server receives messages from agents and sends them to the Soccer Server and vice-versa.

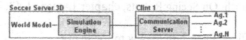

Figure 2 SPADES Components Diagram

4.2 Sense-Think-Act

SPADES implements what it calls the sense-think-act cycle in which each agent receives sensations and reply with actions. That means an agent is only able to react after receiving a sensation message. Of course the agent is capable to request a sensation, but the principle is remained - Always a sensation must precede an action. Figure 3 depicts the sense-think-act cycle and the time where each of its components runs. From A to B a sensation is sent to the agent. After receiving the sensation (from B to C) the agent decides which actions will be executed; then from (C to D) the actions are sent to the server.

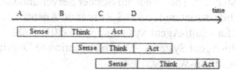

Figure 3 SPADES Sense-Think–Act Cycle

5. Putting All Together: A Complete Simulation

3D Soccer Server is consisted of three important parts: the server, the monitor and the agents. The server is responsible to start an agent process. Agents connect via UNIX pipes to a SPADES Commserver. They use a length prefixed format to exchange messages. The Commserver in turn communicates with the server [11].

In a complete simulation, 3D Soccer Server allows twenty two agents (eleven from each team) to interact with the server in order to play a simulated robotic soccer game. Each agent receives sensations about the relative position of the other players and field goals and other information concerned with the game state and conditions. To reply to each sensation an agent sends actions such as *drive* or *kick*.

6. Conclusion

RoboCup 3D Soccer Simulation Server provides a real-world and challenging domain for AI and MAS research using the game of soccer. Many researchers from all over the world implement their own teams and compete with each other using this simulator in various tournaments to evaluate the outcome of their approaches. However, the development of 3D Soccer Server has not been stopped and is undergoing some new works on a better timing system and more realistic visualization as well as adding more soccer rules.

References

1. Alan Mackworth. On Seeing Robots, chapter 1, pages 1-13. World Scientific Press, 1993
2. RoboCup Official Page, http://www.robocup.org
3. Kitano, H. et al. RoboCup: The Robot World Cup Initiative. In Proc. of IJCAI-95 Workshop on Entertainment and AI/ALife, 1995
4. RoboCup Soccer Simulation Server Official Page, http://sserver.sourceforge.net
5. Stone, P. Layered Learning in Multi-Agent Systems. PhD Thesis. School of Computer Science, Carnegie Mellon University, 1998
6. Kolger, M. and Obst, O. Simulation League: The Next Generation. In Daniel Polani and Brett Browning and Andrea Bonarini and Kazuo Yoshida. Springer Verlag, Volume 3020, pp 458-469, 2004
7. Riley, P. and Riley, G. SPADES – a distributed agent simulation environment with software-in-the-loop execution. In S. Chick, P. J. S´anchez, D. Ferrin, and D. J. Morrice, editors, Winter Simulation Conference Proceedings, 2003. 1.3, 2.3, 4.10, 4.11, 6.8
8. Noda, I. and Stone, P. The RoboCup Soccer Server and CMUnited: Implemented Infrastructure for MAS Research. Agents Workshop on Infrastructure for Multi-Agent Systems, pp 94-101, 2000
9. Ferber, J. Multi-Agent Systems – An Introduction to Distributed Artificial Intelligence, Addison-Wesley, 1999
10. Wernecke, J. The Inventor Mentor: Programming Object-Oriented 3D Graphics with Open Inventor, Addison-Wesley, ISBN 0-201-62495-8, 1994
11. RoboCup Soccer Server 3D Maintenance Group. Text Instead of Manual, downloadable from RoboCup Soccer Simulation Server CVS Repository, http://sserver.sourceforge.net

Review of Current Crime Prediction Techniques

Vikas Grover[1], Richard Adderley[2] and Max Bramer[1]

University of Portsmouth, UK[1]

A E Solutions[2]

{Vikas.Grover, Max.Bramer}@port.ac.uk

Rick.Adderley@A-ESolutions.com

Abstract

Police analysts are required to unravel the complexities in data to assist operational personnel in arresting offenders and directing crime prevention strategies. However, the volume of crime that is being committed and the awareness of modern criminals make this a daunting task. The ability to analyse this amount of data with its inherent complexities without using computational support puts a strain on human resources. This paper examines the current techniques that are used to predict crime and criminality. Over time, these techniques have been refined and have achieved limited success. They are concentrated into three categories: statistical methods, these mainly relate to the journey to crime, age of offending and offending behaviour; techniques using geographical information systems that identify crime hot spots, repeat victimisation, crime attractors and crime generators; a miscellaneous group which includes machine learning techniques to identify patterns in criminal behaviour and studies involving re-offending. The majority of current techniques involve the prediction of either a single offender's criminality or a single crime type's next offence. These results are of only limited use in practical policing. It is our contention that Knowledge Discovery in Databases should be used on all crime types together with offender data, as a whole, to predict crime and criminality within a small geographical area of a police force.

1. Introduction

In recent years police forces have been enhancing their traditional method of crime reporting with new technological advancements to increase their output by efficiently recording crimes to aid their investigation (Adderley and Musgrove 1999). Data is not just a record of crimes, it also contains valuable information that could be used to link crime scenes based on the modus operandi (MO) of the offender(s), suggest which offenders may be responsible for the crime and also identify those offenders who work in teams (offender networks) etc.

It is not an easy task for a Police analyst to manually unravel the inherent complexities within police data and this problem is compounded when the analysis is undertaken by a team, as each member is not in possession of all relevant facts and relevant information could be lost. For a long time, criminologists and statisticians have been applying their skills and knowledge trying to predict when and where the next set of crimes will occur, with varying degrees of success. The volume of crime and the greater awareness of modern criminals put a strain on the existing methods. Human reasoning fails when presented with millions of records. Therefore, there is clearly a requirement for a tool kit to assist in analyzing the data which will make the best use of limited resources. Knowledge Discovery in

Databases (KDD) techniques can be used to reveal knowledge which is beyond intuition.

The aim of this study is to examine the current techniques used in crime prediction.

2. Crime Facts

We have categorised crimes into two types; Major crimes: Murders, rapes etc. and Volume crimes: Burglary, vehicle crime, robbery, theft, damage etc. The cost of volume crimes, both in financial and emotional terms, makes their effective targeting essential.

2.1 Crime Recording Process

Whenever a crime is committed, a police officer visits the crime scene or the report is taken by telephone, which is known as the crime report. All UK police forces record their crime reports in a similar way but in different computer systems. The variables stored may be known in a variety of ways but comprise the following: - Time, day and date of the crime; Offence type (there are in excess of 800 different Home Office crime codes); Location of crime to include post code and Ordnance Survey grid references; Victim information; Modus operandi (MO) identifies how the crime has been committed.

Depending upon the crime recording system used by each individual force the data fields will be a mixture of free text and structured (and often) validated fields. The free text may not even contain key words or phrases and will contain non standard abbreviations, mis-spellings and, on occasion, contradictory information. The quantity and quality of information recorded varies considerably from case to case. It is often imprecise, and is almost certainly at times inaccurate. Unstructured and inconsistent data formats make it very complicated to automate the analytical processes.

2.2 Environmental Criminology

Understanding Environmental Criminology and the behaviour of offenders plays a significant role in understanding and predicting crime and criminality (Brantingham and Brantingham 1991, Rhodes and Conly 1991, Cohen and Felson 1979; Clarke and Felson 1993, Adderley and Musgrove 2003).

3. Current Crime and Offending Prediction Techniques

The 'holy grail' in policing is to be able to predict when and where the next crime or set of crimes will occur. This, of course, in a holistic sense is not currently possible. Many attempts have been made in the crime prediction arena, each of which has had limited success. Most of these attempts have been either concerned with the crime and criminality relating to either a single offender or a single crime type. The sections below discuss the current crime prediction techniques.

3.1 Statistical Methods

Canter (1994) found that scene of a crime is a key feature to the address or home base of an offender which has been confirmed by Rossmo (2000) and there is a distance decay pattern for crime trips (Brantingham and Brantingham 1984).

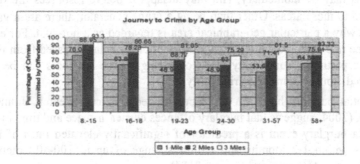

Figure 1: Distance travelled by age

Using West Midlands Police crime data, Figure 1, we have confirmed the statement mentioned in academic papers listed above. The left hand column of each age band clearly demonstrates that a large proportion of offenders commit their crime within one mile of their home address. The figures in the chart are accumulative.

If there is a lack of physical evidence, the behaviour of an offender has been used to suggest that the offender may be responsible for other undetected crime. In these instances the main emphasis is on the MO i.e. offender's 'way of working' (Davies 1992; Grubin et al 2001). The search for a common behavioural thread linking the offence of a single individual may be like searching for a needle in a haystack that is not there. Here data mining could help to find the links.

3.2 Miscellaneous Methods

Several academic ventures have made an abortive attempt to use artificial intelligence (AI) to identify volume crimes such as burglary (Lucas 1986 and Charles 1998). This has engendered suspicion within policing regarding the usefulness of AI techniques. There are only few examples of using data mining on crime data (see Adderley 2004; Brown 1998).

There are several other techniques that have been used by several researchers. Chau et al (2002) has used entity extraction to discover the patterns that identify person names, their addresses, vehicles and other characteristics. Some of the approaches, such as string comparator, social network analysis and deviation detection are described in Chen et al (2004) to use on crime data in understanding criminal behaviour. Hauk et al (2002) have used the concept space algorithm on crime data to detect abnormal activities. Once these activities are identified it may be possible to predict the next occurrence of such activity. Several algorithms have been used by Oatley et al (2004) to match and link burglary crimes together into a crime series. Having ascertained that a series is occurring it is possible to suggest, from that data, where the next crime in that series will occur. Repeat victimisation has also been used to assist the prediction (Ewart and Oatley 2003).

3.3 Geographical Information System Methods

(Brantingham & Brantingham 1995) propose that crime hot spots are developed in areas of the community that can be labelled as crime generators, such as entertainment areas and shopping malls. The techniques used by police forces to identify hot-spots are not always consistent. Crime problems in areas designated as hot-spots may be momentary, and may disappear before resources are officially allocated to those areas. Other than being a crime generator, there are a variety of reasons why a particular geographical area is regarded as a hot-spot. For example, the crime rate could be caused by a prolific offender being released from prison or due to a particular community event occurring. These hot-spots can be used as good predictors of crime and criminality.

Residential burglary has been the focus of geographical research. Johnson and Bowers, (2004) suggests that burglary offences cluster in space and time in affluent areas, "a burglary event is a predictor of significantly elevated rates of burglary offences within 1-2 months and within a range of up to 300-400 metres of a burgled home" (Johnson and Bowers 2004).

4. Discussion

Current prediction techniques have had limited success in operational policing. Many researches have spent time analysing large amounts of police related data with a view to predicting either where the next crime or set of crimes will occur. There are two main areas where these prediction techniques have been concentrated: - An individual crime type and an offender's movements. There are two subsidiary areas where these techniques have been concentrated; Repeat victimisation and Hot-spot analysis.

In our view by limiting the research to a single crime type or offender or geographical area the ability to predict has limited value to operational policing. In order to effectively prevent crime and arrest offenders, it is necessary to effectively target the geographical area where crimes are occurring or will occur. This is ALL crime and not just an individual crime type. Therefore, we suggest that KDD could be and should be used on all crime types together with offender data, as a whole, to predict crime and criminality.

References

Adderley, R. (2004) The Use of Data Mining Techniques in Operational Crime Fighting, *Intelligence and Security Informatics, Second Symposium on Intelligence and Security Informatics*. Springer, ISBN: 3-540-22125-5

Adderley, R., and Musgrove, P.B., (1999) Data Mining at the West Midlands Police: A Study of Bogus Official Burglaries, *BCS Specialist Group on Expert Systems, ES99*, London, Springer – Verlag, pp191-203, 1999.

Adderley, R., and Musgrove, P.B., (2003) Modus operandi modeling of group offending: a data mining case study, Accepted by: *The International Journal of Police Science and Management*, 2003.

Brantingham, P., & Brantingham, P., (1984) *Patterns in crime*. New York: Macmillan.

Brantingham, P., & Brantingham, P., (1991), Notes on the geometry of crime, *in Environmental Criminology*, USA: Wavelend Press Inc.

Brantingham, P, & Brantingham, P., (1995) Criminality of place: Crime generators and crime attractors. *European Journal on Criminal Policy and Research 3,3*, special issue on Crime Environments and Situational Prevention, 5-21.

Brown, D.E. (1998) The Regional Crime Analysis Program (RECAP): A Framework for Mining Data to Catch Criminals. in *IEEE International Conference: Systems Man and Cybernetics Society.*

Canter, D.V. (1994) *Criminal Shadows* London: Harper Collins.

Charles, J., (1998) AI and Law Enforcement, *IEEE Intelligent Systems*, pp77-80.

Chau, M., Xu, J., and Chen, H (2002) Extracting Meaningful Entities from Police Narrative Reports. In: Proceedings of the National Conference for Digital Government Research (dg.o 2002), Los Angeles, California, USA.

Chen. H., Chung, W., Xu. J. J, Qin. G. W. Y, and Chau. M (2004), Crime Data Mining: A General Framework and Some Examples. *IEEE Computer Society.* 50-56.

Clarke, R.V., & Felson M. (1993), Introduction: Criminology, Routine activity, and rational choice *in Routine activity and rational choice: Advances in criminological theory, volume 5.* Clarke, R.V., Felson, M. (eds.) New Jersey, USA: Transaction Publishers.

Cohen, L.E. and Felson, M., (1979), Social Change and Crime Rate Trends: A Routine Activity Approach. *American Sociological Review*, Vol 44, 588-608.

Davies, A. (1992) Rapists Behaviour: A three aspect model as a basis for analysis and the identification of serial crime. *Forensic Science International*, 55, 173-194.

Ewart, B. W., and Oatley, G.C. (2003) Applying the concept of revictimization: Using burglars' behaviour to predict houses at risk of future victimization. *International Journal of Police Strategies and Management, Vol.5 (2).*

Grubin, D., Kelly, P., and Brunsdon, C. (2001) Linking serious sexual assaults through behaviour. Home Office Research Study 215. ISBN 1-84082-560-X

Hauk, R.V., Atabaksh, H., Ongvasith, P., Gupta, H., and Chen, H. (2002) Using Coplink to analyze criminal justice data, *IEEE Computer*, 35(3), pp. 30-37.

Johnson, S.H. and Bowers, K.J. (2004) The Burglary as Clue to the Future: The Beginnings of Prospective Hot-Spotting, *European Journal of Criminology*, Vol 1 (2): 237-255: 1477-3708.

Lucas, R. (1986) An Expert System to Detect Burglars using a Logic Language and a Relational Database, *5th British National Conference on Databases, Canterbury.*

Oatley, G.C., Zeleznikow, J., and Ewart, B.W., (2004), Matching and Predicting Crimes. In: Macintosh, A., Ellis, R. and Allen, T. (eds.), Applications and Innovations in Intelligent Systems XII. Proceedings of AI2004, *The Twenty-fourth SGAI International Conference on Knowledge Based Systems and Applications of Artificial Intelligence*, Springer: 19-32. ISBN 1-85233-908-X

Rhodes, W.M., Conly, C., (1991), *The criminal commute: A theoretical perspective in Environmental Criminology*, USA: Wavelend Press Inc.

Rossmo, D. K (2000) *Geographic profiling*: CRC Press. ISBN 0-8493-8129-0. pp 97-110.

An extended version of this paper is available as Grover, V., Adderley, R. and Bramer, M. (2006). A Review of Current Crime Prediction Techniques. University of Portsmouth, School of Computing, Technical Report.

Data Assimilation of a Biological Model Using Genetic Algorithms

Manoj Thakur, Kusum Deep

Department of Mathematics, Indian Institute of Technology, Roorkee (India)

manojdma@iitr.ernet.in, kusumfma@iitr.ernet.in

Abstract

In this paper the calibration of well known biological system namely Lotka-Volterra model is done using Genetic Algorithms. The problem of parameter estimation is formulated as an optimization problem, which is highly non linear and multimodal in nature. Binary Genetic Algorithms as well as Real Genetic Algorithms have been used to obtain the results. The comparative study shows that the Real Genetic Algorithm is more promising.

1.   Introduction

The problem of parameter identification of a system is an inverse problem and is often very difficult to solve. The main difficulty comes with the development and implementation of the algorithm that uses the sampled data from the system to identify it without a priori significant knowledge of the system.

Previously dynamical system models were measured using trial and error process by taking different sets of parameter values and comparing the results obtained graphically. Unlike the trial and error procedure, where the process of calibration of parameters used to be very expensive in terms of time and often unreliable and inaccurate result were obtained, numerical optimization techniques are more accurate and less time consuming and do not depend upon the modeler's knowledge to adjust the system parameters.

In the formal assimilation studies Fasham and Evans [3] and Prunett et. al. [7, 8] has used conjugate gradient method. On the other hand other researchers [10] used different kind of trust region methods. These kind of methods do not guarantee to locate the global optimal solution of the problem under consideration but are less time consuming because less number of function evaluation are required.

In the recent past, probabilistic techniques like simulated annealing [5], genetic algorithms [9] and genetic programming [1] have been applied to solve the inverse problem. All of these methods are of great importance because they do not use the information about derivatives of the function and are able to locate the global optimum of the function. However they turn out to be more time consuming due to more function evaluations.

2. Mathematical Model of the Problem

Let us assume that the system under consideration can be characterized by a system of n first order differential equations of the type

$$\frac{dy}{dt} = f(t, y; a) \text{ , With initial conditions } y(t_0) = y_0. \tag{1}$$

Where $y = (y_1, y_2, ..., y_n) \in R^n$ and $a = (a_1, a_2, ..., a_k) \in R^k$ are the state-vector and vector of the parameters to be estimated respectively. $t \in R$ is the independent variable.

Let $y(t; a) = (y_1(t; a), y_2(t; a), ..., y_n(t; a))$ be the solution of the system defined in equation (1) and y_{ij} $(i = 1, 2, ..., n, j = 1, 2, ..., l)$ be the response of the system parameters measured at time t_{ij} $(i = 1, 2, ..., n, j = 1, 2, ..., l)$ for some unknown set of parameter values a^*. Then the parameter identification problem is to get an estimate of a, such that the solution of (1), with this estimated parameter value fits the data closely. In this paper, we use the classical least square method in which the square of the deviations between the predicted and measured values is minimized. So the optimization problem corresponding to the system identification problem could be stated as

$$\text{Minimize } f(a) = \frac{1}{2} \sum_{i=1}^{n} \sum_{j=1}^{l} (y_{ij} - y(t_{ij}; a))^2 \tag{2}$$

In the present study we consider the classical Lotka-Volterra model given below

$$\frac{dx}{dt} = a_1 x - a_2 xy, \frac{dy}{dt} = a_3 xy - a_4 y, \tag{3}$$
$$x(0) = x_0, \quad y(0) = y_0 \text{ (Initial conditions)}$$

where x and y are state variable and t is time and a_1, a_2, a_3 and a_4 are growth rate of prey, predation rate, growth rate of predator and mortality rate of predator respectively. In [10] it is found that the simple looking Lotka-Volterra model is an appropriate problem to compare parameter estimation approaches. It is important to note that in the absence of initial conditions the initial population of the parameters is also considered to be parameters. So the parameter set to be estimated is given by the vector $a = (x_0, y_0, a_1, a_2, a_3, a_4)$.

In the real life situation the response of the system should be measured at different time steps and then to be used to estimate the parameters of the system. However, in the present work a twin experiment [4, 10] is done: a reference solution of the model is obtained with some set of reference parameters (for details refer [10]).

3. Experimental Setup

The optimization problem formulated in section 2, is solved by two different kind of genetic algorithms.

1. Binary GA
2. Real GA

In Binary GA, binary strings of length 10 are used to represent each of the parameter. Whereas In Real GA, the variables are taken to be real numbers. The fitness function $F(a)$ in both the GA is defined as follows

$$F(a) = \frac{1}{(1 + f(a))}, \text{ Where } f(a) \text{ is the objective function value.}$$

Tournament selection with tournament size 2 is used for both the GA. For binary GA, two point crossover and bitwise mutation [2] is applied to produce the new generation and for Real GA, whole linear crossover with non-uniform mutation [6] is applied. In all the experiments population size of 60 is used. The crossover probabilities $p_c = 0.9$ and mutation probability $p_m = 0.05$ is used in both the Binary and Real GA. Maximum number of generations is fixed to 500 and with each run 100 runs with different initial population are performed.

The lower and upper bounds for parameters are taken as follows $a_{lower} = (0.5, 0.5, 0.1, 0.05, 0.05, 0.01)$ and $a_{upper} = (1.5, 1.5, 0.6, 0.5, 0.5, 0.3)$.

The experimental setup described above is used to test the potential of both the Binary and Real GA. Figure 1, 2 and 3 shows the results obtained by Binary GA and Real GA.

In Figure 1 the graphs between the prey and predator populations are plotted. Figure 2 and Figure 3 show the prey and predator population with respect to time respectively. The response values are shown by circles ('o').

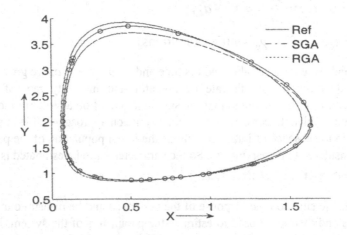

Figure 1

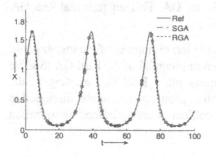

Figure 2

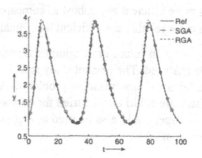

Figure 3

4. Numerical Results and Discussions

The statistics of all experiments with above mentioned parameters is given in Table 1. The table shows the percentage of success and average number of generation required for successful runs in all the experiments. A run is considered to be success if the optimal solution obtained lies within 1% of the true optimal solution ($f^* = 0$). In all the cases we have seen that Real GA has outperformed Binary GA both in terms of accuracy and number of generation required to reach the optimal solution

Table 1.

runs	% of Success	Avg. no. of generations for successful
Binary GA	68	326
Real GA	84	257

5. Conclusions and Future Scope

Parameter identification is a necessary and important part of model development in the any field of engineering and science. One of the approaches to accomplish this task is to formulate the parameter estimation problem as an optimization problem. The techniques of parameter identification used in literature are often very demanding in terms of CPU time. This is the reason why we need strong and efficient optimization techniques. GA provides an alternative to solve the optimization problems because of their ease to use and simplicity. In the present work we have applied Binary Coded GA and Real Coded GA to estimate the parameters of Lotka-Volterra model. The results obtained in the present study are very encouraging. Despite highly nonlinear and multimodal nature of objective function, both the GA converges quickly near the global optimal solution. It is also evident from Table 1 that Binary GA has performed pretty well however Real GA is more efficient and robust as compared to Binary GA. This suggests that Real GA is more reliable and efficient than Binary GA.

In future more complex systems having larger number of parameter could be analyzed. The present study is an indication of potential of the Real GA to solve multimodal optimization problems. Also, many other Real GA existing in the literature could also be tried for data assimilation problem. The model discussed in this paper could also be used as a good test problem of unconstrained optimization problem.

6. Acknowledgements

The second author acknowledges Council for Scientific and Industrial Research (CSIR), New Delhi. India, for providing financial support.

References

1. Cao H.-Q., Kang, L., Guo, T., Chen, Yu-Ping, Garis H. D. A two level hybrid evolutionary algorithm for modeling one-dimensional dynamic system by higher-order ODE models, Haris, IEE transaction on System, Man and Cybernatics 2000; 30(2): 351-357.
2. Goldberg, D. E. Genetic Algorithms in Search, Optimization and Machine Learning, Addison-Wesley, 1989.
3. Fasham, M. J. R., Evans G. T. The use of optimization technique to model marine ecosystems dynamics at JGOFS station at 47 deh N 20 deg W, Philosophical Transaction of the Royal Society London 1995; 203-209.
4. Lawson, L. M., Spitz, Y. H., Hoffman, E. E., Long, R. B. A data Assimilation technique applied to a Prey-Predator Model, Bulletin of Mathematical Biology 1995; 57: 593-617.
5. Matear, R. J. Parameter optimization and analysis of ecosystem models using simulated annealing: a case study at station P., Journal of Marine Research 1995; 53: 571-607.
6. Michalewicz, Z., Genetic Algorithms + Data Structures = Evolution Programs, Springer Verlag, 1994.
7. Prunett, P., Minster, J. F., Dadou, I. Assimilation of surface data in one-dimensional physical-biogeochemical model of Surface Ocean: 2. Adjusting a simple trophic model to chlorophyll, temperature, nitrate and pCO2 data. Global Biogeochemical Cycles 1996; 10: 139-158.
8. Prunett, P., Minster, J. F., Ruiz-Pino, D. Assimilation of surface data in one-dimensional physical-biogeochemical model of Surface Ocean: 1. Methods and preliminary results, Global Biogeochemical Cycles 1996; 10:111-138.
9. Roeva, O., Pencheva, T., Hitzmann, B., Tzonkov, S. A genetic algorithm based approach for identification of Escherichia coli fed-batch fermentation, Bioautomation 2004; 1: 30-41.
10. Walmag, J. M. B., Delhez, E. J. M. A trust region method applied to parameter identification of a simple prey-predator model, Applied Mathematical Modelling 2005; 29: 289-307.

AUTHOR INDEX

243